DE
DE

The Baroque Concerto

The
Baroque Concerto

by
ARTHUR
HUTCHINGS

FABER AND FABER
3 Queen Square
London

First published in 1959
by Faber and Faber Limited
3 Queen Square London WC1
Second edition 1963
Third revised edition 1973
Printed in Great Britain
by Western Printing Services Limited Bristol

Copyright © 1959, 1963, 1973 Arthur Hutchings

ISBN 0 571 04808 0

To
MICHAEL BONFITTO

Acknowledgments

I thank the undermentioned for information used in this book, for guiding me to sources, lending music or other materials that were difficult to obtain, or for their advice after reading parts of my typescript. For these services I am particularly indebted to Michael Bonfitto.

Miss Jean M. Allan, Reid Music Library, Edinburgh.
Dr. Peter Evans, Music School, University of Durham.
Dr. Herbert Franke, University of Cologne.
Dr. Francis Jackson, York Minster.
Miss Margaret Johnson, Durham Cathedral Library.
Dr. Walter Krüger.
The Rev. Canon K. J. Meux.
Dr. Oscar Mischiatti.
The Rev. Claude Palfrey, Precentor of Norwich Cathedral.
Professor Sir Jack Westrup.

I also thank those who have enabled me to secure the photographs reproduced within these pages. Their names appear under the relevant plates.

A.H.

Contents

9

Illustrations

Italian cities associated with concertos

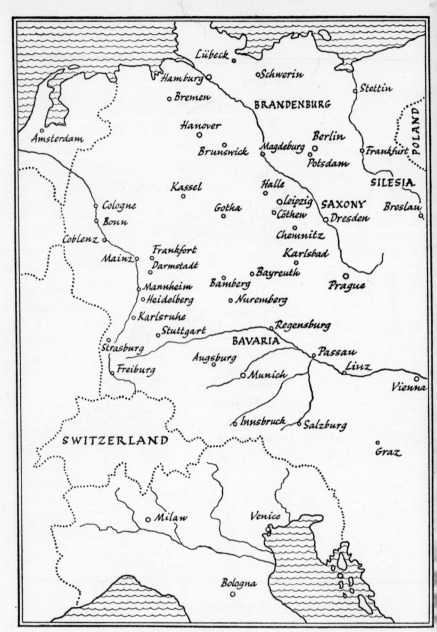

Greater Germany, showing main centres of concerto composition

[14]

CHAPTER I

The Period and the Places

However late or early the year to which different historians may assign the emergence of the concerto as a distinct genre, 1700 is a reasonably approximate year from which to trace the spread of concertos from Italy into the court and church orchestras of German-speaking States, and 1715—just after Roger had printed Corelli's Op. 6 and Vivaldi's Op. 3—a reasonably approximate year from which to observe such a rapid growth in the cultivation of concertos that the printers of Amsterdam and elsewhere issued band parts of hundreds of sets of concertos within a few decades, almost to the exclusion of other kinds of orchestral music. What they printed was no longer performed for aristocratic pleasure only. The concerto was the first orchestral form to be composed expressly for the most popular modern service of serious music—the orchestral concert; London enjoyed public concerts before the concerto was born; other European capitals were to establish regular public concerts during the years which saw the conquest of private court orchestras by the Italian concerto.

People who frequent concerts of purely instrumental music must either be attracted to sound as a moth to light and enjoy it in a kind of hypnosis or trance, or else be satisfied with the forms and processes of music without help from words, dramatic action, or dancing. In the early years of the concerto few commoners except the citizens of London could often hear concerted instruments, but we should remember that they were heard in many of the greater Italian and German churches. Cities as far apart as Bologna and Hamburg were famous as much for instrumental as for vocal music before 1700, yet Italians and Germans were slow to demand regular public concerts. When the San Cassiano Theatre first offered public opera at Venice in 1637 the popular demand for one kind of music that had formerly been a princely pleasure was enormous; new opera houses were quickly opened for the general public in Venice and elsewhere; but only in London, Hamburg, Vienna, and perhaps one or two places concerning which I lack relevant information, did large numbers of citizens show themselves eager to enjoy the chamber music of the privileged until the eighteenth century was well advanced.

On returning to their estates, many of the princes and dukes who visited France during the grand epoch sought to recapture their enjoyment of the first famously disciplined orchestra—the royal band selected and trained by Lully to outshine the Twenty Four. They increased their own musical establishments, some to a larger complement of players than Lully's, sent their musicians to study the French methods, imported enough overtures and suites to provide an immediate French repertory, and expected their composers to augment it. At the beginning of the eighteenth century the largest orchestras in the royal, ducal or episcopal courts were those of Dresden, Stuttgart, Darmstadt, Vienna, Munich, Gotha, Grosswardein, Regensburg and Passau. Within a few years some hundred feudal rulers had augmented or bettered their orchestras by seeking leaders and trainers from Italy, whether they had set up an opera theatre or not. During the century a small orchestra sometimes became a large and fine one when a highly musical employer succeeded to the throne. Stuttgart, Dresden, Hanover, Potsdam and Mannheim in turn were famous for their court orchestras.

Ensembles of few or many instruments in Italian courts and churches were more affected by 'the French style' than some of our standard histories suggest, for the rhythms of many of Corelli's movements (even in church sonatas and concertos) were of French origin. Although the concerto came from Bologna and Rome, it was enriched when German musicians applied its principles and style of performance to the French overtures which they already knew how to compose. What they called an overture was a suite. Its opening was the composite slow-fast movement which we still call a French overture, after which there followed from three to as many as nine dance movements, the last of which might be a chaconne or a march but was usually a gigue. Sometimes other movements than the first were quite long and ambitious, no longer the simple organisms that accompanied a ballet or divertissement.

Neither the concert-goer nor the discophile hears much of the early orchestral repertory in 'the French style'. The part of it that was imported from the ballets and operas of Lully, Campra, Destouches and other French composers became chamber music by the transfer; but the German court composers produced it specifically for concerts, for listening to an orchestra, and their workmanship was often superior to the French. The only works often heard in modern concerts to represent their efforts are the last and finest examples—Bach's suite in D with the trumpets and drums, his concerto-like suite in B minor for flute and strings, together with Handel's *Water Music* and *Fireworks Music*.

When 'the Italian style' shared programmes with 'the French style'—in short when concertos joined overtures—music for instruments alone was still classified under a name that associated it with grand residences. Unless it was played in church or theatre it was called chamber music. Overtures, chaconnes and other dances had come from the theatre; the Italian concertos had come from church sonatas and were used at High Mass. We speak of concerts and recitals, but in the seventeenth and eighteenth centuries music was named after the places in which it sounded—church, theatre, chamber—and according to that classification we do not hear church music when we listen to Bach's organ works in a concert hall, to theatre music when one of Handel's overtures is played in a cathedral, or to dance music when we play jazz records. Church sonatas became chamber music at sessions of the Bologna academies, in court music rooms or in London taverns. Within a church sonata or concerto, sober movements derived from sarabands, gavottes and other measures of the French suite would not openly be labelled with the names of the dances yet such a sonata or concerto became chamber music in the Ottoboni Palace or the Queen of Sweden's music

B [17]

room. The rapid ascent of the concerto in the eighteenth century testifies not only to the number and quality of chamber concerts given by private orchestras but also to the inauguration of regular public concerts, of music societies, academies and *collegia musica* in cities and universities which had rarely heard an ensemble of more than a few instruments.

We shall devote a chapter to the spread of concerts in various European countries and the conditions in which concertos were first performed. We are concerned here only to notice that the occurrence of a novel idea in Corelli's imagination was not alone responsible for the rise of the concerto grosso between 1680 and 1700. Concerti grossi had not suddenly grown after privileged visitors to the court of Louis XIV heard Lully's orchestra, nor did Englishmen compose a treasury of works on the scale of concertos for the English royal band. Purcell's overtures which include a trumpet (for instance the famous one in *The Indian Queen*) are not unlike the contemporary Bolognese trumpet concertos which they outshine, and of course there were listeners who enjoyed Purcell's overtures, chaconnes and dances as absolute music, just as there were English listeners to sonatas and string fantasias; but the fully orchestral works came within dramatic conceptions.

The time during which the concerto first appeared was not accidental; nor were the places associated with its emergence. The foremost devotees of sonatas had been members of the university and city of Bologna, ducal families who maintained chamber musicians, and the aristocracy of Rome, especially Cardinals Panfili and Ottoboni, and Queen Christina of Sweden.[1] Ottoboni's Academy of Arcadians, though enrolled for the avowed purpose of furthering the sciences and humane letters, especially poetry, was far more interested in music. Corelli lived and worked in the Ottoboni Palace but he had been taught in Bologna, and he called himself Bolognese on title-pages. He was thus associated with the city which, during the last quarter of the seventeenth century, produced more sonatas and instrumental works than any other in Europe. The immediate forebears of the concerto grosso

---

[1] Daughter of Gustavus Adolphus. In 1654 she became a Roman Catholic and abdicated in favour of her cousin Charles X. She lived in Rome and was generous to the musicians whom she engaged for the splendid concerts given in her palace.

were trio and violin sonatas rather than works called concertos—
a name usually denoting an association of voices with instruments.
Works for five, six or seven stringed instruments with continuo,
which might be called sonatas or concertos, were very often far
more like canzonas and far less like the first concerti grossi than
were the usual trio sonatas or sonatas for violin and continuo.
The huge success of the concerto grosso was prepared by the
cultivation of that kind of sonata which composers gradually
omitted to designate as *da chiesa*, for it was not intended only
for the church, and as it developed it owed to the suite its form
of three or four distinct long movements instead of the many
tempo changes of the canzona. The last characteristics of the older,
canzona-like church sonata were the frequent slow opening, the
counterpoint in an initial slow-fast movement, and the transformation into staid, dignified movements of dances which were
openly named in chamber or court sonatas.

Although in Italy the orchestra had previously been associated
with the theatre, the first concerti grossi did not come from the
opera composers of Venice and Naples, but from Corelli and the
musicians associated with Bologna—the university, the basilica of
St. Petronio and the famous *Accademia Filarmonica*. An account
of their origins and emergence can be misleading if it begins by
tracing previous connotations of the word 'concerto' and suggesting a direct chain of evolution. Misleading also is the application of *post hoc ergo propter hoc* to some notable feature of the
concerto grosso. For instance, before Corelli's tutti-concertino
pattern, the most remarkable contrasts of texture and density to
be used consistently as part of a musical design were those between instrumental groups in the *symphoniae sacrae* and grand
canzonas composed by Giovanni Gabrieli; but there is no more
direct connexion between Gabrieli and Corelli than between
Schütz and Bach. Even if we discover that Corelli heard or saw
music by Gabrieli and Bach music by Schütz, we can surely say
that the later masters would have composed as they did if the
earlier ones had never existed. The grand instrumental music at
St. Mark's declined rapidly soon after Gabrieli's death. Its decadence continued through the middle years of the seventeenth
century until Legrenzi was appointed director, while the music
for string ensemble was ascendant at St. Petronio. Moreover the

[19]

splendour of Bologna was of quite a different order from the splendour of Venice; it was less idiomatic, and to modern ears it sometimes sounds dry, suggestive of a proud academic and ecclesiastical community. Yet the Bolognese concerto was more directly beholden to the opera sinfonia of Venice than to any music associated with St. Mark's, for when the music of Bologna reached its zenith during the last decade of the century the most magnificent pieces heard in St. Petronio, and probably at sessions of the *Accademia Filarmonica*, were the *sinfonie con due trombe, concerti per trombe* and *sonate con trombe* by Torelli, Perti, Domenico Gabrielli[1] and Jacchini.

The kind of concerto that was destined to precede the classical symphony and to share its honour did not grow from previous large ensembles at all, except indirectly from Lully's string orchestra. Even under Legrenzi, who must have taught some of the concertists of the early eighteenth century, including Albinoni, large ensembles were often of mixed soloists—violins, viols, trombones, perhaps an oboe, often a bassoon, organs and instruments of the lute family. Concerti grossi were aggrandizements of the more integral sound of the trio sonata for violins and 'cello, which Corelli incorporated into his concertos by making it persistent in the fabric and exposed as a concertino. The nurseries which had cultivated sonatas for nearly half a century produced in the concerto grosso what stood to the sonata as a standard rose stands to a bush, the leaves and flowers being similar. A new rose is widely grown only if thousands of amateur and professional gardeners share the first grower's ideal; they do not share his precise desire, for they lack his knowledge, imagination and laboratory, but their favour affects his experiments. During most of the seventeenth century no composers except those in England were deeply concerned with a wide general public if they had secured the favour of privileged employers or patrons in the church or aristocracy. The first exceptions were the Italian opera composers after 1637. Half a century later a considerable general public was ready to enjoy chamber music and to acclaim from Corelli onwards a series of increasingly marvellous violinists as a former public had acclaimed opera singers.

[1] Though also spelt 'Gabrieli', this composer's name is best written as at St. Petronio, thus distinguishing him from the famous Venetians.

London already enjoyed plenty of public concerts, and Londoners had only themselves or their incomes to blame if they knew little about sonatas; but London concerts rarely mustered an instrumental ensemble of the size used in an Italian opera or concerto grosso, and London programmes were largely of songs interspersed with instrumental airs and solos. Not everybody who likes instrumental music in church or playhouse can enjoy it for hours at a concert where it does not assist other forms of expression, and the attitude implied by Fontenelle's 'Sonate, que me veux-tu?' was by no means peculiar to France. The public for absolute music is always limited, and its taste depends upon its opportunities. Like the boy Verdi, it may form its first judgements from the village band or church organ, and its later judgements of symphonies and concertos are then more than the acquired gloss of fashionable education. There is, however, a wider concert public which does not quickly like music that is unemphatic and gently coloured. It immediately loves the orchestra, the fine singer or virtuoso, and perhaps the sound of a chorus with orchestra, but it acquires slowly a taste for string quartets. Such listeners among the nobility and burgessy swelled audiences for chamber music when it became orchestral, so that during the second decade of the eighteenth century the presses of Amsterdam, London and Paris outran those of Venice and Bologna in the supply of printed parts of concertos.

Consideration of this wider audience may incline us to believe that the title of the new concerto was no more accidental than the time and place of its emergence. Corelli, Gregori, Valentini and Torelli—all the early concertists except Dall'Abaco—called their works concerti grossi to distinguish them from instrumental concerti sacri or concerti ecclesiastici and from concerti da camera, which might employ five or six instrumental parts but were not orchestral conceptions. The more parts, the less orchestral the sound; for the sound most associated with the orchestra in Italy was that of the ritornello to an opera aria, or of the opera sinfonia and dance movements. The composers did not wish concerti grossi to produce the sound of single instruments except when, by writing 'solo' on the parts, they deliberately recalled the sonata during concertino sections.

Albinoni, Vivaldi and the Marcellos—the immediate successors

[21]

of the Bolognese concertists—did not use Corelli's title even when they used his outlay of instruments, and it was not generally favoured by the many German concertists who were inspired by Vivaldi and the Venetians. The title and opus number of the finest baroque concertos, Handel's 'Twelve Concerti Grossi, Op. 6' seem to have been chosen as a tribute to Corelli in the country which continued to honour him by verbal panegyric and sedulous imitation for some fifty years after his death; yet Corelli's closest imitators in England, Geminiani who was his pupil and Avison who was Geminiani's, called their publications 'Six Concertos in Seven Parts', not 'Six Concerti Grossi'. Plainly the adoption of the Corellian model with its contrasts of tutti and concertino within the string texture did not necessarily induce the eighteenth-century composer to adopt his title. On the other hand we know from Handel that concertos with no concertino sections could be called concerti grossi.

Because of a widespread mistake it is desirable to say again that Corelli and the others did not intend 'Concerto Grosso' to designate a work with a concertino, but an *orchestral* conception, distinct from the *concerto a quattro* or *concerto a cinque* which we should call a string quartet or quintet with continuo. A concerto grosso for the church was more than a *sonata da chiesa* in many parts; a concerto grosso for the concert room was more than a suite of dances on too grand a scale to be called a *sonata da camera* or *trattenimento*.[1] It was the equivalent and rival of the sinfonia, the grand overture at the opening of a Venetian opera, or of the sinfonia that was heard on church or university high days at St. Petronio.

Hence the pendants to 'Concerti Grossi' on title-pages, telling the buyer that he required more than one player to each violin part, that a double bass was desirable to complete the orchestral sonority although the organ and archlute served as fundament instruments, that many players could swell the ripieno but that none should double any part in the concertino. These works were not to be tackled indiscriminately by as many players as happened to attend in the organ gallery for High Mass or in the palace concert room after dinner. When the concertino sounded alone,

---

[1] Bolognese and Venetian composers sometimes published suites of dances as *Trattamenti* or *Trattenimenti*, i.e. entertainments, diversions, or 'courses'.

the fine texture of a trio sonata emphasized the richer texture of those sections wherein it was no longer exposed. Corelli's design was a pattern of textures which differed from former concertos as an embossed fabric like brocade differs from a cloth of uniform thickness.

The habit of referring to the orchestral ensemble as the concerto grosso prevailed in parts of Germany and also in England, where professional pride, not stooping to the native 'full' used by cathedral musicians, could have been satisfied with the single Italian word 'ripieno' or 'tutti'. The ambiguity of 'concerto grosso' may have prevented composers from using it as a title, but it has not prevented historians from referring to 'the period of the concerto grosso' instead of 'the baroque concerto period' when they are dealing with composers from Corelli to Quantz. We loosely include among concerti grossi all Bach's Brandenburg Concertos and all his concertos for harpsichord and for violin. Bach, Handel and other late baroque composers still regarded the concerto as an essay in orchestral texture when part-writing took precedence during a fugue or a slow middle movement.

The first concerti grossi crowned more than half a century of Italian devotion to violin playing that followed and reflected a former devotion to singing, for the sonatas and concertos played by the Vitalis, Torelli, Valentini, Corelli, Vivaldi, Geminiani, Veracini and others upon Amati's and Stradivari's instruments mark a golden age of the string ensemble that is comparable with the previous golden age of vocal ensemble. For Corelli and Vivaldi, as for Mozart, the violin was a wordless voice of superhuman compass and range of expression, with clearer attack and greater agility than a human voice, and free from the strain of human fatigue. The second generation of concertists in Italy, notably the Venetians, introduced wind instruments. Their concertos are rarely like sinfonias for string and wind instruments; instead the oboe, flute or bassoon receives the affection elsewhere bestowed on the solo violin; but in Germany especially the technique and expression of wind instruments developed as the concerto developed, and the liberal inclusion of wind instruments into the ripieno prepared the larger court orchestras for the classical symphony.

[23]

The history of the baroque grosso may be somewhat crudely summarized thus:

1. *The Sonata Concerto*, emerging chiefly through a Bolognese-Roman School: Corelli, Torelli, Dall'Abaco, Albicastro and, in the next generation, Bonporti.

2. *The Suite Concerto* of the first German or Austrian School: Muffat, Aufschnaiter, Pez. (Certain composers classed under Nos. 4 and 5 below, e.g. Telemann and Handel, are partly 'suite' concertists.)

3. *The Operatic or Dramatic Concerto* of the second Italian (Venetian) School, comprising the opera composers in Venice—Albinoni, Vivaldi, Alessandro Marcello, Benedetto Marcello. (Later followers: Tartini and, in France, Leclair.)

4. *The Kapellmeister Concerto* of the main German School. Chief composers: Pisendel, Heinichen, Fasch, Graupner, J. S. Bach, Telemann, Stölzel, Molter, Hurlebusch, Birkenstock, J. A. and K. H. Graun, Quantz, Hasse.

5. *The Public Concerto* of the English School. Chief composers: Geminiani, Avison, Handel, Stanley, Festing, Babell, Barsanti, St. Martini, Defesch and Hellendaal.

6. *The Symphonic Concerto*, including some of the later works by Vivaldi and by composers who were also symphonists, e.g. Locatelli and G. B. Sammartini.

CHAPTER II

'Concerto' and 'Sinfonia' during the Seventeenth Century

Ideals held in Palestrina's time would ultimately have found expression not unlike Corelli's even if there had been no cult of the violin. It is mistaken to think of the high renaissance as epitomized by one kind of music. Ascetic and voluptuary face us from its canvases, and its music includes passiontide motets and gay lute songs; but it is no mistake to regard musicians of the high renaissance as much concerned with ensemble, not just with securing ensemble. Marenzio and Victoria, Byrd and Wilbye no more *forged* a vocal style than Corelli and Vivaldi forged an instrumental one; they mastered an inherited style while they were scarcely more than boys, and its use in long works gave them no unusual task. They secured distinction and have maintained it because they transcended the facility which many practitioners could display without distinction—the condition which tells us that a style is decadent. Like composers of concerti grossi, they often achieved melodic beauty, but their instrument was the choir itself. *Ensemble as an entity was their medium of expression.*

Another word for 'ensemble' is 'concerto', and the term 'concerto grosso', meaning simply 'full choir', must surely have been used when only voices were present. There are instances of its application during the sixteenth and seventeenth century to works in which the voice or voices are accompanied only by the organ or lute. It may have been used as a title (at least to part of a work) even earlier than the sixteenth century, but the first printed music on which the present writer has seen it is Ercole Bottrigari's *Il Desiderio . . . Concerti di varij Strumenti Musicali* published at Venice by R. Amadino in 1594. 'Concerto' was used with increasing frequency during the last years of the sixteenth century; but so also were 'concerto', 'symphonia' and, in England, 'consort', When did any of these synonyms acquire a special application?

Several recent writers affirm that early in the seventeenth century 'concerto' became attached to the particular kind of ensemble wherein there was an element of contrast—between solo voice and organ, trombones and viols, loud and soft sections, many and few voices. ('Voci' was used for instrumental parts and 'chori' for groups of instruments.) Their authority is Praetorius who, in the third part of his *Syntagma Musicum*, 1619, derived 'concerto' from *concertare*, to compete, instead of from *conserere*, to consort; but both in classical and medieval usage *concertare* has a second meaning, to act together, to work with a common purpose, and we strain imagination if we suppose that the idea of rivalry was widely or frequently entertained by listeners to concertos. More than one eighteenth-century writer compares the texture in a concerto with chiaroscuro in a painting, but none speaks of strife or competition among the participants. Praetorius merely says that some listeners once regarded participants in forms of concerto as engaged in harmonious contention.

Franz Giegling and Hans Engel, the contributors of the articles 'Concerto' and 'Concerto Grosso' to *Die Musik in Geschichte und Gegenwart*, suggest that Praetorius himself was mistaken. They mention the spelling 'conserto' during the sixteenth century and occasionally afterwards, and they suggest that 'concerto' is a transformation. This is convincingly countered by David Boyden[1] who notes that 'concerto' is not only the commoner but also the earlier spelling. Praetorius took care to say that the word did not *necessarily* refer to music in which there was the kind of disputation (*Streiten*) which he exemplified by the opposition of a few

[1] David D. Boyden. 'When is a Concerto not a Concerto?' *The Musical Quarterly*, vol. xliii, 1957.

picked performers to a large ensemble, and he expressly stated that the Italians sometimes used 'concerto' as an alternative to 'concentus' or 'symphonia' when referring to the smoother kinds of ensemble.

When or where listeners to music imagined contention, warlike or friendly, matters little; when and why they discriminated between synonyms matters considerably. Fortunately 'concerto' and 'symphony' were disjoined very soon after they came into frequent use. Long before the growth of public opera 'sinfonia' might refer to one of the introductory, connective, descriptive or incidental pieces played in theatres, including what were called in England curtain tunes and act tunes. Symphonies belonged to the theatre or to dramatic conceptions like oratorios and serenatas, and they retained this association in the time of Bach and Handel. Yet sometimes a fully scored sinfonia was used in church. Several of the St. Petronio trumpet pieces composed during the last decade of the seventeenth century were called sinfonias, perhaps because they resembled Venetian opera sinfonias or overtures in the employment of trumpets. Some of the festal preludes to Bach's cantatas are called sinfonias and so are many pieces more ferially scored, such as the one which opens part two of the Christmas Oratorio. Before the advance of the concert symphony in the middle years of the eighteenth century, orchestral sinfonias or Italian overtures entered the concert room as visitors from the theatre and became chamber music just as the corresponding French overtures had done. The orchestral symphony was not born in the concert room—that is the point to emphasize, since many seventeenth-century sonatas for only three or four players, both of church and chamber type, were entitled sinfonias. Here we are discussing only the orchestral sinfonia.

'Concerto' on the other hand was *not* of the theatre. Early in the seventeenth century 'concerti' was the title of lute duets by Francesco of Milan, motets for more than one choir by Andrea Gabrieli, sonatas and canzonas for instrumental *chori* by his brilliant nephew, accompanied choruses by Banchieri, music for solo voices and organ by Viadana, madrigals by Monteverdi and others, as well as works for five or six chamber musicians. Until well after 1700 purely instrumental pieces might be called sonatas, concertos or sinfonias without apparent distinction of structure. What Torelli would have called *sinfonie con trombe* at Bologna, and Bach *Konzerte* at Cöthen were called *Sonatae Grossae* by Molter, director of the orchestra at Gotha. The choice of designation was not affected by the number of performers. A concerto might be for one or two voices with organ, a sonata for a large festival orchestra, a sinfonia for a string quartet with continuo; *but before Corelli's concerti grossi became known, 'concerti' was most often used when voices and instruments were combined.* Thus, outside France and England, it was frequently the title given to church music.

This application survived longest in the conservative world of the Lutheran cantor. Bach called his most important music for the church *Kirchenkonzerte*, for his contemporaries associated *Kantaten* with secular and usually amorous words. Because the Bach Society volumes called cantatas what Bach called concertos the misnomer came into general use, and we should be pedantic to shun it. During almost the whole of the last quarter of the seventeenth century 'concerto' denoted purely instrumental music unless the title were qualified, as in *concerti ecclesiastici, sacri concerti, salmi e concerti*, etc. From soon after 1680 a concerto was normally an aggrandized sonata requiring from six to twenty strings with the organ, harpsichord or archlute.

Though distinct from 'sinfonia' as a title, 'concerto' did not designate a definite number, order or structure of movements until the classical era, and some of Vivaldi's concertos are not distinguishable by the ear alone from works entitled by him *sinfonie*. The order and shape of movements in a sinfonia, a concerto, a suite, a partita or an overture could be similar before 1750. The sinfonia which opens Bach's second partita is cast in the shape of a French overture; the ungrouped partita published in the second part of his *Clavierübung* is actually called 'French Overture'; a Handel concerto sometimes resembles a French suite—overture followed by dances; Haydn's symphonies were advertised in London newspapers as Grand Overtures; finally, neither at the beginning of its history nor in the days of Bach and Handel did the concerto grosso necessarily contain solo or concertino sections.

Despite this apparent confusion 'concerto' denoted a distinct genre as soon as concertos belonged to one category of music, *chamber or concert music*, having sloughed voices and association with the church; this they did before Corelli's concertos were printed and long before symphonies acquired a comparable distinction. In 1730 a symphony might still be an Italian overture, a passage for organ in an English anthem, a march, battle, storm or pastoral piece in an opera or oratorio, or a ripieno concerto served under another name; but if a work were called concerto it was intended for 'absolute' listening, for use at a concert. It might be cast in movements like those of a church sonata, but it would not be exclusively for the church even if it were called a Christmas Concerto and used in church; it would also not be associated with the theatre.

From about 1715 very few concertos can have been composed with any thought of church use. Until the middle of the century most concertos except those composed in England were cast in the three-movement form favoured by Vivaldi, Albinoni and the Marcellos, for the Venetians strongly influenced the German musicians who had formerly composed French overtures and suites. When the pre-classical symphony largely ousted both the French overtures and the concerti grossi from orchestral programmes in several of the German courts, the title 'concerto' proved more distinctive than 'symphony', for the word 'concertante' came into use when the older form of concerto was obsolete. It meant simply 'in a concerto style', not 'in competitive style'. There is quite as much competition in symphonies as in concerti grossi.

Although Praetorius's derivation of 'concerto' must be upheld, the determining factor in the emergence of the concerto was a delight in the instrumental ensemble, whether it included strong contrasts or not. If the contrasts had been the chief determinant concertos should have emerged long before the last decades of the seventeenth century. Many who had the rank and wealth to maintain orchestras heard the grand concertato at Venice when Giovanni Gabrieli was composing there, the diverse instrumental groups in Monteverdi's *Orfeo*, or the broken consort that was sometimes used on a grand scale in the English Stuart masques;[1]

---

[1] The mere bringing together of many diverse instruments by Monteverdi was no novelty for a court festivity. In the very year of the first performance of *Orfeo*, Campion's music for *Lord Hay's Masque* required 'on the right hand

yet early in the century the frequent assembling of many and diverse instruments in veritable phalanxes of contenders produced nothing like the concerto grosso.

As will be evident from facts given in other chapters, Venice was not the only city in which, during the early seventeenth century, listeners could enjoy the sound of many instruments and voices arranged in opposed groups; yet in Venice the grand concertato could be heard more frequently and probably on a more lavish scale than elsewhere, if we judge from accounts by French, German and English travellers of the period. The most vivid description of Venetian concerted music is by Thomas Coryate (1577–1617) who, after education at Winchester and Oxford, became a hanger-on at the court of James I. Though a clever scholar he was content to be jester or court fool, even putting to comic use the name of his birthplace and home, Odcombe in Somerset. In the church at Odcombe he hung the boots in which he had walked across Europe. He published in 1611 *Coryate's Crudities hastily gobbled up in Five Months' Travel*, which is now particularly scarce and valuable, though the British Museum owns two copies. Here is the passage concerning music in Venice:

'Sometimes there sung sixeteene or twenty men together, having their master or moderator to keepe them in order; and when they sung, the instrumental musitians played also. Sometimes sixeteene played together upon their instruments, ten Sagbuts, four Cornets, and two Violdegambaes of an extraordinary greatness; sometimes tenne, sixe Sagbuts and foure Cornets; sometimes two, a Cornet and a treble violl. Of those treble viols I heard three severall there, whereof each was so good, especially one that I observed above the rest, that I never heard the like before. Those that played upon the treble viols, sung and played together, and sometimes two singular fellowes played together upon Theorboes, to which they sung also, who yeelded admirable sweet musicke, but so still that they could scarce be heard but by

. . . ten musicians with bass and mean lutes, a bandora, a double sackbut, and a harpsichord with two treble violins; on the other side . . . were placed nine violins and three lutes; and to answer both the consorts six cornets, and six chapel voices . . .'. (Papers of William Trumbull the Elder, quoted in 'Ben Jonson', ed. Herford and Simpson, vol. x, Oxford, 1950.)

those that were very neare them. These two Theorbists concluded
that nights musicke, which continued three whole howers at the
least. For they beganne about five of the clocke, and ended not
before eight. Also it continued as long in the morning: at every
time that every severall musicke played, the Organs, whereof
there are seven faire paire in that room, standing al in a rowe
together, plaied with them. Of the singers there were three or
foure so excellent that I thinke few or none in Christendome do
excell them. . . .'

Coryate says 'in that room', for he does not describe music in St.
Mark's nor, evidently, in a church, but in the hall of the 'School'
of St. Rocco. He merely tells us that it was part of the festivities
in honour of St. Rocco,[1] which were almost entirely musical.
For their participation in these and in civic ceremonies special
payment was made to the musicians of St. Mark's, whom we
should regard 'less as church musicians than as the kapelle of
one of the most brilliant courts in Europe'.[2]

Before the vault of St. Petronio echoed to the trumpets and
massed violins of Perti's and Torelli's most grandiose church
works, and before Corelli's concertos were first heard in Rome,
the grand concertato of Venice provided most nearly the kind of
pleasure that was derived from the concerto grosso. As the concerto grosso had no single creator and no precise origin we cannot
say that these Venetian pieces were not concertos, nor that the
'real' or 'true' concerto began with Stradella, G. M. Bononcini,
Corelli or Torelli. Yet we may understand why different writers
have claimed each of those four as the originator of the orchestral
concerto for church or chamber listening. Each of them helped
to make the concerto grosso a *distinctive* genre, and each lived to
recognize it as such; yet if we placed side by side the first page of
a concerto by Torelli, an orchestral sonata by Valentini, and an
opera sinfonia by Legrenzi or Stradella (wilfully choosing works
of similar style) only someone who already knew the pieces could

[1] The saint came from France to the cities of North Italy during the thir-
teenth century, was beloved for his ministrations to those smitten with the
plague, by which he died. The relics of St. Roch or Rocco were finally taken
to Venice where they received special veneration during August.

[2] Denis Arnold. 'Music at the Scuola di San Rocco', *Music & Letters*, vol. xl,
no. 3, July 1959. This is the first article in English which explains 'School' as
referring to a Venetian guild or sodality.

identify the concerto. No single feature—recurrent solo or concertino sections, an initial tutti closing in the tonic, ritornelli—is
enough to distinguish a seventeenth-century concerto, but many
features persisted when the genre had emerged, and it is profitable to devote a chapter to their origin and growth.

CHAPTER III

Stylistic Features of Baroque
Concertos

Even before 1600 the harmonic tread of a texture was as much part of a composer's thought as the chief melody (tenor or soprano) or the points of contrapuntal imitation. This is proved by a desire to represent on paper the succession of harmony just as the notes on a stave represented the course of melody. Although first the signs and then the figures placed with a *basso seguente* were devised for accompanying instruments, they marked an attitude to composition; imitative counterpoint was no longer the paramount means of continuing a texture, but one of several means. They included sequences of chords, sequences of melody without exact sequence of chords, rhythmic imitations without exact melodic sequences, the division of music into sections by cadences which were the equivalent of punctuation marks in prose, being confirmed by harmonic approaches that were becoming fixed and conventional, and the gradual turning of cadences into modulations in the later sense of the word— changes of key.

Recourse to counterpoint as a means of varying, decorating and enlivening the ensemble of parts was almost a necessity in pieces longer than a metrical psalm-tune, a chorale, a short dance or a song when the stuff of music was conceived by what Bukofzer calls 'a polarization of the uppermost melody and the bass'. The counterpoint could be reserved for contrasting sections or it could leaven all parts of a piece, but the continuously contrapuntal texture of certain organ pieces and certain movements in church sonatas and concertos had no general influence upon concerto style; the contrapuntal section had, because it enabled the composer to make extra contrast between thematic and transitional material, or between tutti and solo (or concertino) passages. With this form of contrast we shall deal under the wider heading 'concertato'.

1. CONCERTATO

One counterpart of the vivid colour-relief in renaissance painting was the opposition of polyphonic and familiar style in vocal ensemble. Though one does not deny that the familiar style, often in jubilant block chords set to a staid dance rhythm, was symbolical of leaping joy (for it frequently occurred at *alleluya* or at *osanna in excelsis*) one must also assert that even the decorous Palestrina introduced contrasts both of style and of vocal registers for purely musical reasons. The words of the famous Advent motet, *Surge, illuminare*, justify the change from interweaving phrases when they reach climax at the words *et gloria Domini super te orta est*, and explain why Palestrina uses jubilant dactyls without contrapuntal overlaps. The words of various items in the Mass give no such clue to Palestrina's vocal scoring, nor always do the words of motets. The last sentence of the motet *Assumpta est Maria* is simply factual—*Maria Virgo cum Christo regnat in aeternum*; Palestrina, however, divides his six parts into contrasting groups of four, those of higher and those of lower pitch, and repeats the sentence three times, once for each group and finally for the six voices in brilliantly sonorous outlay.

This purely musical effect we shall call concertato, though the word had other meanings early in the seventeenth century. Concertato of the kind already used by the vocal masters of the renaissance survived in orchestral music and is noticed in the opening tuttis, as well as in other sections of classical concertos. Mozart devised sections in contrapuntal style, often lightly scored, within more weighty sections for the ensemble of strings and wind, sometimes with trumpets and drums. In the sixteenth century this technique was naturally most abundant in light-hearted vocal ensembles such as frottole and balletti; but because the greater churches had the largest musical resources the contrasts had the strongest impact in compositions for *cori spezzati*, divided choirs or broken consorts. ('Coro' was a complement of instruments, or of voices, or of both.) In Italy the effect was much weightier than the English antiphony of decani and cantoris, or decani and 'full', for in Venice at St. Mark's, in Bologna at St. Petronio, in several churches at Rome and elsewhere, the musicians were placed in facing galleries above the chancel bays or in transepts. Each side had its organ, and when other instruments such as cornetts and trombones were associated with one vocal choir and strings with another there was opportunity for brilliant concertato.

The most vividly juxtaposed sonorities conceived before 1600 were in the sumptuous pieces by Giovanni Gabrieli.[1] The best known of these is the *Sonata pian' e forte*[2] from the *Symphoniae Sacrae* of 1597; it opposes a 'first chorus' of a cornett and three trombones by a 'second chorus' of a viola da braccio and three trombones. (The compass is that of the viola, and though Gabrieli wrote 'violino' we can of course discountenance the idea that he meant 'violin'.) In the same set is Gabrieli's *Sonata Octavi Toni* with two *chori* of six players, but most of his polychoral pieces were called canzonas. Praetorius tried to distinguish their titles, and discovered that the sonatas were the more solemn works. The most brilliant concertato effects by Gabrieli are in the works produced after 1600, including the famous *In ecclesiis* for two vocal choirs, soloists, organ, brass and strings.[3] This work is a compendium of the Venetian cult of concertato that began with the purely vocal compositions for more than one choir by Adrian Willaert and other Flemish musical directors at St. Mark's, and

[1] We await a new edition of Giovanni Gabrieli's works, edited by Denis Arnold for the American Institute of Musicology as the twelfth issue in the series 'Corpus Mensurabilis Musicae'. At present the best collection of Gabrieli's works in grand concertato style is still vol. iii of Winterfeld's three-volume *Johannes Gabrieli und sein Zeitalter*, Berlin, 1834.

[2] Printed in *HAM*, vol. i, no. 173. The *Symphoniae Sacrae* are included in vols. i and ii of *Istituzioni e monumenti dell'arte musicale italiana*. Recorded in *Anthologie Sonore* and also commercially.

[3] Printed in *HAM*, vol. i, no. 157, and recorded in Vol. IV of *A History of Music in Sound*.

reached its climax of the vocal stage with Andrea Gabrieli's pieces for three or four vocal choirs.

2. FIGURATION IN CONCERTATO

Recourse to chains of figures, rarely sequences of long phrases, and to sections of contrapuntal imitation contrasted with plainer texture can also be observed in the work of Giovanni Gabrieli. The quotation at Ex. 1 is from his *Sacrae Symphoniae, Part ii*, which consists of two sets of works—*Canzoni e sonate* and *Reliquae sacrorum concentum*. This posthumous publication of 1615, which testifies to the esteem in which the composer was held by other musicians, contains the most grandiose of all these early forms of purely instrumental concertato, for some of the pieces require four *chori* and one requires five. It also contains a *Sonata con tre violini* which is the most modestly scored and also the most prophetic of Gabrieli's known works, for it uses real violins, has only four staves (the lowermost, presumably for organ, labelled 'Basso se piace') and is remarkably like many later church sonatas and concertos before Corelli's. The passage quoted at Ex. 2 might have been written at least two decades later. It well illustrates the main points of style that succeeded renaissance polyphonic methods—a bass that guides a progression of harmonies towards a cadence, a series of sequences, decorative pseudo-counterpoint. A glance at the bass in the closing bars of the *Gloria* in Palestrina's *Missa Brevis* will show how nearly the sixteenth-century composer thought in terms of continuo harmony, but Palestrina never used Gabrieli's figure development, and he very rarely wrote a sequence.

Minor composers at Venice and as far off as Vienna imitated Gabrieli's grand concertato, which was developed no further at St. Mark's after Gabrieli's death. Indeed it is difficult to imagine any further development that would not weaken the very effects for which it was and still is admired. Judging by modern attempts to revive some of Gabrieli's pieces for more than two *chori* one cannot imagine how, even with St. Mark's acoustics and the placing of performers well apart in the transepts and other parts of the building, some of these works failed to lose brilliance and clarity because of their sheer weight and thickness. One of the

1.

G. Gabrieli. Sonata a 8. [Winterfeld]

[Notes halved]

2.

Gabrieli. Sonata for 3 violins. [Wasielewski]

1615 sonatas uses twenty-two parts, four *chori* of four parts each, surmounted by one of six. Whether the musical result is worth the preparation we cannot judge, for we do not know what instruments were required for some of the parts; but the effect of another sonata in this set, which requires one *chorus* of four trombones and another two with three trombones and two cornetts, is not as fine as that of some of the canzonas or of the *Sonata pian' e forte* which require only two *chori*. As we have

[37]

already remarked, the Venetian polychoral concertato had no direct effect upon the Venetian concertos of Albinoni and Vivaldi for whom a texture of many voices would have been encumbering.

A more interesting point of early baroque technique is the juxtaposition of level and broken texture, for this persisted in various forms of sonata and became a feature of concertos. We have noticed it in Gabrieli's work, but it occurs also in simple monodic pieces of the early baroque, and it can be observed better in many of Monteverdi's madrigals than in the earliest compilations to bear the title 'Concerti'—Gabrieli's *Concerti per voci e stromenti*, 1587, Malvezzi's *Intermedii et Concerti*, 1591, Banchieri's *Concerti ecclesiastici*, 1595, and Viadana's *Concerti ecclesiastici*, first volume 1602, second 1607. Some of these contain no dramatic concertato. Much of their music is a dignified and sometimes dull monody of one, two, three, or four solo voices with organ *basso seguente*. In Monteverdi's madrigals, as in some parts of his *Magnificat* and *Vespers*, brilliant solo figuration and coloratura are contrasted with plain choral or instrumental sonority, and it seems hardly accidental that Monteverdi uses the title 'Concerto' in his seventh book of madrigals (1619) precisely when he offsets a virtuosic vocal solo by a tutti of no fewer than nine instruments.[1] Similar contrasts are found in pieces for soloists. They were, of course, a feature of lute music, and we find them in many Italian and German collections of organ pieces, for the organ lends itself to solid full chords offset by rapid passages of scales and figurations for one hand. This form of concertato is notably demonstrated in Gabrieli's *Intonazioni d'organo* of 1593. Its survival in the classical concerto is noticeable where bravura work for solo violin, harpsichord or piano is offset by solid orchestral texture.

Particularly vivid concertato can be found in the *Symphoniae Sacrae* (1629, 1647 and 1650) of Gabrieli's pupil, Schütz, especially the specimens which use strings and brass as well as the organ. Like the *Geistliche Konzerte* of Schein (1626) and Scheidt

[1] The word 'concertato' appears in the sixth book of madrigals in the title of No. 7—'*Una donna fra l'altre*', *concertato nel clavicembalo*. Each setting in 'Scherzi Musicali' (*c.* 1607) has an instrumental introduction, but 'Non così' has small instrumental interpolations. The eighth book of madrigals first shows instrumental insertions in extended imitation of the vocal exposition (i.e. No. 1, with 6 voices, 4 viols and 2 violins).

(1631) these works are in some respects conservative, whereas Gabrieli's and Monteverdi's had been modern enough to arouse such literary attacks as those of Artusi. When Hassler, Schütz and other German composers returned from Italy they introduced what soon became old-fashioned in Italy; and though we possess Schütz's transcription to German words of Monteverdi's 'Zefiro torna' he declined to imitate fully the more arresting features of his new hero's music. The 'Three S's', though outstandingly admirable, are not important in the pre-history of the concerto, to trace which our regard is focused on Italy from about 1630 to 1680. These dates roughly enclose the period during which Italian music in church, theatre and concert room was moving towards the styles of Corelli and Scarlatti.

3. SEQUENCES

We have mentioned 'chains of figuration', small-unit sequences which prescribed a texture of sections that were juxtaposed to weightier sections. The growth of sequences of all kinds is of importance in the history of a genre which would not have become important unless it had been the vehicle of ambitious musical thought—in short, unless it had ultimately gained long and integrated movements. What is development? The answer: 'Continuation chiefly by sequences from proposed ideas', though too summary, would not be less silly than the question, for sequences cover a large part of classical concertos and symphonies when ideas are not being stated or fully repeated. Sequences are perhaps the chief vehicles of development although they do not account for its quality. Albinoni, the first concertist to produce three long movements in concerto after concerto, notably and judiciously made a very extensive use of sequences where Corelli and Torelli had continued by other means, some almost improvisatory.

Sequences, rare in Palestrina, are almost an obsession in Gabrieli, who needed a forward-carrying technique whenever he discarded the overlapping phrases of counterpoint. In Gabrieli's sequential developments of short motives, the bass often moves by the rising fourths or falling fifths of a cadential formula; and his fondness for finishing each unit with a major chord (by a picardy third if needed) leads him to incidental modulation. Composers of the generation after Gabrieli used longer sequences and introduced them without breaking the flight of a whole musical paragraph. The following examples are from *Canzoni da suonare a tre*, op. 9, 1639,[1] by Tarquinio Merula, who was then director of music at the cathedral in Bergamo, though he belonged to the Bologna *Accademia dei Filomusi* and published in Venice. Ex. 3 is not unlike music by Gabrieli, but the broad melody of Ex. 4 could be imagined in a sonata or concerto by Corelli, and so could its underlying chords of the seventh. (It is worth mentioning that Ex. 4 begins a section of the canzona marked *tremolo*.)

By the next generation, as Ex. 5 from a work given in 1667 serves to show, sequences were used as freely and naturally as by Corelli and Handel, and there is little purpose in quoting more examples of a process that is very obvious as we turn the pages of anthologies. It needs no advanced musical culture to recognize that the airs and instrumental passages in Carissimi's oratorios or Cavalli's and Cesti's operas belong more to Corelli's time than to Gabrieli's. By the middle of the seventeenth century most Italian composers wrote whole passages which could belong to sonatas or concertos of the following century. The theorists used the terminology of the past, but from about 1630 the melody and harmony of Italian, French, even English composers belonged to the two classical scales, the major and minor, and their weft of rhythm to a warp of bar lines, of regular metrical stresses. When to this basis of musical thinking they added regular phrasing, melodic or rhythmic sequences, figure-patterning, and a series of key changes by clearly marked cadences, they had clarified design and style in a way that was essential to the making of lengthy sonata movements. Until the sonata was established the concerto had to wait.

4. ECHOES AND REPETITIONS

We now reach a non-contrapuntal means of continuing a musical texture which, though belonging like the others to a general history of style from late renaissance to high baroque, was

---

[1] Printed by J. W. Wasielewski in the supplement ('Instrumentalsätze') to *Die Violine im XVII Jahrhundert*, Bonn, 1874. Reprinted as a separate book, Berlin, 1905. The canzona from which Ex. 3 comes is printed in *HAM*, vol. ii, no. 210.

specially useful in concertos. Unless combined with concertato in some form it would have been retrograde. Repetition is more primitive than sequence, and even in fine rhetoricians like Liszt it may often weaken the expression it tries to enforce. Plain repetition can halt the advance of musical thought, but even a simple soft-loud or loud-soft contrast within the same medium prevents the repetition from being plain, and quotations from

Corelli are unnecessary to prove that the right musical idea may be repeated to advance the movement almost as much as does a sequence.

Until the birth of the concerto grosso the *p-f* repetition was rarely used except as a ritornello; on the other hand the *f-p* repetition came into widespread favour during the seventeenth century. Sometimes it was used for dramatic point, as in the spelling lesson of Blow's *Venus and Adonis* or the witches' cavern scene of *Dido and Aeneas;* but it was also used in purely instrumental works where there could be little other reason for its existence than delight in its effect. Long after Monteverdi had introduced dramatic echoes into Act V of *Orfeo* he employed them in sacred works, for instance in *Audi Coelum,* where they lovingly prolong the name 'Maria' and in the 1610 *Vespers,* though the word 'echo' is not actually written. The *Sonata sopra Sancta Maria* in the *Vespers* is, of course, an instrumental concerto of great splendour, showing an early example of what later became developed into a recapitulation.

Echo effects persisted well into the eighteenth century, for instance in J. M. Molter's *Concerto con l'echo*[1] (Carlsruhe, *c.* 1730), in the last movement of Bach's *French Overture* (1735), and in Mozart's *Notturno en echo* (1777). The first noted example of highly developed echo music is a piece in Lassus's *Libro di Villanelle* (1581) where the effect is humorous. Serious recourse to a technique like an echo was much advanced by double choirs and the contrast between strings and wind; but it came into very great favour with the construction of two-manual organs and harpsichords, and we find its most extensive employment in pieces by Sweelinck (Ex. 6), Scheidt and Gigault.

As early as 1621 echoes are found in purely instrumental works by Dario Castello, one of the masters of the orchestra in St. Mark's. The quotation at Ex. 7 is from his *Sonate concertate in stilo moderno,* bk. i, no. 1,[2] published in Venice. He was appointed to St. Mark's eight years after the sonatas appeared, but as many of them are for mixed string and wind instruments we may suppose that they were used at Venice.

[1] Molter's spelling.
[2] Reprinted by L. Torchi in Vol. VII of *L'Arte musicale in Italia*, and by Wasielewski. (See note on p. 40.)

5. KINETIC RECURRENCE

I apologize for coining the term 'kinetic recurrence' to name a musical procedure which I have not seen described elsewhere. It is a special kind of repetition, either of melody, or of melody with supporting harmony, which certainly does not retard rhythm but actually seems to add energy and shapeliness. Obviously there must be contexts and conditions in which it can be used effectively and others in which it cannot, but I should not like to define them. I merely note that, in the examples I have observed, this form of repetition includes no long rest in a melody, and usually goes with a bass that moves inexorably in crotchets or quavers. An illustration from Albinoni (Ex. 8A and B) shows that kinetic repetition may occur either in thematic or in connective tissue. It will be noticed that the repetition within the main theme of the movement (Ex. 8A) includes the full close—a fact that led me to discard the term 'oscillation' which I had adopted when I mistakenly supposed that repetitions with this forward thrust were usually built upon a harmonic formula that resembled an interrupted cadence, so that they could be used any number of times in succession without halting the flow of melody or the tread of harmony. Such a harmonic formula nearly always goes with this kind of repetition when it occurs in connective tissue; but the full close seems to give extra strength and emphasis when it recurs in main themes, and the Venetian concertists, especially Albinoni and Vivaldi, seem by this method to have anticipated the classical symphonic practice which has been called 'presenting arms in the tonic'.

Kinetic recurrence was far from new to music in the early years of the concerto. It can be found in folk songs and dances but it was not part of renaissance ensemble technique, and I know of no instance in Gabrieli or Monteverdi. It may have come into the Italian sonata and concerto through French overtures and dances. We take notice of it here because it is manifestly contributory to the art of achieving length with integrity. Its importance may be judged by trying to imagine the themes quoted in Ex. 9 without their internal repetition. At Ex. 10 are shown several specimens of kinetic repetition from a wonderful and long movement by Handel which makes frequent recourse to this device both in the

main theme and in the passages which lead it to various keys. In Ex. 11 the principle is combined with concertato or echo.

Albinoni, Handel and, of course, Haydn often produce a delightful effect of irregular phrasing, especially in fast movements, by kinetic recurrence of a small unit within a flight of melody. In Albinoni's Op. 5 and Op. 7 concertos this phrase-extension is a rule rather than an exception.[1]

6. RITORNELLO

Ritornelli are a distinguishing characteristic of the classical concerto. Tovey pointed out half a century ago[2] that the function of the initial tutti is misunderstood if it is regarded as an otiose

[1] Perhaps the device of kinetic recurrence is most fully demonstrated in the *Essercisi* and other keyboard sonatas of Domenico Scarlatti.

[2] 'The Classical Concerto', included in *Essays in Musical Analysis*, vol. iii, Oxford.

parade of expository ideas. After the solo has entered in a classical first movement the tutti sections are chiefly ritornelli, partial ritornelli, or variants and developments of ideas from the opening tutti. They may, however, be echoes or continuations of solo materials. Songs, dances with refrains and other pieces of the rondo type originate the ritornello, which takes an important step towards the organization of a classical concerto directly it is not an exact or complete recurrence but an allusion or part-quotation which leads to new material. An example of abbreviated ritornello occurs during the prologue of Monteverdi's *Orfeo* (1607). Before the singer begins, the viols play a short introduction of eight measures, but each time the singer rests they play only the last

[45]

six measures. Monteverdi and his disciples used the words 'ritornello' and 'sinfonia' as synonyms. Heuss[1] supposes 'sinfonia' to designate musical scene-painting and 'ritornello' to designate what merely integrates vocal sections and clinches the form and sentiment of a scene.

With the opening of a great number of public opera houses in Italy after 1637 came a demand for more and longer solo arias, rather than for madrigal-like choruses or musically complex scenes in which recitative, arioso, ensemble and orchestral music were mixed to gain dramatic realism. The simplifiers of opera who favoured many bel canto arias—Rossi, Cavalli, Cesti, Carissimi, Stradella and others—used ritornelli to give these pieces dignity and length as well as to put the voice into high relief. Long-range composition was difficult until musicians became familiar with a scheme of modulation which did not lead them too quickly back to the tonic. Even a genius like Purcell cannot at first have found length easy to maintain without recourse to ground bass or contrapuntal texture, and minor composers of the seventeenth century are decidedly short-winded, shuttling their choruses between the dominant and tonic keys and making their canzonas patchy because only fugued sections are prolonged. Even by the time of Cavalli's *Ercole amante* (1662) and Cesti's *Pomo d'oro* (1666) the more impressive pathetic songs are slow chaconnes or airs interrupted by declamations and ritornelli. (Handel sometimes used this technique; a supremely lovely example is Cleopatra's 'V'adoro pupille' in *Giulio Cesare*.)

The Italian melodic and harmonic style that spread across Europe was mature long before most composers were inclined to spin it at length. Carissimi's well-known 'Vittoria! Vittoria mio corde' (*c.* 1650) might belong to 1680, even to 1700 or later. It is longer than most arias of its time. Accompanists sometimes play its first phrase as an instrumental prelude, for the composer himself did not supply one; if he had done so, and also used it as a ritornello, he would have spoilt the aria, for until a broader conception of composition by key change had evolved, ritornelli, which mark the excursions to different keys, would have emphasized the fact that the aria uses only two tonalities. We reach

---

[1] 'Die Instrumental-Stücke des Orfeo' in *Die venetianischen Opern-Sinfonica* (Sammelbände der Internationale Musikgesellschaft, Leipzig, 1903).

the composers of sonatas and concertos with long movements before we find long and elaborate developments in the ritornelli of arias. Before about 1710 even Alessandro Scarlatti rarely repeated any portion of his orchestral introduction except at the main cadence in the dominant. He is associated with the device of repeating the first vocal phrase or of interrupting it by the orchestra so that the singer repeats it before continuing. German critics call this double announcement *Devise*, and Riemann speaks of *Devisenarie*. Other writers describe the procedure as a 'Scarlattian opening motto', but it was used before Scarlatti could have popularized it, for instance in Purcell's 'Hark, the ech'ing air'. (Albinoni regularly uses the *Devise* in his oboe concertos.)

Arias by Scarlatti and others of the Neapolitan School wherein the voice

(a) first repeats the main orchestral theme and
(b) proceeds to other music but
(c) is punctuated by references to the orchestral opening in other keys than the tonic

show us one of the generating principles of those concerto forms in which the tutti sections are mainly ritornellos. Albinoni, Vivaldi and the other Venetian concertists were the first to use them in all types of movement. These forms had to wait for opera composers who were accustomed to quoting parts as well as wholes of an initial tutti, combining them with echoes of the solo melody and introducing them in any key they had reached.

An example of this development is provided by Francesco Provenzale, the most important composer of the Neapolitan School before Scarlatti, in an opera performed in 1671 (Ex. 12). After the voice has entered, the reference to the opening bars is not an echo or Scarlattian 'motto', for the voice enters before the orchestral prelude has finished. In Scarlatti's *Griselda* (British Museum) which was performed in 1721, long after concertos had become popular, only one aria uses the *Devise*, but in many arias the vocal line is punctuated by partial ritornelli and the whole work shows the influence of concertists. Among the eighteenth-century classifications of aria (*d'agilità, parlante, di bel canto*, etc.) histories mention the *aria concertata*, but the instances given in *Grove* and other reference books (without mention of authorities)

[47]

suggest not an aria like a concerto movement but one with a very full instrumentation, or one in which horn, trumpet or other wind obbligato parts took much of the listener's interest.

For arias in which ritornello technique is elaborately organized we must study composers who lived *after* the concerto grosso and solo concerto had become popular. Often in arias by Handel, for instance, the orchestral echo of a vocal cadence is also a ritornello. The reader is asked to examine 'He was despised' in *Messiah*, wherein echoes and ritornelli are as beautifully organized as in any classical concerto. In the A section of this ABA aria Handel uses between vocal sections each of five phrases from the orchestral prelude, not only as echoes but also as advances; yet at no moment does contrivance make this music sound less than spontaneous.

We need recall only the unisons in the adagio of Vivaldi's first Op. 3 concerto, in the first movement of Bach's third Brandenburg concerto, or in the slow movement of Beethoven's fourth piano concerto, to recognize the importance of ritornelli and to understand why nineteenth- or twentieth-century concertists could not easily compensate for loss of the introductory tutti or what it implies. Our interest in their piano concertos, which one does not wish to disparage, rarely involves appreciation of the concertist's art, for these works are more like accompanied piano sonatas or symphonies with piano.

The truncation or omission of an initial tutti is in itself of little importance. Some of Bach's and Handel's choruses in concerto form dispense with the orchestral prelude but carry out its implications. The first movement of another Brandenburg concerto could have been made from Bach's 'Cum Sancto Spiritu' or his 'Et resurrexit' without changing the voice parts. Yet so important in the later evolution of the concerto was the conception of an opening tutti from which ritornelli would be drawn that some writers regard it as a *sine qua non*, and so reject Schering's claim that certain pieces by Stradella (called sonatas or sinfonias but consistently scored for concertino and concerto grosso) are as much concertos as several of the works published by Corelli forty years later. Even Bukofzer held the opinion that the 'so-called concerti grossi of Stradella . . . are not concertos in the strict sense of the word', and added: 'Self-contained tutti sections closing in the

[48]

tonic can be found only in compositions beginning with Torelli, so far as I am aware, and they became the rule with Vivaldi.'[1]

An initial tutti which closes in the tonic puts a seventeenth-century concerto in the evolutionary stream of the classical solo concerto. It is found in many of the Bologna trumpet sonatas to which Torelli was the most notable contributor. If, however, such an opening tutti is the *sine qua non* of a 'genuine concerto' then most of Corelli's Op. 6, regarded by contemporary musicians as 'the models', and most of Handel's Op. 6, the greatest of concerti grossi, most church concertos, and even Nos. 2, 4 and 7 of Vivaldi's Op. 3 must be excluded from the genus.

The church concerto may have four, five or six sections, some of them contrapuntal and asymmetrical, instead of three long movements of broadly binary or ternary design. It would be difficult to conceive a closed tutti of ritornello materials at the beginning of the slow prelude or fugued allegro of a church concerto. Bukofzer's true observation that 'the formal aspects of Corelli's concertos seem . . . primitive and tentative' is arresting because Corelli is such an elegant and assured stylist.[2] Even in chamber concertos Corelli was sparing with ritornelli, and but for his superb sense of style the music after the double bar in some of his movements would sound improvisatory; yet directly we reach the ninth of his concertos, which is the first chamber concerto in the set, we find a closed initial tutti. Moreover the first ritornello, finishing in the dominant, quotes only the portion from B (Ex. 13), while other short tutti sections quote A or C. These facts do not make the concerto a better one than any of the first eight, but in the light of subsequent history they show a development that distinguished the concerto from the symphony.

[1] Letter to the present writer, 4 August 1952.
[2] *Music in the Baroque Era*, pp. 223–5.

CHAPTER IV

Stradella. Sonata and Concerto

Stradella composed at some time between 1670 and 1680 a *Sinfonia a Violini e Bassi a Concertino e Concerto grossi distinti.* It is the second of a set of twelve *Sinfonie a più instrumenti,* and the twelfth piece in a neat album of Stradella's orchestral works in the d'Este Library at Modena. Roncaglia found a second copy in the Foà Collection at Turin with the title *Sonata di Viole, cioè Concerto grosso di Viole e Concertino di 2 Violini e Leuto.* The beginnings of the movements in this work are shown at Ex. 14.

In 1905 Schering declared certain works by Stradella in the Estense Library at Modena to be concerti grossi, and said that they were composed 'after 1670'. As Stradella was murdered in 1682 they almost certainly antedate the performance of Torelli's and Corelli's concertos, and therefore they antedate the publication of Torelli's by more than twenty years and Corelli's by more than thirty. Stradella's probable use of these pieces as overtures to operas or cantatas, or as interpolations in them, does not alter their musical form. If they are not in the form of concerti grossi then neither are Corelli's church concertos. The concertino effect alone does not warrant disagreement with Bukofzer's opinion that these are merely 'incipient concertos', but the musical design does, and it is upon an examination of the movements as wholes that Roncaglia[1] considers them to be concerti grossi in all but title.

[1] Gino Roncaglia, Le Composizioni Strumentali di A. Stradella, *Rivista Musicale Italiana*, vol. xliv, 1940.

Concertato was common in theatre music during the second half of the seventeenth century. Lully, for instance, was fond of alternation between the string ensemble and a wind trio—the oboes (or flutes) and a bassoon—which Scarlatti and other Italians called the *concerto di oubuoè*. The French and English theatre composers, notably Purcell, sometimes introduced a solo trumpet, and in the Venetian theatres parts for two or more trumpets were in high favour, especially in the initial sinfonias; but what we

[51]

notice in Ex. 14 reveals quite a different plan from the usual overture with concertante effects, or the usual sonata for double orchestra.

Alessandro Stradella (1645–82) is the most vital composer between Carissimi and Scarlatti, and a book about his music in the Modena and Turin libraries, together with the publication of the most impressive specimens, is much to be desired.[1] His father was governor of Vignola, but he studied in Modena under Uccellini and the elder Bononcini and was also influenced by Vitali. We shall mention some of these musicians later as members of the Bologna School. We do not know if Stradella was ever in Bologna for longer than a short visit, but he was certainly influenced by the trend of music in that city, and his work must have been known and discussed by the Bolognese musicians of Torelli's generation. It is noteworthy that Stradella composed at least one trumpet sonata (i.e. concerto) which could easily pass for one of those by Perti or Torelli, and though there is no identified copy of it in the St. Petronio archive, it may have been played at Bologna.

But Stradella belongs to no school. His manuscripts found their way into the ducal library at Modena because, after his death, they were sold on behalf of his son (still a minor and probably needing money) by Stradella's elder brother, an Augustinian friar.[2] Stradella worked in Modena, Naples, Rome, Venice, Turin and Genoa. Like Handel he was a free-lance in an epoch when outstanding opera singers were among the few musicians who would risk freedom from a regular appointment. Nearly a century later Leopold Mozart hoped that his son would secure a lucrative kapellmeistership. Handel himself took care to hold a similar appointment to the Duke of Chandos at Cannons in case his London enterprises proved too precarious.

What is told of Stradella by Bourdelot[3] and retailed by Burney

[1] The first nineteenth-century musician to draw attention to it was A. Catalani, who issued a catalogue, *Delle opere di Alessandro Stradella esistenti nell'Archivio musicale della R. Biblioteca Palatina di Modena* (Modena, 1866). The best monograph on his chief work is still Heinz Hess's *Zur Geschichte des musikalischen Dramas im Seicento Die Opern Alessandro Stradellas* (Leipzig, 1906).

[2] Hess, *op. cit.* See also *Stradella* by F. Marion Crawfurd (London, 1908).

[3] Pierre Bourdelot (1610–85) was physician to the King of France. He began a history of music that was expanded by other members of his family.

presents him as a romantic philanderer, but their conception of
his character is conjectural and their explanation of his assassina-
tion mistaken. He was certainly an industrious and serious composer. That is no vague appreciation of his fecundity, but a
natural comment upon the evident care with which he conceived
the exact sounds of his music and tried to commit them to score.
Despite imaginative use of their instruments, Monteverdi,
Legrenzi, Cavalli and other seventeenth-century composers left
posterity, which they may rarely have considered, the task of
guessing many of their intentions with regard to other orchestral
parts than those for the soprano and those for the bass of their
harmony. Stradella clearly defines each part in textures which
use as many as eight or nine parts, and this is of particular
value to our judgement of his works in concerto grosso style. On
the other hand, he does not consistently mark the speed and style
of his movements. In the work quoted at Ex. 14 the initial
'Adagio' is written on the score, but not the supposed 'Allegro'
four bars forward, nor any further changes of movement which
would have been obvious to the performers. (Some of his intentions, for instance that the finale is *Allegro alla giga*, are obvious
even to us.)

To Stradella most changes of speed required no verbal indication, but he showed 'great concern for dynamic effects' in his
operas and serenatas, in which the 'aria forms are so fresh and
inventive as to baffle analysis'.[1] Both these comments suggest the
kind of musician who, had he lived longer, would have left us at
least one whole set of concerti grossi. He may, however, have
further developed his application of concerto technique to opera
and oratorio, for his most careful written directions (e.g. '*Man-
cano a poco a poco gli stromenti*') are prompted by the circumstances of a drama or the meaning of a text. In several of his
works for voices with orchestra an evident desire that the voice
and the words should be clearly heard induced him to accompany
the singer with a concertino and to mark the ritornelli and other
purely instrumental sections 'concerto grosso' or 'tutti'. Since
the first works in the form of a classical concerto are arias with an
opening tutti and ritornelli, those in which Stradella uses the

[1] Edward Allam, 'Alessandro Stradella', *Proceedings of the Royal Musical
Association*, vol. lxxx (1953–4).

concertino are undoubtedly the closest prototypes of Torelli's and Vivaldi's concerti da camera. As we have already noted, the term 'concerto grosso' had often been used previously, and it is strange that Roncaglia adds 'according to Schering' who quotes its use by Malvezzi in his *Intermedii et Concerti* of 1591. (Viadana wrote only 'ripieno' on the organ part of his *Concerti ecclesiastici* of 1602.) In oratorios, operas, cantatas and the instrumental pieces to be described here, Stradella wrote 'Concertino' and 'Concerto grosso'; but after Corelli had used the latter term as a title it was rarely written in Italy except as a title. Vivaldi wrote 'Tutti' instead of 'Concerto grosso', though he kept 'Concertino'.

The three purely instrumental pieces by Stradella which have been claimed as concerti grossi are all in the key of D. The first has already been quoted. The second comes from p. 84 of the same collection and bears the same title, but the Turin copy is called *Sonata a quattro, due Violini e due Cornetti, divisi in due Chori, ciascuno col basso.*[1] It is more concise than the other work and more like a chamber concerto than a church concerto, for it has no fugued sections. It advances by echoes, sequences, ritornelli and the contrast between dialogue and ensemble. There are two movements, the second changing to 3/8 after twenty-eight bars of 3/2. No speeds are indicated; those shown in Ex. 15, which gives the openings of each section, are suggested by Roncaglia.

The third work of particular interest in this collection is found at p. 112, and is called *Sonata a 8 viole con una tromba.* The strings are divided into two four-part orchestras instead of concertino and concerto grosso, the 'Primo Choro' and 'Secondo Choro' being equal in weight and constitution. Beneath their eight staves is one for the solo trumpet and one for the *basso seguente.* Each of the four movements bears a written indication of style rather than speed. Noticing the saccadé formula we should probably be right to interpret the second movement as Bach did his fifth fugue in 'The Forty-Eight', which is in the same key— *Pomposo, all'Overtura francese*—for Stradella's is also a prelude to a fugal movement. The openings of the movements are shown at Ex. 16.

[1] Like the work mentioned previously this is 'Sonata' in the Turin copy and 'Sinfonia' at Modena.

15.

Unusual antitheses of instruments, concertato effects and elaborate instructions to players are found in the overtures and sinfonias of several of Stradella's oratorios, serenatas and operas, and the concertino-tutti division is used by him in certain arias—not always so that the concertino shall make a light accompaniment for the voice, but for purely instrumental effect. Both this fact and Stradella's work in general leads to an interesting question. In the previous chapter we discussed stylistic developments which were bound to affect the instrumental ensemble as soon as it was an orchestra, not simply the *più stromenti* mentioned on title-pages between 1620 and 1700. Why did not the orchestral concerto appear earlier? The orchestra was no new invention of the St. Petronio musicians or of Corelli. It made a brilliant debut in France, and when Corelli's concertos were first heard (during the 1680s) an orchestra larger than the minimum he required was available in the opera houses of Venice, Naples, Rome, Milan and even smaller cities. Indeed the most perfect prototypes of Vivaldi's concerto movements were the various kinds of operatic aria with ritornelli, and it is to the opera that we look for advances in orchestral style, since the opera composer does not 'think up' new orchestral techniques; they are demanded by dramatic situations and words. Why did not the first sets of concerti grossi come from Stradella and other opera composers? Why did 'the models' come from Corelli, who is not known to have published music for the theatre?

It is sometimes difficult to read the evidence of history and recognize that men whose thought and taste differed so much from ours were quite as intelligent as we are. Although a genius like Stradella could compose instrumental pieces for the theatre (for oratorios were theatre music) in the form and style of concertos, and though such pieces might be discussed and even played by members of the Academies which existed before the *Accademia Filarmonica*, neither musicians nor public of that age could think of them as concert works. The sinfonia, even a *sinfonia di concerto grosso*, was part of a dramatic entertainment, and it was only as the seventeenth century turned to the eighteenth that listeners in general were growing accustomed to the interchange of the three types of music they knew—church, theatre, chamber. Church and chamber music were greatly indebted to theatre music, but the

church concerto and chamber concerto came directly from works of their own class, from church and chamber sonatas.

Ideally the pre-history of the concerto as a distinct genre should include the pre-history of the sonata as a distinct genre, but even if the present writer were qualified to provide it these pages would be swollen disproportionately. It is necessary, however, to comment upon the broad evolution of sonatas until their movements were similar to those of the first concerti grossi. We should exclude from consideration sonatas composed before about 1665 because their separate movements were rarely long enough to be comparable with the movements of concerti grossi; but for two reasons at least we should comment upon certain composers of sonatas who published in the first half of the century.

The first reason concerns titles. Biagio Marini (*c.* 1597–1665) whose Op. 22, *Diversi generi di Sonate, da Chiesa, e da Camera*, was published at Venice in 1655, has been mentioned by some historians as establishing by this title the contrast between church and chamber sonatas, for he deliberately replaces 'canzona' by 'sonata'. Tarquinio Merula called his Op. 12 of 1636 *Canzoni, overo sonate concertate per chiesa, e camera*. The interesting word here is not 'concertate', for it is frequent during the period, and Merula's own Op. 6 of 1624 is called *Motetti e sonate concertati*, but 'overo'. It tells us that nearly twenty years before Marini's publication Merula equated canzonas and sonatas whether they were performed in church or at a concert. During the second half of the century in Italy an unqualified 'Sonata' usually meant a church sonata, which did not always begin with a slow movement nor include a fugato. Moreover there was a distinct tendency to add 'da camera' when sonatas were not thought suitable for church, or to call them by an entirely different name such as 'Balletti e Correnti' or 'Trattenimenti'.

The second reason for mentioning earlier composers of chamber works is to comment upon their travels. Like some of Corelli's contemporaries, many of them command our admiration for a measure of that adventurous spirit which took Coryate on foot from England to Italy, Constantinople, Agra and Lahore. Marini worked first in Brescia, then took appointments in various German cities and finished in the Venice to which he always seemed most attracted. Merula always published in Venice but he travelled at least as far as Warsaw. These men represent dozens of Italians who incurred risks and hardships comparable with those of modern explorers to remote tracts and primitive peoples, but their migrations were of the utmost importance to our subject of study. Sonatas composed in Italy did not alone prepare the way for the conquest of northern countries by the concerto.

Passing by the Modenese virtuoso, Marco Uccellini, we reach the composer whose sonatas first strike us as having a stature fit for concertos like Torelli's or Corelli's. For sheer quality of workmanship Giovanni Legrenzi (1626–90) outshines all other immediate predecessors of Corelli and Torelli. Handel copied his *Intret in conspectu*[1] and, like Bach, borrowed subjects from him. The fact that he was an organist at Bergamo and Ferrara before his double appointment in Venice (at the Conservatorio dei Mendicanti and at St. Mark's) was no special guarantee that he would be a fine contrapuntist and unwilling to publish trivial music. There is plenty of jejune baroque organ music that is also solemn and contrapuntally stolid, but Legrenzi's mind did not turn constantly to the keyboard. At the Mendicanti he worked as did Vivaldi a few years later at the Pietà, and from 1685 he evidently intended to bring the instrumental music at St. Mark's back to a state worth comparing with that of music at St. Petronio. We know the constitution of the orchestra at St. Mark's after it had been reorganized by Legrenzi—'*8 violini, 11 violette, 2 viole da braccio, 2 viole da gamba, 1 violone, 1 fagotto, 2 cornetti, 3 tromboni, 4 tiorbe.*'[2] The many operas he wrote for Venice and the general excellence of his music link him with Stradella as one of the finest Italian artists between Monteverdi and Vivaldi. Outside the churches a successful composer in Venice had to cater for the taste of Europe's pleasure resort. Chamber music was cultivated, but not as at Bologna. The main musical attractions were the opera houses and St. Mark's. Visitors may already have begun to take an interest in players and singers in the conservatories, for there were Sunday concerts before Vivaldi's day; but the musical atmosphere of Venice was not at all like that of Bologna and Rome. Otherwise Legrenzi and not Corelli might have gone

[1] Royal Library MS., British Museum.
[2] G. Benvenuti, *La musica strumentale in S. Marco*, Milan, 1932. (Istituzioni e monumenti dell'arte musicale in Italia.)

down to history as the patriarch of the concerto, and in that case the concerto would probably have been less distinct from the sinfonia than was Corelli's.

Legrenzi composed a great number of trio sonatas, but some of his sonatas are in as many as seven 'real' and fine parts; and when their design is most ambitious they are often similar to the trumpet pieces and sinfonias composed by Vitali, Colonna, Torelli and Perti for St. Petronio. They have a similar vigour and frequently angular ideas, and they enable us to imagine what the high baroque Italian style might have been if Corelli had not published nor Scarlatti's operas had so great an influence. Only the elder Vitali among the musicians at Bologna approached Legrenzi as a contrapuntist—in the making of fine subjects for fugal treatment and of vigorous countersubjects to go with them.

Legrenzi composed four books containing over sixty sonatas. All except the second book are called *Suonate a due, a tre*, etc. (meaning church sonatas which can also be used at concerts); the second book, Op. 4 of 1656, is called *Suonate da chiesa, e da camera, correnti, balletti, allemande, e sarabande a tre*, and to the general title Legrenzi adds in the last book, Op. 10, Vivaldi's later title, '*La Cetra*' (The Lyre). The only purely chamber sonatas in all Legrenzi's published works are those which share his Op. 4 with church sonatas and independent dances, and each consists only of a 'first' movement. The court musician was expected to make a suite by following this movement with a selection of the dances offered in the same book—one of the allemandes, one of the sarabands, and so on. It is interesting to note that in Muffat's *Florilegium* concerti grossi of 1701, a revision and re-scoring of his *Armonico tributo* sonatas, the composer called a first movement either an overture, a praeludium, a Vorspiel or a sonata, as he wrote his preface respectively in French, in Latin, in German and in Italian.

Though there were minuet-like movements before Legrenzi, the minuet itself, favourite among French dances and often used in vocal airs by Lully, did not seem to be acknowledged in Italy until Vitali introduced it. Vitali's titles are similar to Legrenzi's. His Op. 1 of 1666 reflects his work as director of concerts for the d'Estes at Modena, for it is called *Correnti, e balletti da camera;* his Op. 2 of the following year reflects his work at St. Petronio and is called simply *Sonate a due violini*. (Later he published sets called *Sonate da chiesa* and *Sonate da camera* when the 'da chiesa' was becoming infrequent.) Legrenzi and Vitali have been chosen to represent the tendencies of two generations because both write long movements, bring dignified dance forms into church sonatas, see between them the obsolescence of viols in favour of violins and instruments like them, and show as plainly as does Corelli that pieces suitable for the church, and much needed in the larger churches where instrumental music was played on week-days as well as Sundays, were not composed exclusively for the church. Italians were not alone in this development of the more dignified type of sonata. To go as far north in Germany as possible, we find that sonatas and sinfonias by Buxtehude, composed between 1680 and 1700 partly for use with organ and vocal music at his evening concerts in church, and partly for the delectation of Hamburg and Lübeck merchants, contain dance forms, especially gigues. Pirro[1] tells us that the title of the 1684 set ended with the phrase 'suitable as church or dining-hall music'. (*Tafelmusik*, the description well known to us through Telemann.)

The church sonata gradually absorbed movements based upon the various dance measures that had been first issued with a *nil obstat* from the Louvre. The dance forms attracted serious church composers like Cazzati, Biber, Reinken, Legrenzi and Vitali who were fine contrapuntists, and finally they appeared in church sonatas and concertos by Corelli. The names of dances are not usually mentioned in works of the church type as they are in those of the chamber type, but there are exceptions. For instance in Sonata III of Corelli's Op. 5 the sequence of five movements with an initial adagio and fugued allegro is as expected in the church type, but the final allegro is labelled 'Giga'. Considering the composers just mentioned, we seek a better explanation of this phenomenon than that there was a general trend of taste towards alluring tunes and away from church counterpoint, or that Corelli's pen slipped.

First we should remember that these composers witnessed the final displacement of other instruments by the violin; the majority and the best of their works are for violins, and when violins first came into great popularity they were associated with dances.

[1] André Pirro, *Dietrich Buxtehude*, Paris, 1913.

Lully's brilliant violin ensemble was trained specifically for the performance of ballets and suites of dances while the voices were still accompanied by the viols and lutes which did not rival them. Directly the violins accompanied arias in Italian theatres there was an element of concertato. The orchestra was to the fore in ritornelli and it retired during the sung sections to the position of accompanist except when there was a musical equivalent of stichomythia. The ballet suites of Lully, Campra, Colasse, Desmarets and Destouches spread from France as 'theatre-chamber' music. Their binary or rondo designs with broad key schemes made these dance movements longer than the movements of canzonas, string fantasias and keyboard ricercars, for the Bachian spread came into fugues only when composers had learnt the leisurely key-scheme of sonata and concerto. Movements derived from the dances gave them freedom to spread, to vary their points of climax, to balance their phrases, develop figuration and modulate.

It must have been apparent to Legrenzi and others that, for instance, the first movement of a church sonata could accommodate fugato and counterpoint yet have almost the pace and spread of a staid allemande. Such was the nature of many an initial allegro in a concerto. We can observe this trend in the length and design of movements by inspecting the few sonatas and concerti grossi that are given in the pages of Davison and Apel's anthology. As we turn the pages from Cazzati's *La Pellicana*, No. 219 (with two movements combining imitative counterpoint with the pulsation of dances in 12/8 and 3/8 respectively) to sonatas of the early eighteenth century, the movements grow steadily longer; so they do in concertos—the first allegro of No. 246 by Torelli is sixty-five bars long while that of No. 270 by Vivaldi is ninety bars long. Particularly striking is No. 220, Legrenzi's magnificent *La Busca*, in seven real parts containing much fine counterpoint; in order to secure three fast movements of impressive length Legrenzi interpolates two adagios, the first being five bars long and the second four. Nos. 252 and 253 show contrasted sonatas from Corelli's Op. 5. The word 'Sonata' appeared in all editions at the head of each work in Op. 5, but the Second Part of Op. 5 was issued as *Preludii, Allemande, Correnti, Gighe, Sarabande, Gavotte e Follia*, the First Part as *VI Sonate*.

[62]

Once the concerto grosso had emerged, the contrast between church and chamber types almost disappeared with Corelli, for the orchestra already had its sonata da camera in the French suite; yet the slow-fast opening of the suite seemed to bring in an element of the church sonata. Corelli's, Torelli's, Dall'Abaco's and Albicastro's concertos were all used as chamber music though many of them were used in churches. The prototype of the classical concerto required the confluence of the third species to church and chamber music—theatre music. It came with the second harvest of concertos and with the opera composers of Venice. The shape of the classical first allegro, and of the most frequent form of slow middle movement, awaited the ritornello techniques of the opera aria and various modifications of its ternary scheme of ideas and keys; but we must first examine the kind of concerto grosso that Vivaldi inherited, the sonata-concerto which, without Corelli's sonata-concertino, might have been undistinguishable from a sinfonia with occasional solo parts. From Rome, Corelli produced a form of concerto which we might never have known if he had stayed with the academicians at Bologna; yet in the legacy of Bologna is most fully documented the transition between sonata and concerto, including the transformation of movements from those like canzonas to those like sinfonias.

CHAPTER V

Bologna. School of St. Petronio

Arnold Schering was the first scholar not resident in Bologna fully to recognize the importance of musicians who worked there during the second half of the seventeenth century. Even Sartori considers that 'while Bologna cultivated music with an assiduity that is exceptional among Italian cities, we find there no school of composers to have marked any epoch or any species of composition with striking local idiosyncrasies'.[1] The word 'striking' disarms comment. How idiosyncratic were the symphonies of the elder Stamitz, Holzbauer, Richter and the outstanding founders of what nobody has been unwilling to call 'The Mannheim School' since Riemann first named it? The Mannheimers are thus honoured not because they were highly original but because the classical symphony took many of its characteristics from them. The shape of the classical concerto was largely determined by the trumpet sonatas of musicians working in Bologna nearly a century before the Mannheim orchestra became famous. We should not withhold 'school' because the St. Petronio musicians included no artist of very first rank, nor use it more readily because we now know that Corelli was trained among them. No Mannheimer achieved first rank. In Vienna and outside Germany symphonists rivalled and excelled those of Mannheim even before Haydn and Mozart produced great symphonies.

---

[1] Article on Bologna in *Grove*, 1954.

i. Exterior from the piazza

ii. Interior from the west door

iii. View of the two organs from the corretto

1. BASILICA OF ST. PETRONIO AT BOLOGNA

The two most important centres of composition and performance in Bologna were the basilica of San Petronio and the concerts
and discussions of the Accademia Filarmonica; to them we add an
influential third, the court at Modena. It may well be asked why
St. Petronio, which was neither the cathedral nor the church of a
religious order, became the most important place in an ancient
university city, and why the Accademia Filarmonica, among
many associations for the study and advancement of music,
assumed such authority among local musicians and acquired so
great a reputation throughout Europe that established composers
coveted its diplomas.

Within Bologna, Paris and Oxford, the most famous of the
medieval universities, was a concentration of secular clergy.
Until the nineteenth century all dons at Oxford and Cambridge
were clerics, and even in modern universities there is a tendency
to set up religious communities and colleges within access of arts
and theology faculties. All the important religious orders from
Dominicans and Franciscans to Jesuits had establishments in
Bologna and drew crowds to ceremonies, penitential processions,
preachings, oratorios and plays. The communities maintained
schools, fine churches and musical establishments, and when St.
Petronio rose to outshine the diocesan cathedral and the churches
of the religious orders, its relation to them was in some ways like
that of St. Mary the Virgin at Oxford or Great St. Mary's at
Cambridge to the college chapels and parish churches. In 1700
Bologna had over a hundred and fifty churches.

The humane learning of the renaissance, crowning the medieval and theological learning of Bologna, made it a city of critics
and connoisseurs, many of them genuinely pious but sharing
general pride in the erection of a huge independent church where
the preaching, the music and the setting of occasions and anni-
versaries should be worthy of Italy's oldest and greatest centre of
learning. St. Petronio was planned in the fourteenth century but
not begun until almost the fifteenth. It took 250 years to reach
its present appearance and it was never finished. It immediately
became the chief musical centre of a city which, though associated
with only three famous musicians—Jacopo, Banchieri and Martini—could provide in all epochs the most critical and informed
audience in Europe. A chair of music was set up there in 1450,

E   [65]

and to some of its later occupants, especially Francesco Vatielli, we are indebted for most of the information here.[1]

It was intended that St. Petronio should be larger than St. Peter's in Rome. Lack of money and continual differences of opinion dragged out the work so that only a vast brick nave unfaced by marble was in use until past the middle of the seventeenth century. It must be admitted that the bricks of this area have a beautiful deep red colour which does not turn to drab puce as some of our English red stone does. The warm solemnity of the interior is surprisingly attractive after the gaunt exterior. There was no proper chancel until Cazzati's arrival as director of music, but the high altar stood at the end of the nave, and in front of it on either side were opposed stalls with musicians' galleries for *cori spezzati*, each with an organ. The wish to enlarge the musical establishment was certainly stimulated by the addition of a chancel in the middle of the seventeenth century, though this was not according to the original plan. What was to have been the largest church in Christendom still measures 387 feet. The altar was set under a baldachin at the top of the chancel steps, and the choir was extended behind this altar to an apse which accommodated as many extra players and singers as were desired. Londoners can see the same arrangement on a smaller scale in Westminster Cathedral, though the galleries there lack organs and do not seem to be used for musicians. (They could be so used, and one would like to hear vocal and instrumental *cori spezzati* in that building.)

It was originally intended to face the walls with sculptured marble as at Pisa and Florence, for St. Petronio was to have outshone the cathedral of Florence in splendour. One may be glad

[1] University musicians were put out of office by the suppression of religious educational institutions in the Napoleonic period. To bring into valued employment the *cappelle musicali* and provide for music in the national scheme of education, music schools called *Licei musicali* or *Conservatori* were opened. Unlike the German *Hochschule für Musik* the *Liceo* or *Conservatorio* does not collaborate with a university department of music nor prepare students for university courses in musicology or composition. It deals with what are elsewhere regarded as university courses and music is not a university subject in Italy. Vatielli, for instance, held office in the Liceo Musicale of Bologna, first as Lecturer in Musicology then as Librarian (succeeding Torchi who retired in 1916) and from 1924 as Director until his retirement. The vulgarly misused 'Maestro' is as precise a qualification of the *Liceo* as 'Dottore' of the university.

that the proposed transept, dome and chancel were never built. They would have made the largest church in Europe but not the best for music. By 1425 Della Quercia had enriched the lower part of the western façade with the sculptured doors that are known to many Londoners because of a copy in the Victoria and Albert Museum; but above the doors is still the flat brick wall and plain window. The archives contain fifty of the designs submitted in 1535 for the adornment of an exterior which has remained as attractive as a warehouse or big granary. Inside, however, the wide unadorned piers and dignified vaulting give St. Petronio a grandeur that is striking to eyes that are satiated with more ornate interiors and are unlikely to notice the incongruously tawdry chapels set against the widely-spaced walls. It is difficult to believe that the effect could have been finer if the east end had followed the original plan with dome and transepts separating chancel from nave.

The Pope conferred basilican status upon St. Petronio, and from its opening it became the venue of all solemnities which required music on a grand scale. Its first *maestro di cappella* was Spataro, pupil of Bartolomei Ramos de Pereja, a Spaniard appointed by Pope Nicholas V in 1450 as the first holder of the university chair of music. Early in the sixteenth century lutes and other instruments were used with organs and voices under Spataro's direction, and the music inspired several poets. It is worth mentioning that Cavazzoni came from Bologna, and that though Venice and Rome reaped the creative fruits of the new sixteenth-century art of keyboard playing it was largely disseminated from Bologna. More interesting for our present purposes, however, is Bologna's early love of massed wind instruments. We read of trumpet playing for university, civic and religious functions during the fifteenth and sixteenth centuries. A hundred players of trombones, cornetts, flutes and trumpets, led the wedding procession of Lucrezia d'Este in 1487. (The court of the Este family was at Modena, a short journey to the north-west of Bologna, and its musicians were in frequent contact with those of Bologna. Very often the same musicians served both places for special festivals.) The Bolognese vocal and instrumental 'Concerto Palatino del Senato' became as famous throughout Italy as the concerted music at St. Mark's. It was a public body which

[67]

performed not only for liturgical and academic ceremonial but for pleasure, and its concerts facing the square from the peristyle of St. Petronio continued up to Burney's time.

In Adriano Banchieri (1567–1634) Bologna had an *avant garde* musician who not only admired Giovanni Gabrieli but lived to be a champion and imitator of his successor at Venice, Monteverdi. Banchieri's vast output of dramatic, vocal and instrumental music still remains largely in manuscript, and we should welcome a modern publication of his many literary works. He held no official position at St. Petronio, for he was a monk of 'Monte Oliveto', the popular name for the monastery of San Michele al Bosco, close to Bologna, of which he became abbot. He travelled a good deal, but it is most likely that the basilican cappella performed some of his *concerti ecclesiastici*, especially those which required the *cori spezzati* and the association of instruments with organ continuo, of which subject he was the most notable early exponent. His *Canzoni alla francese* of 1596 and his *Moderna Armonia* of 1612 were influential far beyond Bologna; but probably his most valuable activity for local musicians was his foundation of the first of the Bologna musical academies, the *Accademia dei Floridi*, later incorporated into the *Accademia dei Filomusi* under the St. Petronio director Giacobbi, who gave much attention to the cultivation of the new dramatic recitative. Another institution, the *Accademia dei Filaschisi*, soon superseded it, but in 1666 all were merged into the famous *Accademia Filarmonica*.[1] No musician of Banchieri's calibre adds lustre to the history of Bologna until the ascent of that Bologna School with which we are most concerned here.

Let us begin with a list of its chief members. It is difficult not to include the name of every known member of the St. Petronio cappella, or of the *Accademia Filarmonica*. It is equally difficult to exclude a musician because he is known only as a performer, probably because he printed none of his works. Even if dated evidence does not survive we can assume that every musician mentioned here was a competent composer and a fine string player. Very probably the list should include more names of musicians employed at Modena, but it has been limited to musicians

---

[1] L. V. Tagliavini, *La Scuola Bolognese*, publication of the Accademia Musicale Chigiana, Siena, September 1956.

from Modena who associated with those of Bologna either within St. Petronio for festivals or outside it for private and civic
engagements. The latter explain the publication of *balletti* and
sopnate da camera for many as well as for few instruments. These
would not have been played in church.

Maurizio CAZZATI (1620–77). He was appointed Maestro di Cappella
at St. Petronio in 1657 but had stayed in Bologna before to direct some
of his compositions in other churches. He was born at Guastalla, about
half-way between Bologna and Mantua, and therefore farther north
than Modena. Before settling in Bologna he held a succession of appointments in cities and courts within a short radius of his birthplace—
Mantua, Bozolo, Ferrara, Bergamo. Bologna was fortunate in being able
to offer him the appointment at a time when he knew of none more
attractive farther afield, for instance at Venice where some of his work
was published. On the other hand the Bologna appointment may already
have been held in unusually high esteem or carried unusually good
conditions of tenure. More will be said about Cazzati later, but we may
note here that he published an enormous amount of instrumental music,
and that several of his trio sonatas of the set issued in 1656 are found
in a manuscript collection in the British Museum[1] along with works
by Locke, William Lawes, Jenkins and Christopher Gibbons. He was
almost certainly among the Italian composers with whose work Purcell
claimed acquaintance, and he is mentioned in Roger North's *Memoires
of Musick*.

Giovanni Paolo COLONNA (1637–95). He was born in Bologna,
where his father was an organ builder. He studied first in Bologna,
then in Rome, became organist at St. Apollinare, and returned in 1659
to Bologna as organist at St. Petronio under Cazzati's directorship. He
was four times elected president of the *Accademia Filarmonica* and he
became Cazzati's successor as director at St. Petronio in 1674 when
Vitali went to Modena. His repute as a composer preceded his return
to his native city, for he was the son of an honoured citizen, and his
works, until then liturgical, had all been published by Monti of Bologna.
It is noteworthy that his oratorios and operas were not composed until
after his return. He is sometimes mentioned in connexion with Corelli
because he adversely criticized some of that master's sonatas, the
tediously recurrent point of dispute being some allegedly consecutive
fifths.

Giovanni Maria BONONCINI (1642–78). He came from Montecorona
near Modena and finished his short but brilliant career as director at
the cathedral in Modena. He was the first distinguished musician of a
musical family. Most of his thirteen publications are of chamber works
with such titles as are found just before 'Sonata', 'Concerto grosso' and
'Sinfonia' had become distinct and stabilized. Typical are the following:

[1] Add. 31,431.

Op. 1. *I primi frutti del giardino musicale.* (Sonatas for two violins and continuo. Venice, 1666.)

Op. 2. *Sonate da camera e da ballo,* 1667.

Op. 4. *Arie, correnti, sarabande, gighe e allemande,* 1671.

Op. 9. *Trattenimenti musicali.* (Chamber sonatas for three or four strings with continuo. Bologna, 1675.)

He was for a time at St. Petronio and also a pupil of Colonna. He then became director at St. Giovanni in Monte, and he was a member of the *Accademia Filarmonica* before he returned to Modena where his two sons were born. He is one of the musicians who has been named as 'the creator of the concerto grosso'. None of his printed and numbered publications includes the title 'Concerto', which might have been more frequent if more of the works had been *da chiesa.* There are, however, no general grounds for incredulity at the discovery of a work called 'Concerto grosso' by any composer in this list, nor at the opinion that a sinfonia, sonata, concerto, trattenimento or suite contains movements with the designs and styles of those in a concerto grosso.[1]

Giovanni BONONCINI (1670–1755). He was the eldest son of the preceding and Handel's rival in London, said to have been finally routed by his plagiarism of a madrigal by Lotti. He became chiefly a composer of oratorio and opera, and his work was greatly favoured in Rome and in Vienna. It deserved to be so, but Bononcini's credit has suffered by comparison with Handel's, and by suggestions that he had an arrogant and haughty temper. His bearing in England may have been induced by conditions which he did not seek, for in 1721 he became the hand-somely-remunerated protege of the Marlboroughs and the other families politically ranged against the Hanoverian monarchy and therefore against Handel. On the other hand he may have been spoilt as a youthful prodigy. His first teacher was his father in Modena. He then passed to his father's teacher in Bologna, Colonna, served the St. Petronio estab-lishment as a 'cellist, joined the *Accademia Filarmonica* and, like his father, became musical director at St. Giovanni in Monte. He was in Bologna until the age of 27. He then left for Rome and the first of his operas was composed, but he published through Monti and Silvani of Bologna volumes of chamber sonatas, duets, concertos, sinfonias and suites for many or few instruments, amounting to eight opus numbers, and also wrote three oratorios. His Op. 1 appeared when he was aged 15 (the title-page says 13) and consists of trio sonatas called *Trattenimenti da camera;* but Op. 2 is *Concerti da camera* and Op. 3–6 *Sinfonie* re-quiring as many instruments as a concerto grosso. No doubt this younger Bononcini could be brought forward as 'the creator' of the concerto grosso, or of the symphony, or maybe of the 'true' oratorio!

[1] Bononcini's protectress, the dowager Laura d'Este, regent of Modena, was Mazarin's niece. Her daughter married the future James II of England. Pur-cell's music and Bononcini's have more in common than is easily explained by contemporaneity.

His brother, Antonio Maria Bononcini (1675–1726) went with Giovanni on some of his travels—for instance to Berlin and Vienna—and was also chiefly a composer of oratorios and operas which were greatly admired by Martini. He has often been confused with Giovanni Bononcini and his name is sometimes given as Marc'Antonio. He belongs to Modena (to which he finally returned) rather than to Bologna, in which he is not known to have held any official post.

Giovanni Battista VITALI (1644–92). He was a native of Cremona and had been Cazzati's pupil before Cazzati came to Bologna. He was appointed 'sonatore di violone da brazzo' or, as we might say, leader of the violas, at St. Petronio in 1666. In his day he seems to have been less renowned as a church musician than as a violinist and composer in dance, chamber and secular styles, like the elder Bononcini, for great honour was accorded to the musical director at a brilliant court if he was honoured by his masters. Vitali's appointment at Modena meant more to people outside Bologna than his appointment at St. Petronio, though his church sonatas are as fine as his balletti and pieces in the French manner. He was probably one of Purcell's 'fam'd Italian masters'. When Cazzati left St. Petronio in 1671, Vitali temporarily took over the directorship, but he left within three years to become director at Modena.

Tommaso Antonio VITALI. He was the son of G. B. Vitali and was born in Bologna, where he edited a volume of his father's sonatas and was a member of the *Accademia Filarmonica*. He also worked at Modena and brought the music there to its most brilliant stage under the music-loving dukes Francesco II and Rinaldo I. He is well known to modern audiences by a chaconne which seems to be in the repertory of every solo violinist, but his father's sonatas are much finer works than his own.

Ercole GAIBARA (dates unknown). He was so greatly admired as a violinist and teacher of the violin that he was known by the nickname 'Il Violino'. His pupils include the next two musicians mentioned in this list, who were the teachers of the teen-aged Corelli.

Giovanni BENVENUTI (dates unknown)
Leonardo BRUGNOLI (dates unknown)

They were also the chief instructors in playing and in composition of the two men whose names follow.

Bartolomeo LAURENTI (1644–1726). He published a set of very Corellian sonatas. His son composed concerti grossi.

Pietro degli ANTONII (1486–1720). He was born and died in Bologna, but was director at other churches than St. Petronio. He composed operas and secular ensemble pieces as well as masses, motets and organ works. His importance to other musicians was evidently in leadership, for he was a greatly respected personality, often elected president of the *Accademia Filarmonica* during the years when the concerto grosso spread throughout Italy and Europe. He does not seem to have composed concerti grossi himself, but is important as one of the first to specialize

[71]

in sonatas for a single violin with so rhapsodic and lyrical a melodic line that the organ or harpsichord part is purely a harmonic support. 'Affetuoso' is a characteristic direction on his slow movements.

Petronio FRANCESCHINI (1650–81), b. Bologna, d. Venice. He was a member of the *Accademia Filarmonica* and president in 1673. He was a 'cellist at St. Petronio from 1675 almost until his death in Venice, where he had just gone as musical director at the Ospedaletto. He wrote several operas which were given at Bologna. Perti was his pupil.

Domenico GABRIELLI (1655–90). He was born and he died in Bologna but he studied with Legrenzi. He played in the St. Petronio orchestra and became a member of the *Accademia Filarmonica*. Silvani's title-pages call him 'Sonatore di Violoncello in S. Petronio di Bologna'. His aptitude on the 'cello, like Gaibara's on the violin, earned him a dialectal nickname after the instrument. Alfred Loewenberg in the 1954 *Grove* suggests that one of his manuscripts of 1689 in the library of the Liceo contains what are probably the earliest works for solo 'cello. His published Op. 1 of 1684, *Balletti, gighe, correnti e sarabande*, was for two violins and 'cello with continuo, but like Degli Antonii, he composed well for the solo violin. Some of his oratorios and of his dozen operas were produced in Venice as well as Bologna. He notably contributed to the repertory of the St. Petronio trumpet sonatas.

Giovanni Battista BASSANI (1657–1716). He was born in Padua. After holding an appointment at Modena he came in 1682 to Bologna where he was elected president of the *Accademia Filarmonica*, for he had been a member before he lived at Bologna. He stayed only a short time, for he was director at Ferrara Cathedral from 1688 to 1712 and then at Bergamo, but he probably remained influential in the academy. His compositions include operas, cantatas, oratorios, masses and sets of what were often reprinted as sonatas but were originally called *Suonate da camera* and *Sinfonie a due e tre instrumenti*, the latter being canzona-like and contrapuntal. The statements by Burney and Hawkins that Bassani taught Corelli are now discredited.

Giuseppe Maria JACCHINI. He was a native of Bologna. The date of his birth is unknown, but he served St. Petronio from c. 1690 to his death in 1727 as 'cellist, violinist and singer. Gabrielli and Perti are known to have been among his instructors. He is chiefly interesting for his 'cello sonatas and his friendship with Torelli, and it is noteworthy that all his works, some published in Bologna and some in Modena, are instrumental. They include many sets of sonatas, of which the most interesting are those of his Op. 5 *Trattenimenti per Camera a 2, 4, 5, & 6 strumenti, con alcune a una e due trombe*.

Giuseppe TORELLI (1658–1709). He was born in Verona but came to Bologna and was elected to the *Accademia Filarmonica* in 1684, that is to say before he was appointed at St. Petronio. In 1686 he applied for the post of 'musico di violetta' at St. Petronio. He was violist there when the orchestra was disbanded in 1696 though Burney says he was 'first violin'. After appointments at Ansbach and Vienna he came back to Bologna when the orchestra was reconstituted in 1701 and remained until his death. As much will be said about his concertos no further notes need be made here.

Giacomo Antonio PERTI (1661–1756). He was born and died in Bologna, where he was educated at the Jesuit College and then at the University. After directing his *missa solemnis* at St. Petronio when he was 19, he made his reputation as a composer by some twenty operas which were given at Bologna and Venice, and some even at Milan and Parma. He held an appointment at Modena before being made maestro di cappella in 1690 at St. Pietro, Bologna. He accepted the same office at St. Petronio in 1696—after the disbanding of the regular orchestra, instrumentalists being still engaged on high days. He remained in the post until his death and thus held it for sixty years. Vatielli[1] says that Torelli studied composition under Perti who was the younger. The St. Petronio archives contain a trumpet sonata by Perti dated 1693, thus composed while he was at St. Pietro. He saw the regular orchestra of St. Petronio revived in 1701 but on a smaller scale than formerly.[2] Perti was frequently elected 'principe' of the *Accademia Filarmonica*, and he lived to enjoy the friendship of Martini. His last opera dates from 1717, for his subsequent works were nearly all liturgical.

Pirro ALBERGATI (Count Capacelli), (1663–1735). He was born and died in Bologna, and is a fine example of the aristocratic amateur who had the professional skill of a maestro di cappella. Over a dozen of his oratorios were performed and he benefited from his admiration both of Corelli and of Vivaldi. He published *Sonate da camera* for two violins and continuo in 1687, and *Concerti da camera* in 1702.

Giuseppe ALDROVANDINI (1665–1707). He was born and died in Bologna, being elected 'principe' of the *Accademia Filarmonica* in 1702. His early reputation was as a composer of operas, first chiefly comic; but after 1700 he published trio sonatas in Bologna and Amsterdam, and also concertos, including some with solo violin and some with solo 'cello. He contributed to the trumpet sonatas.

Evaristo DALL'ABACO of Verona (1675–1742). His concertos are often coupled with Torelli's in critical commentaries. He worked at the court of Modena from 1696 to 1701, after which he took up an appointment at Munich where he died. His published works are entirely instrumental. Like Corelli's they reach six opus numbers. Three are sets of trio sonatas (da chiesa and da camera) and three are sets of concertos.

Arcangelo CORELLI (1653–1713). His printed designation 'Il Bolognese' will be discussed later. Let it suffice to enrol him with the Bologna School because he did so himself, having studied under Benvenuti and Brugnoli.

---

[1] *Arte e vita musicale a Bologna* (Bologna, 1927).

[2] Jean Berger's statement in *The Musical Quarterly*, vol. xxxvii, no. 3, July 1951, 'No more trumpet sonatas are found after 1695' should be taken as 'No trumpet sonatas bear a written date beyond 1695'. Several such works were printed in Bologna after 1695, e.g. Alberti's. Torelli also composed several for the reconstituted orchestra.

Giuseppe Matteo ALBERTI (1685–1751). He was born and died in Bologna, but he was so much the junior of composers previously mentioned in this list that we need some justification for including him in it. In fact he lived late enough to compose some popular and somewhat stereotyped concertos which were much played in England in the middle years of the eighteenth century. We mention him here, however, because of his contributions to the Bolognese trumpet pieces, some of which must have been composed while he was still in his teens.

The importance of this incomplete list lies not in its size but in the quality of the musicians. They were, as Burney said of the Mannheim players, 'an army of generals'. Even at the height of Bologna's musical reputation in the 1690s the actual cappella of St. Petronio was not as large as that of St. Mark's, and where we find multiple copies of parts we know that they were for extra players. The music cannot have sounded as loud as some of the music heard in the much smaller St. Mark's, and never as loud as the music in Rome, which by the middle of the century had further inflated the polychoral technique of Venice to the detriment of other qualities than size, and earned a niche in history labelled 'colossal baroque'. The climax of flatulence was reached with Benvoli's Mass for the consecration of Salzburg Cathedral. It required six instrumental *chori*, including three of brass, two eight-part vocal choirs, soloists and organs. (See *DTO*, vol. xx.) In St. Mark's the listener must have been reminded of the wealth and grandeur of Venice, for the musicians were part of the Doge's retinue of state, and it is noteworthy that when Monteverdi, who could have outblazed even Gabrieli (and did so in the 1610 *Vespers*) took over the directorship at St. Mark's, he pleased the clerical curators by such conservative and aptly liturgical works as the Advent mass *In illo tempore* and by restoring staid solemnity to the routine services. The St. Petronio music was that of a religious and academic body. The players wore no grand uniforms and could hardly be seen during service. Outside St. Petronio their reputation was chiefly as composers of chamber music, especially solo sonatas and *balletti*. The Bolognese publishers, Monti and Silvani, reprinted much of their work several times, and at least four of them had further editions issued in Antwerp or Amsterdam.

It would be scarcely an exaggeration to say that the instrumental concerto was produced in St. Petronio at the hands of the *Accademia Filarmonica*, whose activities were largely centred upon the basilica. Until they had their own building near Martini's church of San Francesco they held their meetings in the room at St. Petronio behind the choir, now used as the archive, or sometimes in the *coretto* or chapter room beneath the place for the orchestra in the apse. Undoubtedly, too, the arrangement of the St. Petronio choir and the contrasting characters of the two organs expedited the ascendance of the concerto. The older organ, made by Lorenzo da Prato, dates from 1475, and is on the right-hand side as one faces the apse. (The original pipes are all still functioning in this renowned monument of the gothic organ maker.) A new organ was placed on the opposite side in 1596, being of a lighter and brighter tone 'per maggior commodo, et servigio del choro et della musica'. It was the work of Baldassare Malamini, who was evidently instructed to build an instrument well suited for continuo accompaniment. By 1659, two years after Cazzati's arrival and at the beginning of the famous period of instrumental music, the present high altar had been set up at the top of the chancel steps with the choir behind it, the apse being unfinished until 1666. Then, presumably, the organs were rebuilt and revoiced in their new positions before the fine baroque cases were supplied in 1675.

The spacing of the stalls and music galleries and everything affecting the music were determined by 1675, and they have remained unchanged. Two organists can still play a transcription of a concerto grosso with excellent echo or tutti-concertino effects. It is interesting to note that what had been called formerly the new organ, on the gospel side, was called the *organo del concertino* during the seventeenth century. It was used with vocal or instrumental soloists and for all small groups, for instance in sonatas.[1] The heavier organ on the epistle side was probably used for ripieno sections when there were many players. There are nearly always two figured bass parts for St. Petronio works that require more than a few instruments.[2] No doubt the heavier organ was

[1] Information taken partly from Vatielli's article 'Il Concerto Palatino della Signoria di Bologna' in *Atti e Memorie della R. Deputazione di Storia Patria per l'Emilia e la Romagna*, vol. v, 1939, and partly from G. Zucchini's *Guida della Basilica di San Petronio*, 1925.

[2] For the trumpet pieces after 1680 there are often several cello and violone (double bass) parts and two or three for the *tiorbe* or archlutes, as well as the organ parts with figures. Never were the bass and continuo sections weak.

always chosen for solo organ music and to accompany the full vocal ensemble.

There had for long been dialogues of soloists as well as antiphony of choirs at Bologna before the regular instrumental music became famous, and the terms 'concerto grosso' and 'concertino' were applied to vocal as well as instrumental music. We see them, for instance, on the manuscript of a *Lauda Syon* in the library of the Liceo, regarded as the original copy of a work by Canniciari, who became director at Palestrina's church, Santa Maria Maggiore, in Rome. There are also many references during the seventeenth century, both at Bologna[1] and elsewhere, to full and distant choirs—*cori ripieni* and *cori lontani*.

The decisive event for music in Bologna was the arrival of Cazzati in 1657. He had held several ducal and civic directorships and he enjoyed considerable reputation as a composer in Italy north of Rome. Although his oratorios appeared after he came to Bologna, that city is said by Vatielli to have used his *Salmi e Messa a 5 voci e 2 violini* (Venice, 1641) and his *Canzone a 3, due violini e violone* (1642). He subsequently published sonatas for strings with organ. In the year before his arrival he published his most popular work, *Suonate a due violini*, *Op* 18, and it was re-issued twice during his lifetime. Wise after the events, we might notice a new interest in instrumental music after Cazzati's appointment, but it was not peculiar to Bologna. The almost immediate enlargement of the musical establishment at St. Petronio is understandable as an act of confidence in a brilliant new director, for Cazzati did not apply for the post; he was asked to take it. The old director at St. Petronio, Bertelli, had announced his intention to retire, and Cazzati owed his election largely to his reputation as a choirmaster and to the fact that some of his works had been performed and greatly admired in St. Salvatore at Bologna. Probably Cazzati directed them and secured fine singing and playing, and though under Cazzati the instrumental music became the chief matter for admiration, we could trace from soon after 1660 in many a city of Italy and Germany, in churches and outside them, a growing taste for the instrumental ensemble and for expert solo performance.

[1] An early example at Bologna is the preface to Giacobbi's *Salmi concertati*, 1609.

From records of payment in the St. Petronio archives we may notice that the fine musicians whose appointment Cazzati secured were not engaged just for festivals. Some of the best playing could have been heard on ferial Sundays and week days. For *occasioni*, ceremonies which would not bring the expense of extra musicians upon the church exchequer, and for *funzioni*, chiefly on the high days of the church kalendar, St. Petronio had previously augmented the choir and orchestra, and the practice of hiring musicians continued after the regular orchestra was disbanded (apparently because it was too costly) between 1695–1701. The neatly-kept minutes show that there were sometimes as many as eighteen extra musicians, called either *musici* or *pagati* (paid); but there is another appellation that can easily be misunderstood. In modern English the word 'dilettante' is hardly honorific, but it was so in Italy during the seventeenth and eighteenth centuries. Albinoni did not style himself 'dilettante Veneto' in pride of a private income from his father's paper mill, nor in respectful tribute to Vivaldi, but to claim his rank as a musician by a word almost meaning 'virtuoso'. It is true that 'dilettante' also had the social status of the contemporary English 'gentleman'. Benedetto Marcello, Albinoni's contemporary at Venice, was 'dilettante', but Vivaldi was 'musico', despite his clerical status, until his renown made him 'musicista'. Gaibara, the Vitalis, Perti and Torelli were 'musici'; Count Albergati could take fees yet still be 'dilettante', and it is important to know that this title is not accurately translated 'amateur'. The Count earned it because he was a fine performer, not simply because he was an aristocrat who patronized music. The derivation is from *delectans*, giving pleasure, delighting.

The university, the colleges of religious orders and the noble or wealthy families in and near Bologna abundantly supplied *dilettanti* and pupils of the *musici*. Players of the calibre we know to have been employed in the regular establishment would not have tolerated admixture with players whose intonation or attack spoilt their own. We should not be misled by accounts of large occasional orchestras (for instance those assembled by the Queen of Sweden for Corelli) into supposing that churches, theatres, or even princely musical establishments during the seventeenth century regularly employed more than six to a dozen players.[1] The Twenty Four, the other French royal band under Lully, and the band which Charles II modelled upon it were exceptional. Royal and ducal orchestras in Italy and Germany were nearly doubled during the first decades of the eighteenth century but they remained small during the seventeenth.

Evidently the St. Petronio festival orchestra was a large one in the eighteenth century, though the regular one was smaller than in 1695. Vatielli quotes figures from several sources, including a diary kept by the historian Barilli (Univ. of Bol. Lib., MS. 225), which show the size of the augmented orchestras in Torelli's time, i.e. after the disbanding and reconstituting of the regular orchestra. In 1709 Perti sometimes directed a choir and orchestra of 180; on at least one occasion in 1716 Torelli led 123 players in some of his concertos, and 131 in the following year. There is no record of these huge numbers for the 1680s and 1690s, the great years of the trumpet sonatas, and we may suppose the players very rarely to have exceeded from sixteen to twenty.[2] Even so, Bologna was exceptionally favoured, and Cazzati was the man chiefly responsible for its good fortune. The abnormal output of Bolognese works for string ensemble was in full spate during his directorship.

It would be false to give Cazzati the honour as a composer that he deserves as a leader, or to offer the safely vague opinion that he 'laid the foundations' of the musical style which led to Corelli's or Torelli's sonatas and concertos. Corelli's suave clarity and breadth is anticipated rather in the arias and sinfonias of Cavalli, Cesti and other theatre composers than in canzona-sonatas by church composers; but as a composer Cazzati was more talented than most maestri da cappella and he deserved the esteem that he enjoyed. Two of his sonatas are available in modern editions,[3]

[1] William Klenz's *Giovanni Maria Bononcini of Modena* recently issued by Duke University Press (Durham, N. Carolina) admirably reveals the musical resources and conditions of work at the d'Este court and Cathedral of Modena.

[2] Triplicate first and second violin parts are found for some of the trumpet works but rarely more than three copies. Two or at most three violinists would share a desk. As there are several awkward page turns in the violin parts they can hardly have been taken by single players.

[3] Sonata 9 from Op. 18 (1656) is available from Schott, ed. Danckert. *HAM*, vol. ii, no. 219, gives one of the 'Sonate a due instrumenti cioè violino e violone, op. 55' (1670).

the later of them in Apel and Davison's anthology along with sonatas by Vitali, Corelli and Torelli. By comparison even with Corelli's Op. 1 they reveal Cazzati's age and stylistic conservatism. The short sections, the frequent contrapuntal imitations between the violin and the bass and the themes which, in deference to church tradition or in order to accommodate imitation, are not particularly idiomatic for the violin, remind us of organ canzonas. Yet if some of the movements were played by an organist we should know that his instrument was already influenced by exchange of idioms. (Unfortunately we lack complete parts of the Cazzati pieces in the seventeenth-century collections at the British Museum.)

Cazzati resigned after a distressing feud with the organist, composer and academy president, G. C. Arresti. It began with a pedantic discussion of the *stile osservato* or 'strict counterpoint', the theorist-made rules of which have been wrangling points from Palestrina's day to ours. Arresti objected to a Kyrie by Cazzati, and the quarrel was much publicized in pamphlets issued by both contestants. (These are preserved in the library of the Liceo at Bologna.) The contestants even went to the expense of printed music illustrations.

Cazzati himself contributed to the repertory of the trumpet sonatas which are the most important precursors of Torelli's concerti grossi. Only a few of these works are in score, a fact which Dr. Jean Berger[1] takes as an indication that they were not played outside St. Petronio. Cazzati may have composed more than three, but only three by him have been discovered, and they have the distinction of being in print as the last three of his Op. 35 sonatas of 1665. These are, of course, church sonatas such as were also enjoyed at concerts. The trumpet parts bear the permission: 'Per mancanza di Tromba, si può sonare con un Violino', which suggests that trumpet sonatas were not common outside the basilica. Yet trumpet sonatas were written by at least one composer who was not a member of the St. Petronio establishment, for Monti published in 1682 a set of sonatas in two, three, four and five parts by Andrea Grossi, a violinist employed at the Mantuan court; they are very like the Op. 35 sonatas of Cazzati,

---

[1] Jean Berger: 'Notes on Some 17th-century Compositions' in *The Musical Quarterly*, vol. xxxvii, July 1951.

and the five-part ones include the trumpet. As they were published at Bologna they may, of course, have been used in St. Petronio but there are no copies in the archive. On the other hand St. Petronio seems to have parts of only one of Cazzati's trumpet sonatas.

Even today we use the triadic intervals of the harmonic series to make a trumpet characteristically bold, festive and ceremonious —in short, trumpet-like—and when the notes are not 'open' the natural intervals are imitated if the trumpet is to sound characteristic. Natural instruments in D, the key of all these pieces, can participate in several forms of approach to cadence in the keys of D, A and G. The Bolognese trumpet parts lie in the clarino register, the normal compass being from the D above middle C to the D two octaves higher. Evidently technique was much developed in the last decades of the century, for Cazzati does not exceed the octave from A to A. Nevertheless his trumpet sonatas are markedly less polyphonic, less canzona-like, than his others.

Except chromatic ideas, which were rarely given to trumpets before the nineteenth century, none could be less idiomatic for trumpets than those of the fluid, interweaving phrases of vocal polyphony, viol fantasias and the fugato sections of church sonatas. Moreover the trumpeter needs short rests even in less high and brilliant parts than were written at Bologna. Therefore the traditional associations of the trumpet with fanfares and consideration of its technique gave Bolognese sonatas the short, bold themes which end crisply even when two or more trumpets overlap their phrases. Such themes naturally suggest concertato, echoes and restatements between strings and trumpets, accentual rhythms, developments with the ♪♪ figure (which became ubiquitous in the Vivaldian concerto), strongly metrical basses rather than those to which one mentally adds slurs when playing fugues, and recurrent cadential formulae. In short, the trumpet pieces expedited the drift of style away from the canzona and ricercar towards the military aria, the opera sinfonia and the concerto grosso.

The later and more brilliant Bologna trumpet pieces are usually called *sinfonie*, occasionally *concerti*, but this word should be regarded simply as the alternative to *sonate*. There is yet no proof that it became distinctive until the concerto grosso was recognized

i. Sinfonia con due trombe

ii. Concerto a due chori con trombe

2. MANUSCRIPT SCORES OF TRUMPET PIECES BY TORELLI

as a genre.[1] There may, however, be a reason for Perti's and Torelli's use of 'sinfonia' instead of 'sonata' to designate some of the last among these St. Petronio pieces—not that they use two, three, even four trumpets, but that the first and last movements, those which invariably include the trumpets, 'abandon imitative counterpoint in favour of the presentation of thematic material in the most precise concerted fashion'.[2] When composing for the church Jacchini, Perti, Torelli and Corelli evidently associated 'sonata' with the canzona tradition of fugued sections. Torelli may introduce a fugued section for relief while the trumpet or trumpets are silent.

Whatever name was given to these trumpet pieces at Bologna, many of them were concertos, not merely precursors of concertos. Within the trumpet pieces of one composer we can trace the development from a sonata to a concerto conception. At Ex. 17 are openings of movements in Domenico Gabrielli's *Sonata a sei con tromba*. The first movement is not at all like that of an eighteenth-century concerto nor like a sinfonia, despite the *f-p* effect; it belongs to the church sonata and may be one of the composer's early works. Very different is the *Sonata con tromba* by him from which Ex. 18 is quoted. We show the last few bars of an expectant initial tutti closing in the tonic while the trumpet remains silent. This initial tutti became the rule with Vivaldi and the Venetian composers associated with him, for it was the source of ritornelli. The only conservative feature in this piece is the tenor viol part, as in Cazzati's scores. Presumably tenor parts were written while good violists were still employed.

Perti was quite the most vital composer of the trumpet pieces except Torelli himself. It is difficult for modern ears not to find the harmonic vocabulary of late seventeenth-century and early eighteenth-century minor composers limited, especially if they are English ears which judge by comparisons with Purcell. Without the discords of polyphony even the music of Perti and Torelli seems simple, but this very simplicity was new and exciting when it was first heard. Perti's and Torelli's *Sinfonie con due trombe* (Ex. 19 and 20) are evidently later works than those we

---

[1] It may yet be discovered that the trumpet pieces called concerti were composed after Torelli's concerti grossi.

[2] Jean Berger, Op. cit.

18.

D. Gabrielli. Sonata a sei con tromba.

[From bar 4 of opening Allegro]

TR.

6 6

6 6 6 2

19. Allegro e spicco

G. Perti. Sinfonia con 2 trombe. D. iv. 1.

Piano

Forte

Trumpets

Largo. [Str. & org.]

po.

For.

Allegro

Vns.

Trumpets

Str. org.

[83]

20.

G. Torelli. Sinfonia con due trombe.
St. Petronio, L.15.A.

have quoted from Gabrielli. Both composers often use the initial
tutti and both abandon five-part string texture to secure a clear,
grand harmony of the kind we associate with Vivaldi or Handel.
Five-part texture became infrequent in Italy when their generation passed and tenor violists were scarce. We meet five-part work
notably in Lully, in some of Purcell's odes, and where it persisted
longest in chamber music, the suites of Muffat and other south
German composers. Yet Gabrielli's five parts are not polyphonic;
three of them are conceived as the harmonic middle between a
strong bass and a high-lighted soprano which becomes a brilliantly sharp profile at the trumpet entries. Purcell's solo trumpets
often add a fifth part to his harmony.

The Bologna trumpet pieces which are not only called sinfonias
but have the general design of the opera sinfonia are compressed,
probably to prevent the solo trumpeters from tiring. Dr. Berger
has written of 'Perti's miniature sinfonias'. The Perti sinfonia
quoted at Ex. 19 is as clearly a concerto as any by Torelli for two
violins. The trumpets do not immediately take part in or restate
an idea sonata-wise; with material that has not been heard during
the initial tutti, they flourish precisely as two violins might do in

a Vivaldi concerto until the first ritornello restates the opening bars. This work is in beautiful manuscript score. The bass stave is labelled 'Violone o Tiorba, Violoncello, Trombone, Bissone, Tiorba', and there are figures both under the 'Violone o Tiorba' and the 'Tiorba' parts, probably for the two St. Petronio organs. 'Bissone' is not a misprint for *bassone* or an alternative for *fagotto*, but a dialect form of *biscoine* (a large snake), the same sort of instrument as Handel heard in England. ('That was nod der serpent that did Eve beguile.') The trombone and bissone play in all three movements.

The trumpet parts at the openings of the first and last movements of Torelli's sinfonia approach very closely the introductions to the many cantata choruses by Bach which follow concerto designs, voices replacing the solo or concertino sections. More of the St. Petronio trumpet pieces are by Torelli than by anybody else and, but for Corelli's connexion with Bologna, we should regard Torelli as the key figure in the emergence of the concerto grosso from the church sonata; yet his later trumpet works for St. Petronio advance less towards his concerti grossi for strings than towards the theatre sinfonia. For instance, he introduces pairs of oboes to echo and converse with pairs of trumpets, and some of his sinfonias require four trumpets, working in pairs and combining only at final cadences. Plainly when Torelli wrote concerti grossi another side of his imagination came forward—that of the violinist who was probably disappointed at being forced to serve so long as a violinist. Fortunately there is documentary proof that Bologna was influenced by the concerti grossi of Rome, and therefore the Bolognese string concerto needs a separate chapter.

A critic who inspected the parts for violins and solo trumpet at the opening of the movement quoted at Ex. 21 and assigned the work to the years between 1710 and 1720 could not be thought a poor connoisseur of period style. Vivaldi or one of the Germans who admired him might thus have constructed the opening of a concerto for a solo wind instrument. Indeed as Alberti was one of the younger men of the group with which we have just dealt, this *Sonata con Trombe e Violini* could be an eighteenth-century piece. After 1701 only string players regularly played at St. Petronio but we know that there were occasionally very large augmentations. It so happens, however, that this is one of the many

[85]

Bologna manuscripts upon which the date of composition is written unmistakably in the same hand and ink that wrote the music,
and it bears the date '20.x.1705'. We need no clearer proof that
the whole transition from canzona sonata to solo concerto is
represented by the St. Petronio composers.[1]

Our last quotations from the trumpet pieces are taken from the
'cellist Jacchini because he was the youngest of Perti's and Torelli's outstanding players. He also furnished at least one exception
to Dr. Berger's general rule that the trumpet pieces were not
printed or disseminated because 'they were used only in the
basilica'. They were probably played at sessions of the *Accademia
Filarmonica*, and though the parts of Jacchini's sonatas with one
or two trumpets are preserved in the basilica, they were published
by Silvani in 1703 as *Trattenimenti per camera*. In most of them
the slow middle movement requires a 'cello solo, and many of the
title-pages specify *Violini unissoni, e Violoncello obligato*. The
order of the published sonatas may be the order of composition,
but this seems most unlikely, for the first is very much a concerto
while the fifth is a church sonata with several changes of movement. The quotations can speak for themselves. (Ex. 22, 23.)

Though effective for their setting and occasions, few of the
trumpet works at St. Petronio are thematically memorable or
highly personal. There is no evidence that they were performed
or imitated far from Bologna, for when Lully introduces the solo
trumpet in his operas he seeks the swaggering effect in a march
or finale, not in a piece on the scale of a sonata. English trumpet
tunes or trumpet voluntaries were more likely to have been suggested by French than Italian music of the seventeenth century,
and none of Purcell's trumpet overtures is quite like a Bologna
piece or a Venetian *sinfonia avanti l'opera*. A manuscript in York
Minster Library, entitled 'Sonata by Mr. Hen: Purcell', though
recognizably English in style, resembles some of the earlier
Bologna trumpet sonatas in design. There are three movements,
of which only the second has any tempo indication—'Trumpet
rest all ye Adagio'. The beginning of this work is shown at Ex. 24.

The St. Petronio trumpet works are important because their
movements become as long, and include just as admirable lengths
of paragraph, as those in the first published sets of concerti grossi,

[1] Probably the father of the G.M. Alberti mentioned on p. 74.

23.

Jacchini. Sonata Quinta con Tromba. (Silvani 1703)

24.

the composers of which undoubtedly were influenced by them even if they did not all contribute to them. They have been liberally quoted because they are not widely known, yet they tell us that works which were really concertos were enjoyed long before concerti grossi for strings were in print.

CHAPTER VI

Corelli and His Contemporaries

The St. Petronio trumpet works cover the period during which Corelli performed his concerti grossi in Rome. Sartori and Pincherle[1] collected convincing evidence that Muffat was either correct or not far wrong in declaring that he heard concerti grossi under Corelli's direction in 1682. We do not know that these were the concertos which Berardi heard in the 1680s or the identical concertos issued by Roger in 1714 as Corelli's Op. 6, but we do know that concerti grossi were recognized as a new genre of church and chamber music during the last years of the seventeenth century.

Torelli's trumpet sinfonias do not differ from his Op. 8 concerti grossi in general design and style. Even the idiomatic difference between trumpet and violin is less than it would have been earlier or later in history. Vivaldi used the direction *violino in tromba* (violin like a trumpet) and made double stops sound like a fanfare for two trumpets.[2] Themes in many Italian concertos of the early eighteenth century, seeming to call for the 'quasi tromba' interpretation, so clarified style that listeners forgot the canzona and polyphonic fantasia but may have been reminded of trumpet

---

[1] Claudio Sartori, 'Le quarantaquattro edizioni delle sei opere di Corelli', *RMI*, vol. lv, 1953. Marc Pincherle, *Corelli et son Temps*, Paris, 1954, p. 207.

[2] Dr. Peter Evans drew my attention to *Sonata ad imitatione della trompetta* composed by Matteis, *c.* 1685, copy in Durham Cathedral Library. Eitner mentions a 'Concert for 3 Trumpetts' by this composer.

sinfonias and overtures to operas, or of the trumpet obbligato in arias and choruses dealing with princely or military glory. Openings of concerto movements which were printed early in the eighteenth century are shown at Ex. 25. They are chosen from movements in D, the key of Italian trumpets. This key might have suggested *violini in trombe*, but one could have collected similar ideas from concertos in any major key. Vivaldi alone provides us with hundreds of themes in which occur the repeated notes of trumpet calls or the fanfare intervals; they are found even in the suave Corelli who may never have written for the trumpet.[1]

Pincherle and others missed one interesting and conclusive piece of evidence that Bologna was fully aware of the Corellian form of string concerto nearly thirty years before printed parts of Corelli's concertos were in circulation. At Modena (in the State Archive, not the Estense Library) there is a letter by Perti written to G. B. Gardini. It is dated 10, iii, 1687, and contains the passage: '. . . *l'Oratorio è a 6 voci, con concertino, e concerto grosso, all'usanza di Roma, ed anche vi è obligata la Tromba. . . . Vi è necessario quantità di stromenti, e l'invenzione è nuova nei nostri Poeti.*[2] No musicians in Europe were more likely to discuss new music given in the cities of Italy than the academicians of Bologna.

The following list of publications covers a period of some twenty years during which the title 'Concerto Grosso' was intended to distinguish this disposition of the orchestra:

[1] I am unable to trace 'One isolated work by Corelli at the British Museum (*Sonata con 2 disc. e tromba*) which emphasises Corelli's indebtedness to his Bolognese training' (Jean Berger, op. cit.). In his Walsh bibliography W. C. Smith quotes an entry from *The Post Man*, April 27–9, 1704, advertising 'A Sonata for two Violins and a thorow Bass with a Trumpet part by Arcangelo Corelli, as also a new Solo for a Violin and a Bass by Martino Beity (i.e. Bitti), neither of them before printed.' Trinity College of Music possesses a Walsh publication with the title page dated 1704: 'Sonata in D for violins in 3 parts . . . as also a solo for a violin by Sig. Martino Betti neither of them before printed . . .'. This seems to be what was advertised in *The Post Man*. See No. 150 of Walsh's musical publications in W. C. Smith's *A Bibliography of the Musical Works Published by John Walsh during the Years 1695–1720*, Oxford, 1948. The following advertisement appeared in *The Daily Courant* on 16 March 1712: '. . . Likewise several pieces of musick proper for the Trumpet, particularly a sonata composed by Signior Corelli on purpose for Mr. Twiselton when he was in Rome.'

[2] This letter is quoted by Leonida Busi in his *Il Padre G. B. Martini*, Bologna, 1891.

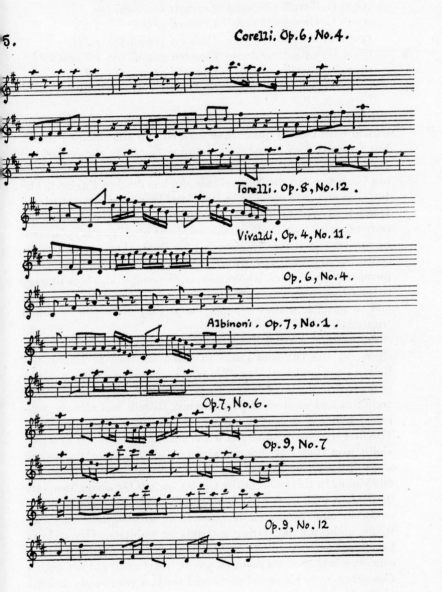

1698, G. Torelli (Bologna) *Concerti musicali, Op. VI.*
      L. Gregori (Lucca)   *Concerti grossi.*
1709, G. Torelli   *Concerti grossi, Op. VIII.*
1710, G. Valentini (Rome) *Concerti grossi, Op. VI and VII.*
1714, A. Corelli (Rome)   *Concerti grossi, Op. VI.*
1715, A. Scarlatti (Naples) *Sinfonie di concerto grosso.*

We notice a change of title when we reach a composer more concerned with theatre music than with church and chamber music, but Scarlatti does include the defining term. By the end of the period thus covered, concertos were enormously popular throughout Germany and the Netherlands and had reached England. The full title was soon dropped in Italy, and its use by Geminiani and Handel, as well as by later Italians than Corelli who were not composing for Italy itself, usually implied Corelli's outlay of instruments—it was normally discarded for flute, oboe and solo violin concertos and retained only with the Corellian concertino. It was never used by Vivaldi, whose most famous collections bore literary titles—*L'estro armonico*, *La stravaganza*, *Il cimento*, *La cetra* and so on; when they did not do so they were simply called 'concerti'.

Following the Stradella pieces, which were surely heard or discussed in the Ottoboni circle in Rome as well as among the Bologna academicians, Corelli and Torelli printed their concerti grossi with prefatory instructions upon the disposition of the orchestra and method of performance. Torelli had already published *Concerti a quattro, Op. 5* and *Concerti musicali, Op. 6*. The first were string quartets with continuo, dominated by a first violin part that was thought virtuosic at the time; the second were distinctly orchestral and some of them included parts for solo violin. In this set as in the Op. 8 *Concerti Grossi* occur square figurations which are a mark of Torelli's authorship. (Ex. 26.)

Corelli and Torelli wished their title to designate works for string orchestra, not string quartets or quintets. The style of Corelli's concertos is that of his sonatas, and the style of Torelli's concertos is that of his trumpet pieces, yet Torelli did not entitle *Concerto Grosso* his most fully scored work, a grand-scale sinfonia of the kind beloved in Venetian opera houses, and evidently in those of Naples too, for we have pieces from Scarlatti of the same type. Scarlatti does not exceed two trumpets; Torelli's sinfonia uses four, along with pairs of oboes and bassoons, the string ensemble and the continuo of both the St. Petronio organs. Yet Torelli's instruments here make their pattern *within or upon the ensemble*, as in a Mannheim symphony, whereas in the texture of the new concerti grossi the solo instruments were *regularly confronted by the ensemble*.

Torelli's Concerti Grossi were printed posthumously but their foreword suggests that the composer had prepared them for publication:

'Gentle Reader: Here is my eighth humble work so far printed which I hope may receive the same approval from you as did previous ones. Let me warn you that in playing these concertos of mine it is necessary that the violins of the concertino be alone, with no doubling, to avoid greater confusion. If, however, you wish to double the other instruments supporting, you can, for actually that is my intention.'[1]

He says that in concertos 3, 5, 6, 7 and 12 there must be violas, but that in the others the viola part is optional. (*Obbligato . . . beneplacito.*) If a double bass (violone) is not available, the archlute may be used instead. On the title-pages of the instrumental parts of the first six concertos are printed the words *con due violini che concertano soli*, and on those of the last six *con uno violino che concerta solo*.

After his Italian tour of 1770, Burney wrote of Torelli:

'This author, who was a member of the Philharmonic Academy of Bologna and the first violin of the church of San Petronio in the same city, published seven different works for violin and left behind him an eighth opera, which was published by his brother Felice Torelli after the author's decease, under the title of *Concerti Grossi con una Pastorale per il Santissimo Natale*, consisting of twelve concertos in eight parts, which has been thought the best

[1] British Museum:
'CORTESE LETTORE, Eccoti l'ottava mia debolfaticha (debole fatica) data sin hora alle stampe, che fidato sù la speranza d'aver riportato un cortese compatimento nelle altre, non dispero d'incontrare simil fortuna in questa. Avvertendoti, che volendo sonare questi miei Concerti, è neccessario, che i Violini del concertino sijno SOLI, senza verun radopiamento, per evitar maggior confusione, che se poi vorrai moltiplicare gl'altri Stromenti di rinforzo, questa si è veramente la mia intentione, e vivifelice.'

of his works and the model of grand concertos for a numerous band.'

We know that Torelli left St. Petronio for appointments at Ansbach and Vienna when the regular orchestra at Bologna was disbanded in 1696. According to the Bologna records he had not played first violin but viola, and at first he was appointed player of the *violetta* which he soon exchanged for the larger *viola tenore*. The St. Petronio pay books note that he was 'often absent', but after his return in 1701 to the reconstituted orchestra under his friend Perti he seems to have become the doyen of Bologna musicians until his death in 1708. The Op. 8 concerti grossi with the Christmas Concerto were published in the following year, and Burney is right in calling the printed sheets posthumous. They were evidently well known already, for it is difficult not to believe that they had an influence upon Albinoni's concertos, published in 1700, as they certainly had upon Dall'Abaco's.

Whatever the esteem in which they were held locally and beyond Italy, according to the last sentence in the extract from Burney's *Present State of Music*, they did not receive the great acclaim with which Corelli's Op. 6 was greeted. There must be many reasons for this—that Corelli had an unprecedented fame as a performer, that he directed concerts in the presence of the most exalted personages and their visitors to Rome, that he lived at the Ottoboni Palace whither notables and music lovers resorted, both Italian and foreign, that he published in Rome, that the concertos were already admired, having circulated in manuscript despite the composer's caution, and having been performed at such notable concerts as that with the Queen of Sweden's special orchestra of a hundred and fifty players. Whether the actual Op. 6 concertos were played on that occasion or not, their publication must have been eagerly awaited.

Surely the outstanding reason for Corelli's huge success is that listeners recognized in each of his publications a quality which is valued for its rarity. We call it classical beauty because its lyricism is not impulsive but spreads with gentle radiance over whole movements. This sensuous loveliness had been specially admired in Corelli's last publication before the concertos, the Op. 5 violin sonatas which bear the date 1700 in their dedication to the Princess of Hanover who was to become Queen of Prussia. Torelli's sonatas lacked this quality, and few copies found their way beyond the Emilian cities, Austria and Bavaria—in other words, where he was known as a player.

Pincherle notes the long interval between Corelli's Op. 5 and Op. 6 and says he was 'restrained by his own fame' from releasing the concertos until they had an irreproachable finish. They were almost certainly composed before Torelli's and they were justly preferred, yet Torelli's show a greater stylistic advance. One might suppose Torelli's concertos to be ecclesiastically conservative because the number of their movements varies from four to six; in form, however, the movements are less conservative than Corelli's, for their only archaic feature is the almost Monteverdian modal flavour in some of the adagio melodies. It does not follow that Torelli's music is best where its style is most advanced. For all his importance and competence Torelli rarely wrote a movement of striking originality, and most musicians would be willing to lose the bulk of his work if thereby they could save the best of Albicastro or Muffat.

Early eighteenth-century German musicographers compared a *Stylus phantasticus* with a *Stylus symphoniacus*, and placed in the first category canzonas and sonatas with many changes of texture and much asymmetrically phrased counterpoint. Gabrieli's polychoral pieces were thought to be in this style, and if the writers had lived to hear the organ fantasias of Bach, which seem like the summit of fine improvisation, they would have deemed them also to be in the *Stylus phantasticus*. Patchwork, however interesting and well contrasted, lengthy development of little motives which are not subsidiary to main ones in a broad ternary design of keys and materials—no technique could be less classical, less suited to a large and balanced orchestral conception, less in 'The French Style'. That is why many seventeenth-century pieces which happen to mix solo instruments with ensemble, or wind instruments with strings, are almost irrelevant in the pre-history of the classical concerto. G. Valentini of Rome produced in 1639 a sonata for violin, cornett, trombone, bassoon and organ,[1] and composers as late as Legrenzi left works specifically for a mixture of timbres, works in which a cornett *or* violin might take

[1] Described by Eitner and attributed by him with three other MS. sonatas at Kassel to Giuseppe Valentini.

the soprano. Because solo passages are not related to a tutti or to an organ part in a concerto-like design none of these pieces is of importance to us here.

It is noteworthy that Mattheson in *Das beschützte Orchester*, Pt. 2 (1717), regards concerti grossi as in the *Stylus symphoniacus* yet relegates sonatas with several alternating solo instruments to the *Stylus phantasticus*. Just as the chief kingdom of the *Stylus phantasticus* was the church gallery with its organ ricercars, its canzonas and contrapuntal sonatas, the kingdom of the *Stylus symphoniacus* was the theatre with its arias, sinfonias and pieces in binary or ternary dance forms. Lully and other French composers supplied the models. The important work of the Bolognese musicians and of Corelli did not consist in abandoning the church designs for the theatre designs. That change came with Albinoni and Vivaldi, the concertists who were themselves opera composers. The Bologna School from Cazzati to Torelli *transformed* the church designs and styles, worked their traditions into long movements, clarified their detail and gave precision to their musical ideas by sequences and other methods which we have examined. The trumpet pieces helped them to accelerate the process.

If we turn to those concerti grossi by Torelli which, being in minor keys, are least likely to resemble the trumpet sonatas, and if we choose the very sections which earlier composers—Torelli himself in his church sonatas—would have filled with a polyphonic texture and unpatterned lines, we shall find a dominating violin line in precise sequences, an articulated accompaniment, a clear tread of harmony towards cadences which clinch sections in a definite tonality. (Ex. 27.) We find in none of Torelli's last concertos the slow and luxuriously solemn counterpoint which made Corelli's concertos the perfect music for a princely High Mass. (Ex. 28.) Torelli seems to have wished, in his last publication, to compare old with new styles. The first six works are largely ripieno concertos and the last six are what came to be known as violin concertos. They follow the fast–slow–fast order of movements in the Scarlattian sinfonia or Italian overture. The incipits of movements from two sample minor-key concertos by Torelli are shown at Ex. 29. They imply a wide contrast of styles, and there can be little doubt that the composer regarded the brisk movements as the ideal ones for concertato.

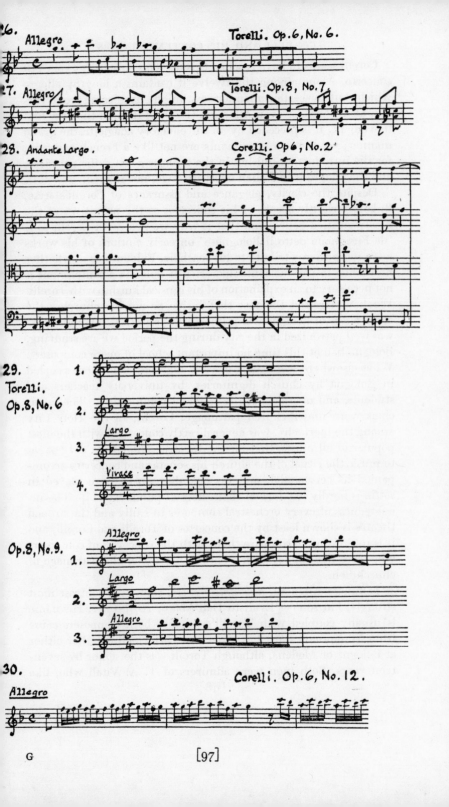

Corelli seems to have reached this decision only by his very last concerto. Alone among the twelve it contains a lengthy allegro which, but for certain mannerisms, might have come from Torelli, Dall'Abaco, or even Albinoni. (Ex. 30.) It is not the very first movement; it is preceded by an introductory adagio in the grand manner; yet the two movements are not like a French overture, for the introduction finishes in the tonic as a self-sufficient piece, and the allegro is in Italian overture style, not fugued.

Despite the clarity, elegance and assurance of Corelli's style, Bukofzer rightly speaks of his concertos as the primitives of the newly entitled genre, and that is why we deal with Corelli as if 'da Fusignano detto il Bolognese' on early editions of his works were more than a tribute to his teachers. Evidence as to whether he wished to pay his contemporaries at Bologna a compliment is not necessary to an explanation of his musical kinship with Torelli. We have stressed the fact that inside or outside churches the atmosphere of Bologna was primarily ecclesiastical. Though opera was well patronized in the city during the period we are studying, Bologna had at this time no important school of opera composers. What elsewhere were court or civic high occasions were peopled in Bologna by church dignitaries, by university teachers and students, and members of the religious communities. The musicians were under church patronage. Corelli, in the Holy City among the hierarchy, was never directly concerned with the most popular of all music, that for the theatre. Though he did not set to music the ritual of the church his sonatas and concertos accompanied its ceremonial, and his chamber works were played in settings hardly less formal than those of public worship. The indebtedness of every orchestral composer to Lully and the French theatre is shown least by the concertos of Torelli and Corelli, and it is interesting to compare them with the concertos of composers who were not employed in a church nor under the patronage of churchmen.

Tommaso Albinoni, *dilettante Veneto*, shows the contrast most strongly, but so does Evaristo Dall'Abaco, 1675–1742. His name is usually coupled with Torelli's because both composers came from Verona and must have met and performed together either at Bologna or Modena, although Torelli was the senior by seventeen years. Both men were admirers of T. A. Vitali who, like

[98]

Dall'Abaco, served the court at Modena. Dall'Abaco's *Concerti a quattro, Op. 2*, published by Roger *c.* 1712, are not orchestral, and they no more concern us than do the similar works of Torelli; but Dall'Abaco's *Concerti a più strumenti*, of which there are two sets, challenge comparison with Torelli's concerti grossi. They are decidedly less *da chiesa* and therefore very unlike Corelli's. It would hardly be convincing to show the comparison by quotation from Dall'Abaco's Op. 6, the later set of *Concerti a più strumenti*, since they were not published until 1730; but the earlier ones Op. 5, appeared only three years after Corelli's, and they serve to distinguish a composer at the Bavarian court from composers who associated with churchmen in Bologna or in Rome. The contrast is quite clear from the mere incipits quoted at Ex. 31 and 32.

Dall'Abaco does not use the title *Concerti Grossi*. Were his first

concertos composed before he had played Corelli's or before the new title was familiar in Munich? By the time he published his Op. 6 was *Concerti Grossi* restricted to works with a Corellian concertino? Whatever the answers, Dall'Abaco wrote chiefly ripieno concertos or *Konzertsinfonien*,[1] their string parts doubled by oboes and bassoons as was usual in German orchestras. His main contrasts are not between solo and tutti but between sections marked *piano* and *forte*. He frequently silences the bass instruments to make their re-entry eventful. A closed initial tutti will be seen in the concerto quoted at Ex. 29, but it is not needed where there are no concertino or solo sections. Dall'Abaco's openings usually move without a close to the dominant key, as in the Italian overture.

Dall'Abaco always begins with a fast movement which, like his other movements, is usually in binary form with a double bar. So were the French pieces played by German orchestras before concertos demanded a large share of the repertory. The 'rondeau' finales and the nature of themes in other movements show an influence of the French suite upon Dall'Abaco such as is not recognized in concertists who remained in Italy. Dall'Abaco normally used four movements and favoured the chaconne form in

[1] The name invented by Schering, not quite happily since he took pains to teach that composers before *c.* 1690 discriminated between a concerto style and a sinfonia style.

most of his slow movements. This was not an occasional choice like Handel's. Subsequent history shows Torelli to have been in advance[1] of Corelli and of Dall'Abaco in his decision to cast all his later concertos in the three-movement order, fast–slow–fast, and to use in them the kind of materials and designs that were favoured by Vivaldi and the next generation of concertists; but the precision and detail of Dall'Abaco's fast movements, despite the double-bars and French features, puts them in advance of Torelli's. Moreover the best of Dall'Abaco's concertos are decidedly more attractive melodically and harmonically than Torelli's.

Turning to Albinoni at Venice, who had no need to please any-body but himself and whatever society he chose to entertain,[2] we find the Vivaldian conception of a concerto. To it Vivaldi had only to bring his particular novelties of scoring and sonority, his magi-cal understanding of violin technique and his embroidered aria-like slow movements. Like Vivaldi, Albinoni was a prolific opera composer living almost entirely in Venice, the city of theatres and opera. No traces of the church sonata and concerto are found in his work after the first decade of the eighteenth century, and even if we chose solo violin concertos as late as Bach's we could hardly find a stronger contrast with most of Corelli's and Torelli's con-certos than is provided by some of the six concertos in Albinoni's *Sinfonie e Concerti a cinque, Op.* 2, printed by Roger in 1700. The Venetians belong to another chapter, but Albinoni, the first of them to publish concertos, should be mentioned here as a remin-der that before Torelli's best works were issued Venice heard concertos in a clearer and more forceful style than any by Bolo-gnese composers.

The comment that this or that composer stands half-way be-tween Corelli and X, the second being one of the Venetians, is utterly misleading unless applied to anyone but F. A. Bonporti, whom we shall discuss in a later chapter. (Much of Bonporti's style is like that of Corelli, from whom he had lessons, but he seems to have been acquainted with the Venetian concertos des-pite the fact that he worked in isolation at Trent.) If we spoke of

[1] To be in advance is neither to a composer's credit nor his discredit. The least advanced of the composers discussed here, Corelli, was the finest artist.

[2] For a short time, Albinoni chose to serve as chamber musician at Mantua. He was obviously more industrious than many musicians who had to earn a livelihood.

a set of concertos as half-way between such disparates as Corelli and Albinoni we should surely be referring to music written before 1700, for Corelli's style scarcely changed between his Op. 1 and his Op. 6, and if his concertos had appeared as sonatas in 1670 nothing in them would now seem out of period. To speak of concertos standing between *Torelli's* and Albinoni's (or Vivaldi's) is plausible enough, and we may so describe the twelve works which form the Op. 3 of Francesco Manfredini, father of the Vincenzo Manfredini who became court composer at St. Petersburg.

Manfredini's dates are not known, but he was born in Pistoia *c.* 1685 and spent his apprenticeship and professional life in Bologna. On the title-pages of his three publications, all issued by Silvani of Bologna, he styles himself 'Suonatore di Violino nella Perinsigne Collegiata di San Petronio di Bologna' and 'Accademico Filarmonico di Bologna'. He must therefore have associated with Perti, Jacchini, Alberti and the other composers of trumpet sinfonias and concertos, though his appointment in the reconstituted orchestra began only in the year 1700. He was thus Torelli's successor in employment as well as in musical style.

Manfredini's *Concertini per camera Op. 1* and *Sinfonie da chiesa Op. 2*, of 1704 and 1709 respectively, are simply trio sonatas the 'sinfonie' including a Christmas sonata or, as it is called, pastorale. He is best known today for the Christmas Concerto, the last of his Op. 3 concertos of 1718 which are not called concerti grossi on the title-page, but *Concerti con due violini e basso obbligati, e due altri violini, viola, e basso di rinforzo*. The pastorale is the opening movement of three, for though Manfredini sometimes precedes his allegros with the slow introduction of the church style, all his published concertos are cast in the three-movement form. As the set proceeds the component movements become longer and more complex. The first four are ripieno concertos with the violins in unison; the next four prescribe 'un violino obbligato' and some of the solo episodes are more virtuosic, especially in their fast arpeggiando passages, than any of Torelli's; the last four are 'con due violini obbligati'. All Manfredini's concertos are remarkably neat, for he avoids thick textures and likes short, compact movements. Indeed he seems to have a aclerer grip of form than Torelli himself, and though it would be foolish to call him a great or highly original composer one is grateful that 'I Musici' have issued a record of six of these Op. 3 concertos.

Soon after the publication of Dall'Abaco's concertos there was issued another set of twelve which were widely popular, and they deserved to be so. The instrumental parts of *XII Concerti a quattro, Op.* 7[1] by Enrico Albicastro who, like Albinoni, called himself *dilettante* on his title-pages, are found in several continental libraries and are known to have been played in Vienna, Munich, Dresden and the Netherlands. No copies seem to have survived in English public archives, but there are several sets in Holland, for the composer was living in Holland when these concertos were published in Amsterdam, *c.* 1703. He was a Swiss of German ancestry despite the Italian name by which he is generally known. He may have liked it because it associated him with the Italian composers and string virtuosi, for he himself was a greatly admired violinist and probably hoped to be thought Italian. The dates of his birth and death are not known, but Van der Straeten discovered in the registers of Leyden University for 1686 both 'Rittmeister Henricus Albicastro' and 'Heinrich Weysenbergh', and he is described as 'Musicus' as well as 'Rittmeister'. He had a private fortune and served as Rittmeister (cavalry officer) in the Wars of the Spanish Succession.

Albicastro's concertos are richer, more emotional than Dall'-Abaco's, but they so resemble them in general design as to suggest that the composers were friends. Dall'Abaco left Modena for the Munich orchestra in 1701. Austria was saved by the conquest of Bavaria after Marlborough's march on the Danube and the battle of Blenheim in 1704. The conquest of the Spanish Netherlands followed after the battle of Ramillies in 1706. It is known that Dall'Abaco was with the Munich musical establishment when the court went to Brussels after Blenheim, and it is most likely that he played Albicastro's concertos before he published his own. The influence of the German-French suite is as noticeable in Albicastro as in Dall'Abaco, but there is one significant difference. Though the earlier concertos were plainly intended by their composer for concert performance, each having four movements beginning with an allegro, most contain fugal passages and a good deal of contrapuntal writing. This does not mean that they *revert* to

---

[1] The whole set is now available from Bärenreiter.

older types of concerto; nor are they forms of church sonata such as were formerly called *concerti a quattro e cinque*. They are fully orchestral and in some places suggest massive tone and very strong contrasts, for Albicastro is fond of forte-piano repetitions which are separated by dramatic rests. His are ripieno concertos like Dall'Abaco's, and include movements with short solo passages for the leading violin. The counterpoint is not of Corelli's luxuriant type, but is a means of achieving length of movement—in short what was later called 'development', except that it may occur as part of an exposition—and of making strong contrast with solid homophony. Most remarkable of all features in Albicastro's work is his composite type of movement, illustrated in the concerto quoted at Ex. 33. We meet nothing quite like this first or last movement until Scarlatti's *Sinfonie di concerto grosso*. The procedure is quite erroneously regarded as a reversion to the canzona type of church concerto, for it has quite a different effect.

Harmonically Albicastro's music is richer than any other by the early concertists. Like Muffat he is an admirer of the Italians yet reveals that he is not an Italian by his teutonic part-writing and his interest in the kind of harmony beloved of cantors and teachers of counterpoint. His style is admirably clear even when his ample use of chromatic notes, especially to produce diminished triads in slow movements, suggests turgid emotions. His progressions so remind us of Bach's organ fantasias that we wonder if he was an organist, or if he used the keyboard when composing. There seems to be no thematic unification of his composite movements yet they sound perfectly integrated and balanced when they are performed with spirit. Quotation from the composite movements conveys little more than the quotation, especially as Albicastro's movements use a good deal of continuation-technique instead of the clear-cut Albinonian differentiation between main theme and sequential connective passage; for this reason only one concerto is quoted here, but as all twelve are available in a modern edition and some of the best can be bought separately the reader is assured that they are very well worth exploration—far more so than Torelli's concertos—and can be well played by local orchestras.

Early concertos should not be valued according to their advance towards the classical concerto, nor according to any single feature. If solo-tutti contrasts were the main criterion then some of

i. Violin part of Torelli's Op. 8, No. 10, printed by Silvani of Bologna 1709

ii. Violin part of Torelli's Op. 8, No. 1, printed by Roger of Amsterdam 1709

3. EIGHTEENTH CENTURY MUSIC PRINTING

(These two first examples explain the Italian musician's desire to publish in Amsterdam.)

Score of Geminiani's Op. 3, No. 1, engraved by Mlle. Vandôme
for the composer, 1755

4. Eighteenth Century Music Printing

Albinoni's concertos would be absurdly regarded as less advanced than some of Corelli's. Composers do not grope towards an ideal that is better perceived by their successors; they are concerned with immediate expression, and they do not suddenly change the way in which they take and give pleasure with a change of title from 'sonata' or 'sinfonia' to 'concerto'. When we have selected concertos for orchestra, not *voces intimae*, we should not set up '*the* concerto style' or '*the* concerto form'.

Certainly one or two composers before 1700 consciously sought to define a concerto style, but they were not consistent. Most members of the Bologna School, and especially Perti, composed a large number of Lenten oratorios. It was by an oratorio that Torelli himself hoped to make an impression at Vienna and secure a court appointment.[1] Some of the sinfonias in these oratorios were cast in three or four movements which one cannot tell from later works called concertos or even concerti grossi. Many of these sinfonias contain solo passages; many open with allegros like those of Torelli's last concertos, that is to say like those of Venetian opera sinfonias—and this at a time when the sinfonias used as preludes for High Mass normally began with a solemn introduction followed by a fugato. Examples mentioned by Schering are from *Maddalena pentita* by Gianotti, the Modena choirmaster (1685), Colonna's *Moisè* (1686) and Albergati's *Convito di Baldassare* (1691).

We cannot always tell concerto from sinfonia by style and form alone. Unfortunately sciolism has magnified into generalization some deductions made by Schering (after careful research) about a particular school. Schering's comment was that Torelli seemed to distinguish sinfonia from concerto. In his *Sei sinfonie a tre e sei concerti a quattro*, Op. 5 (1692) the sinfonias were in three parts, because Torelli wanted their part-writing to be clearly audible, but the concertos were in four parts (the viola part being obbligato) because their texture was conceived as a prominent first violin, supported by a small orchestra as in a violin sonata with a figured bass. From Venice in 1699 Giulio Taglietti of Brescia

[1] Letters written during 1700 from Torelli to Perti are in the Liceo at Bologna. Though Torelli had been happy at Ansbach he was downcast by his disappointments in Vienna, and was advised to take a month's rest after his return to Bologna in order to avoid serious illness.

(about a hundred miles north of Bologna) issued his *Concerti a quattro e Sinfonie a tre, Op. 4*, and again the sinfonias contained the contrapuntal part-writing of the church style while the concertos had a lively first violin part that was merely accompanied by the other instruments. Taglietti expressly stated in a note that the viola part, 'often regarded as optional' (*beneplacito*) was to be regarded as obbligato in the concertos. He had probably seen Torelli's work.

There is thus good reason to believe that in at least much of Lombardy and Emilia, with leadership from performances and discussions at Bologna (Quantz says that Torelli's concertos were 'first played at meetings of the Bologna Academy'), composers were attaching 'Sinfonia' and 'Concerto' to distinctive styles before the eighteenth century, for these were the two concert forms regarded as orchestral when sonatas had become associated with one or two violins. Yet at Bologna, the Mecca of these very composers, the St. Petronio men who cast their finest trumpet pieces most markedly into the designs and styles of Torelli's Op. 5 concertos called them sinfonias on the manucript parts and occasional scores. Their attempt to associate title with style evidently remained local, for Alessandro Scarlatti is known to have begun composing in June 1715 the twelve works which he called *Sinfonie di concerto grosso*.

It was not the most advanced but the most respected and persuasive composer who taught musical Europe the glory that could be expected from the title 'Concerto'. Corelli's concertos were regarded as 'the models'. Too frequently one reads that they 'pointed the way' or 'laid the foundations' for later concertists. The only truth in such phrases lies in the fact that many listeners, including some who later composed concertos, first enjoyed the antithesis of a string orchestra and a concertino when they heard Corelli's concertos. But men set up as a model what they suppose cannot be modified for the better. Models inspire; they do not propagate; they are imitated, not treated as parent organisms for new shoots. Corelli's models inspired some of the least vital of English concertos and also the greatest concertos before Mozart's, not excepting even Bach's, but we shall see later that Handel's Op. 6 was far from a mere imitation or modification of Corelli's Op. 6.

33.

Corelli's concertos were an elaboration of the Corellian sonata, its projection upon the texture of the orchestra. Vivaldi's concertos were of a new musical species cultivated first by Albinoni and further cultivated by Bach and his sons as well as by Mozart and Beethoven. The first and still the best known of Vivaldi's concertos, *L'estro armonico*, were already cast in the parent designs. This truth does not prevent one from deploring the fact that while musicians seem to have awakened to a recognition of Vivaldi's genius, few seem to have recognized the rare order of Corelli's judgement as a composer (in the strict sense of the word) or the steady glow of musical imagination that is enshrined in his last beautiful undertaking.

Hawkins wrote about Corelli's music: 'Amidst all the innovations which the love of change had introduced, it continued to be performed and was heard with delight in churches, in theatres, at public solemnities and festivities in all the cities of Europe for near forty years.' This might be taken as grandiosely imaginative, coming from a country in which Corelli was more popular than Vivaldi. In most parts of Germany Vivaldi became the favourite, for Venice had been a Mecca of German music lovers throughout the seventeenth century and continued to be so in the eighteenth. Yet instrumental parts of Corelli's sonatas and concertos in several German libraries are known to have come from the music galleries of Protestant churches, and works like Couperin's *Apothéose de Corelli* as well as written comments by Frenchmen testify to veneration for Corelli even in a country which produced no direct imitations of his concertos.

To recognize the immediate and unusually wide success of Corelli's concertos we should note that Albinoni's and Vivaldi's were printed first and that Vivaldi's Op. 3 was so enormously successful as to induce Roger to print as many new works as Vivaldi sent, and to reprint some that had been originally published in Venice. Vivaldi's Op. 3 was first issued either in 1712 or 1713, and Corelli's Op. 6 appeared posthumously in 1714.[1] The date of Corelli's dedication to the Prince Palatine of the Rhine, 1712, was until recent years mistakenly regarded as the date of

---

[1] For conclusive evidence that the Amsterdam edition of Corelli's Op. 6 was the first, and that it was posthumous, see Pincherle's *Corelli et son temps*, pp. 169–70.

publication. Many reasons have already been offered for the European popularity of Corelli's concertos despite the merits of Torelli's, Dall'Abaco's, Albicastro's, above all Vivaldi's, and their considerable popularity in the very years when orchestras were increasing (some of the German ones doubling their numbers within two decades) and when public concerts were beginning in cities of Germany, Holland, France and elsewhere than London.

The man himself was liked. Like Fux and Haydn, Corelli was able to elicit the respect of other musicians without incurring their envy, though there seems to be some truth in the suggestion that in later life, finding himself eclipsed by younger performers, he feared to play in public any unfamiliar music more advanced than his own. We lack corroboration of the stories about this matter in Mainwaring's life of Handel or even in Burney and Hawkins. Much that is told about Corelli by English writers probably came from Geminiani who was at pains not to over-praise him. Mainwaring expects us to believe that Handel, whose highest recorded attainment as a violinist made him a second violin at the Hamburg opera, 'snatches the instrument out of his (Corelli's) hand, and, to convince him how little he understood them, played the passages himself'. Other writers suggest that Corelli was 'a person of great modesty and meekness', and these virtues would be compared with the arrogance or temperamental awkwardness of other notable players or singers. This modest one was received honourably by royalty and sought by distinguished people when they visited Rome. He himself was of patrician descent. The meek Corelli could leave a Breughel to Ottoboni. Crowds came to his funeral, cardinals officiated, and a grand marble tomb was ordered by Ottoboni for the remains of a mere musician who dressed in black and collected pictures by living frugally.

The reception of Corelli's concertos was delayed by the composer himself. Five sets of sonatas had been received from him at intervals from 1681 to 1700 with increasing acclaim, the greatest of all greeting the last set, those for a single violin with a figured bass. They were republished within a few years in Italy and in many cities outside Italy. Vatielli shows by parallel quotations,[1] one of which is copied at Ex. 34, that in this last set of sonatas

[1] F. Vatielli, 'Il Corelli e i Maestri Bolognesi del suo Tempo', *RMI*, 1916.

more than in previous ones Corelli's ideas often resemble the music which he had played under his teachers at Bologna; yet the 'detto il Bolognese', which he either allowed or requested to be printed on his title-pages, does not appear after the Op. 3 sonatas.

Corelli's first and last title-pages are worth comparing. The church sonatas of 1681 are announced as *Suonate a tre, due Violini, e Violone, o Arciliuto, col Basso per l'Organo*. They were no more restricted to the church by mention of the organ than disqualified by substitution of an archlute. All Corelli's sonatas, church or chamber, were welcomed as concert music while he was still living. The title-page of the concertos introduces them thus: *Concerti Grossi con duoi Violini, e Violoncello di Concertino obligati, e duoi altri Violini, Viola e Basso ad arbitrio che si potranno radoppiare*. The first eight are church concertos, but no organ or archlute is mentioned. The concertino takes the top three of seven staves; the concerto grosso the four lower. Figures beneath the 'cello stave of the concertino form a row which continues even where the figures are duplicated beneath the *basso*. This may mean that Corelli wished concertino and ripieno to sit apart like instrumental *cori spezzati*, each with its organ or harpsichord or archlute. We may interpret the title-page thus: 'Concerti grossi, combining a concertino which *must* consist of two violins, one 'cello, and one continuo instrument, with a ripieno of at least two other violins, a viola, and the bass instruments of the string ensemble, which should have its own continuo instrument. You may increase the ripieno to taste, but not the concertino.' A Corelli orchestra therefore requires at least ten players unless the same keyboard instrument accompanies both concertino and tutti.

Despite the Queen of Sweden's taste some of the concertos are spoilt by a much larger orchestra than the specified minimum.[1] Important notes played by the second violin of the concertino in No. 8, the Christmas Concerto,[2] are swamped by more than two

[1] Pepusch has been accused of adding a viola part to Corelli's concertino in the Walsh and Hare edition of 1732. He merely transcribed Corelli's own viola part from the ripieno, though it is hard to imagine the arrangement of desks and players for which he thought it was needed.

[2] Several sets of concertos include one *Fatto per la notte di Natale* (Corelli) or *Per il Santissimo Natale* (Torelli). They were specially associated with the Midnight Mass of Christmas Eve, and Corelli may have set an example which

first violins. Large forces make gracing ineffective where it was plainly intended, as in the last movement of the Christmas Concerto, which is called *Pastorale ad libitum* and marked *Largo*. As the notes of the first chord are tied to those of the previous movement, the *ad libitum* can hardly mean: 'You may omit this movement if you want to play the concerto at some other time than Christmas.' Here is the very kind of movement in which the violinist was expected to show his taste and training in the extempore addition of ornaments. There are a few even in the deliberately simple pastoral symphony of Handel's *Messiah*. With too large an orchestra such movements—not just their ornaments— surely lose the very effect for which they were intended.

It is rightly said that what marks the chamber sonatas or concertos is their similarity to dance suites. Corelli had not the kind of personality that advertises unconventional procedures and original ideas. We do not easily speak of him as a genius, but a very high order of imagination conceived, in church and chamber concertos alike, movements which can be traced to French dances yet have been taken from the dancing school to the church or the palace. Corelli minimizes the contrast between church and chamber works. The parent forms of the two movements before the pastorale in the Christmas Concerto are the minuet and the gavotte; yet Corelli's twelfth and last concerto, the most obviously *da camera* of the set, opens with a slow-rolling contrapuntal texture over an inexorable quaver bass—the kind of movement which may recur in church concertos and so limit the number of movements derived from dance forms.

In charge of a less-assured stylist such movements would sprawl like certain organ pieces of the period. If Corelli had been less than a rare self-critic even some of his dance movements would sound improvisatory. Symmetrical phrases assure mechanical formality but Corelli rarely invents and develops an arresting initial phrase; instead he lets his continuations maintain the moderate interest and smooth tension of his openings. His musical thought is thus quite different from Albinoni's, Vivaldi's, or even Torelli's,

made such concertos popular. As early as 1637, however, there was printed by Vincenti of Venice *Pastorali Concenti al Presepe* (Pastoral music at the Crib), the Op. 3 of Francesco Fiamengo. Sartori gives the list of its contents, which are all vocal except a *Sonata pastorale*.

and quite different from Handel's. His is the antithesis of a technique in which an idea with a striking shape or rhythm is immediately foiled by the bariolage or brisures of the solo violin, and then forced further into the listener's memory as a tutti ritornello. That is why so many of his movements begin with the concertino and could just as well begin with the tutti. Corelli's solo-tutti changes break only the homogeneity of the texture; they do not break the continuity of materials. This is one of the points which prevent us from declaring that Handel, though inspired by Corelli, composed similar concertos. Nowhere in Corelli's Op. 6 is there any parallel to the heavenly entry of the solo violin in the seventh bar of Handel's first concerto in Op. 6— an effect which has been prepared by the insistence upon another idea during the six previous bars. The difference is not just the obvious one of genius, though it is unkind to play Handel before Corelli. It is the difference between two conceptions of a concerto grosso, two treatments of the solo-tutti relationship.

If Corelli's concerti grossi were played as trio sonatas by putting the viola part into the organ or harpsichord support and by making a marked antithesis of *piano* and *forte* they would sound as satisfactory as his other sonatas. Perhaps that is how Pepusch thought small groups would like to use them. The only changes between concertino and tutti which are not continuations are repetitions, some by variation, like the specimen quoted at Ex. 35. A brief and very broad analysis of the first concerto, mentioning only what happens in each movement at the first change of texture, will show that not a single movement contains a ritornello.

Concerto grosso No. 1 in D major

1. *Largo.* An ensemble introduction.
2. *Allegro.* Concertino begins, tutti continues.
3. *Largo.* (Minuet style.) Concertino begins, tutti repeats. (Later in the movement concertino begins, tutti continues.)
4. *Allegro.* An ensemble movement.
5. *Largo.* Concertino begins, tutti adds cadences (i.e. continues) and occasionally punctuates in unison.
6. *Allegro.* Concertino begins a fugue which is continued by tutti. Concertino also leads the stretto.
7. *Allegro.* (Gigue style.) Concertino begins, tutti continues each sentence to its cadence.

To say that Corelli did not advance the forms of concerto movements but simply enriched those of his sonatas is not to deny that he had a sense of form so acute that he had no need to *rely* upon sequences, motives, ritornelli or other devices in order to make improvisation sound like careful workmanship. He used various devices when they were the best means of procedure but he could express himself with assurance when he dispensed with them, for instance in the fugal ensemble of the Christmas Concerto. One of the seven movements in the first concerto, the second allegro, is frequently interrupted by a change of speed to adagio; yet the whole concerto sounds integral and satisfying. Unlike many a greater genius, Corelli knew when a movement was long enough for its ideas. To us his ideas are not of a calibre to treasure in anthologies, and the experience of practising only Corelli's works for a day or two is enervating; but the influential composer of his own time is he whose contemporaries find themselves expressed by his expression—would have composed what he composed if they had his ability and imagination. Because Corelli cast his most ambitious sonatas in the form of concerti grossi he did more than any composer except Lully to make a wide audience love orchestral texture and love concertos.

CHAPTER VII

The First German (Austrian) School

The concertos of the first Italian School grew from the sonata; those of the first German School, associated chiefly with Muffat, grew from French suites composed by men who had first studied and admired Lully but were then fascinated by the Italian style of ensemble playing, especially in concertos. Although they were court composers they had little traceable influence upon the *second* German School of concertists from Pisendel to Bach and Quantz. The first German or Austrian School were too early to be influenced by Vivaldi. Their inspiration came chiefly from Corelli and from Italians like Torelli and Dall'Abaco who had been active in Bavaria and Austria.

At the beginning of the eighteenth century some three hundred sovereign principalities existed between Alsace and Austria, and we include them all when we speak of Germany in a comment upon baroque music. German was their vernacular tongue, but the acquired or affected tongue of their nobility was often French, especially in the north. The favourite music for concerts or for keyboard instruments was also French, especially in the south. What was composed by German chamber musicians in the years before concertos arrived from Italy and were imitated? Some dates and titles of French-style 'Overtures' or suites, either for ensemble or keyboard, will give the best answer. The works mentioned are only a few published within about twenty years before the arrival of manuscript parts of concertos. The influence of France dates from much earlier. For instance, Rosenmüller's first publication, *Paduanen, Alemanden, Couranten, Balleten, Sarabanden mit 3 Stimmen und ihrem Basso pro Organo*, was in 1645.

1678 *Arion Sacer* by R. I. Mayer.
1682 *Composition de Musique* by J. S. Kusser.
1692 *Pythagorische Schmids-Füncklein* by Mayer.
1693 *Sechs Ouvertures* (sic) *nach französicher Art* by P. H. Erlebach.
1695 *Florilegium Primum* by G. Muffat.
   Concors Discordia, Amori et Timori by B. A. Aufschnaiter.
   Le Journal du Printemps by J. K. F. Fischer.
1696 *Duplex genius sive gallo-italus instrumentorum concentus* by J. C. Pez.
1698 *Zodiaci Musici* by J. A. Schmierer.
   Florilegium Secundum by Muffat.
1700 *Apollon enjoué* by Kusser.
   Festin des Muses by Kusser.
   La cicala della cetra d'Eunomio by Kusser.
   Musicalisch Divertissement by Johann Fischer (not J. K. F.).
1702 *Tafel-Musik* by Johann Fischer.
1704 *Feld- und Heldenmusik* by Johann Fischer.
   Lustige Feld-Musik by J. P. Krieger.

Where musicians were the retainers of princes who wished their courts to resemble Paris or Versailles architecturally, socially and artistically, the seventeenth century witnessed a French musical conquest of Germany more thorough than of London when, after the Restoration, the royal band played French airs and dances, the theatres served music in the French style with their plays, and French music could be enjoyed with native music in London taverns and music rooms.

The suites mentioned above and many others composed by Germans contain better music than much by Lully, Colasse, Campra and Destouches which inspired them, and better music than we find in most of the Italian sonatas and concertos we have so far discussed. It is not suggested that Campra's dances or Torelli's concertos are not worth hearing, but that music by

Muffat, Krieger and J. K. F. Fischer is even more worth hearing, and it is a pity that so little of it is generally accessible. Even the pieces by them which appear in the historical anthologies stand out among comparable pieces for their workmanship—their melodic, harmonic and rhythmic interest. Indeed one regrets that so many of the German concertos composed after 1720, which we must consider later and are available in miniature scores, seem less attractive than the earlier German court music which we examine in this chapter.

Aristocratic ears were not the only ones charmed by the neat French style. It affected, for instance, the suites for wind instruments by Johann Pezel or Petzold, 1639–94, a virtuosic trumpeter who composed for the Stadtpfeifer or city waits of Leipzig and Bautzen. Though of higher social origins (his name sometimes appears with a 'von'), and though chiefly a theatre and church composer, J. P. Krieger, 1649–1725, the first of a family succession of fine musicians, emulated Pezel in his *Lustige Feldmusik*. It is for oboes and bassoons, not chiefly brass like Pezel's, and as the suites are also marked 'strings ad libitum' they may be regarded as popular serenade music that could also serve as aristocratic chamber music.

We know from the life of Schütz what havoc the Thirty Years War made in the lives of court musicians, but at Dresden Schütz was with one of the courts most thickly involved in the strife, and it is matter for wonder that so many establishments revived and quickly became larger soon after the war. In Austria, numbers of fine German musicians were ready to rival the migrant Italians. The composers and performers in the Imperial service of whom we hear earlier in the century are Priuli, Valentini, Arrigoni and Bertali; during the ascent of the Bolognese sonatists and concertists J. H. Schmelzer (c. 1623–80) at Vienna outshone even the Venetian P. A. Ziani (c. 1620–1710) as violinist and composer, and at Salzburg H. I. F. Biber (1644–1704) acquired a reputation to which Burney paid tribute nearly a century after the composer's death. Biber was the high musical light of the Salzburg archiepiscopal court, where from 1678 to 1689 the music came under the driving personality of an organist who was also the apostle of Corelli's concerto grosso, Georg Muffat (1645–1704). Despite his service under ecclesiastical grandees and despite our association of Austrian music chiefly with Biber's splendid *Mystery* or *Rosary* sonatas, we should remember that the taste of most south German courts was for dance movements and melodically attractive keyboard suites. Among the composers with whom Muffat may be grouped, those who had not gone to France were influenced by such German composers as Rosenmüller, Kerll, J. J. Walther and J. P. Krieger.

The first publication of Johann Rosenmüller (1619–84), was a set of dances with organ continuo. He was at that time (1645) a master and the cantor's deputy at St. Thomas's School, Leipzig. When accusations against his moral conduct led him to quit Leipzig for Venice he republished his *Sonate da camera cioè Sinfonie, Allemande, Correnti, Balletti, Sarabande* for five-part string ensemble; and when the musical Duke of Brunswick, who was in Venice and to whom the sonatas were dedicated, had secured for Rosenmüller his return to Germany and the Kapellmeistership at Wolfenbüttel, this composer's last and best French suites, called sonatas, were published at Nuremberg. Rosenmüller's are among the finest German works for string ensemble before those by the first composers who made German ears familiar with concerti grossi. In the year of Rosenmüller's Nuremberg publication (1682) there was published a set of very French orchestral suites by the musician who became his successor at Wolfenbüttel. These were the *Composition de Musique* by the Hungarian Johann Sigismund Kusser, or Cousser (1660–1727), chiefly known as a composer of operas.

Kusser, Fischer, Muffat, Aufschnaiter and Pez, or Petz, may be regarded as a school, although the first two of them did not publish concerti grossi. Being by birth or adoption south Germans who worked and published in Nuremberg, Augsburg or Austrian towns, we should expect them to be among the first Germans affected by Italian music; but it was accident rather than proximity which made them Corelli's apostles. Although Vienna in the late seventeenth century was musically a second Venice, what distinguished the first from the later German concertists was the lack of noticeable influence from Venice. Their work just missed the impact of Albinoni's, and therefore of Vivaldi's concertos. Natural it may have been for musicians in the imperial and other Austrian employment to go to Venice either through Klagenfurt or over the Brenner, yet the latter route seems to have attracted north quite as much as south Germans, and to this day Venice seems to be the city which most fascinates them. It received a constant pilgrimage of chamber musicians and orchestral directors following the previous one of Protestant church composers in Schütz's generation. Albinoni's concertos were among the first to be popular with north German orchestras, and Vivaldi conquered Germany as Corelli conquered England; but Muffat, Aufschnaiter and Pez composed concertos under Corelli's influence before Corelli's own concertos were published.

All the concertos of Muffat's school are expanded suites. The materials of their movements are either of the *Fortspinnung* or continuation type or they are largely cast in dance forms varied by the tutti-concertino contrast. They do not anticipate the ritornello types or the symphonic types of concerto that we associate with Vivaldi and with the later German concertists.

Muffat had only to write the signs T and S (Tutti and Solo) upon his *Armonico tributo* suite-sonatas in order to include some of them in his volumes of concerti grossi. Where orchestral sonorities and orchestral discipline were already loved, and where French overtures and dance music had been developed into finer and more expansive concert movements than any by Lully and Campra, the concerto already existed *in posse*, especially in the suites of Kusser, Muffat and Fischer which were not called concertos. Unless an imaginative and literary title was used the most common German names for a French overture and several dances were *Parthey*, *Partie* or *Partita*. Kusser, Muffat and Fischer had actually visited Paris in order to study with Lully, though all wrote 'Sonata I, Sonata II', etc., above each suite.

Kusser's complete title was *Composition de Musique suivant la méthode Françoise*. Muffat's *Florilegium* volumes could have borne Kusser's title, though the tutti-concertino effects came from the composer's new enthusiasm for Corelli. We have seen that in 1702, after the issue of Muffat's 1701 concerti grossi but before the publication of Corelli's, Fischer published his last set of orchestral French suites as *Tafelmusik*. This title, or its French form *Musique de table*, was not new in Germany, though we remember it chiefly because of the concertos for various combinations of string and wind instruments which were later published by Telemann and well picked by Handel. It is a great pity that the general musical public hears only the orchestral suites of Bach in B minor and D major to represent a whole century of the German orchestral repertory except concertos. True, Bach's are the greatest German representatives of both types, but now concert-goers seem aware that the orchestra was enjoyed before there were classical symphonies they should have the opportunity to know why it was enjoyed before there were concertos. Suites by Rosenmüller, Muffat and Fischer should be part of the general repertory.

The most attractive of all their works are perhaps those of Muffat, whom Eitner notes to have been 'of Scottish descent'. The statement has not been contradicted because Moffat is a familiar Scottish name and not a German one, but nobody has discovered the time or circumstances of the family migration. Among composers of the second rank whose works deserve revival Muffat stands high. He avoided the formulae of his times unless he could invest them with life which grew to a musical organism. He seems to have been incapable of slovenly or even mediocre work and never to have fallen below a certain level of melodic charm and rhythmic invention. His best is far better than Torelli's or Geminiani's, and better than second-rate Vivaldi. He was by nature an apostle, either persuasive enough or in high enough favour to secure leave and money for travel to the places where he could satisfy his enthusiasm for French and Italian music. First he was attracted by Lully. Having spent six years as Lully's pupil in Paris he became organist at Strasbourg Cathedral which he left in 1675. He was then musical director for the Bishop of Salzburg, but he paid long visits to Vienna and to Rome, in which city he came under Corelli's spell. Finally, he was appointed organist (1690) and then Kapellmeister (1695) to the Bishop of Passau, and while he was at Passau he published his concerti grossi. Muffat's publications are as follows:

1682, Salzburg.   *Armonico tributo*. Sonate di camera.
1690, Augsburg.[1] *Apparatus musico-organisticus*, dedicated to
                    Leopold I, and including twelve toccatas,
                    a chaconne and a passacaglia.

[1] This publication is reprinted in the *Trésor des pianistes*, the two *Florilegium* collections in D.T.O. I and II, and the 1701 concertos in D.T.O. XI.

1695, Augsburg. *Suaviores harmoniae—Florilegium I.*
1698, Passau. *Florilegium II.*
Both the Florilegium volumes contain an autobiographical preface printed in four languages—Latin, French, German and Italian.
1701, Passau. *Auserlesene mit Ernst und Lust gemengte Instrumentalmusik.* Six concerti grossi.

True to Lully's practice, the *Armonico tributo* sonatas are in five strands—two for violins, two for violas and one for violone with cembalo. The preface says that they can be played as four-part or five-part sonatas with one instrument to each part, or by the full orchestra throughout (*concerto grosso durchaus*); but they 'can be played with varied texture by forming two groups, a concertino of two violins with a 'cello or a gamba to be used wherever the letter S occurs on the parts, and the concerto grosso wherever T is written'. Muffat also says that the violins should not be heavily doubled unless the orchestra contains a double bass. He acknowledges that 'the concerto (or concert) style cultivated in Rome' stimulated him to compose his *Armonico tributo,* and certainly the materials of these pieces, especially their openings, almost prove his acquaintance with Corelli's concertos over thirty years before their publication. Muffat shows the French influence far more obviously than Corelli does, but like the Italian master he admirably transforms the French dances into concert movements that are much more than copies. The Lullian admixture is so strong that one of the concertos actually ends with a march. Samples of his French-style movements are shown in Ex. 36, which includes the openings of a gavotte that was evidently among Handel's borrowings.

As Muffat enjoyed the role of evangelist as well as apostle we should summarize his multi-lingual *Florilegium* preface:

'While in Rome I conceived the idea of studying the Italian style of organ and clavecin playing under Pasquini. I heard with wonder some of A. Corelli's concertos splendidly performed by a large ensemble. . . . Noticing the rich variety of sounds with which this sort of work is filled I set to imitating it, and am beholden to Corelli himself for several useful observations on the way to obtain the right effects, and for kindly giving my works his approval. I was the first, after my return from France, to bring the style of Lully's ballets to Germany, and now after my return from Italy I bring these first essays in a new texture . . . I have brought their number up to twelve, and hope that the mysterious titles which I have added (in Latin) may suggest the occasions when each is most suitable, though they refer to the kindness of Their Imperial Majesties to me in the past. . . .'

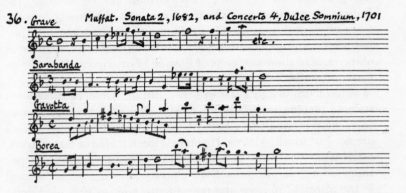

Muffat leaves us wondering if he delighted in loquacity or if remarks which seem otiose should be treasured as documentary evidence of the state of music and stupidity of musicians in south German States. Why did he labour in four languages to give examples of the size and constitution of bands which *could* play the concertos?

'If you have a great number of players you may add several clavecins, theorbos, harps, regals or similar instruments. . . . You should use the three best players in the trio or concertino and limit their accompaniment to a single harpsichord or theorbo.'

To which one says: 'Of course. Did he expect some directors to be puzzled by the appearance of his scores or parts?' He certainly expected his pieces to be tackled with inadequate resources, for he says that the ensemble cannot possibly sound majestic without a double bass, and that the trio of double reeds, two oboes and a bassoon, may in some movements replace or echo the string concertino, especially in airs and galanteries. This last remark reflects his experience in the French theatre.

On the other hand, some of Muffat's comments which ought to be unnecessary sound like the admonitions of a modern trainer. The first note of a tutti should be well attacked unless the word or sign *piano* forbids this treatment, but even then 'to play first notes timidly or raggedly spoils the style'. Inequality of tone is so unpleasant that each player should produce the same degree of *p* or *f* and be sure of the exact note from which a change of dynamic is to be made. Listeners should be 'surprised at the grandeur of a *forte*'. Let German players imitate the Italians by making the style and tempo of a movement (adagio, largo or vivace) immediately evident, and far more obvious than has been customary outside Italy. 'It is the exact and unanimous observance of these contrasts of slow and fast, vigour and suavity, tutti and simple trio, which delight the ear in Italian playing . . . as chiaroscuro delights the eye in painting.' Observe the Italian style of playing especially when you deal with syncopations or fugal movements; use a firm, detached bow. These instructions are not just for the violins. If you find some stupid or lazy players, teach what you want to a few of the better musicians and put them among the laggards. Secure precision in the release as well as the attack of phrases and movements, and see that final notes are exactly counted and unanimously quitted. Attention must not flag in the middle of a movement, and there should be no long waiting from one movement to the next. Unmarked rallentandos spoil a concerto. Finally, these new pieces should not be played too often or too many at a concert. Two are enough. Hackneyed music bores players.

The preface to Muffat's last publication contains a portrait of the dedicatee, Maximilian Ernst, Count of Scherffenberg, Archbishop of Salzburg, etc. He must have been as handsome in heart as in visage, for it was through this apparently comely grandee that the composer was 'enabled to travel during the previous twenty years, and so combine Italian pathos (*Tieffsinnige Italianische Affecten*) with French lightness and grace (*Lufsbar und Lieblichkeit*)'. Having in 1695 and 1698 published plenty of French pieces the author now offered the first German concertos in the Italian style. The airs and galanteries ruled them out of church and the solemn and pathetic movements made them unsuitable for dancing. 'They have been composed solely for the satisfaction of cultivated ears, for noble receptions and music makings, and for the evening concerts of connoisseurs and lovers of music.'

Only half of these concerti grossi were new works; the rest were new versions of sonatas from *Armonico tributo*. The process of revision would have been harder if Muffat had followed Vivaldi instead of Corelli. Only a few of Corelli's movements foretell the kind of concerto in which the solo instruments are confronted by a tutti—not merely with the contrast of tone but with contrasting musical materials. Muffat was willing and anxious to show himself in advance with stylistic change but like Corelli he was a cautious and not a prolific composer. A comparison between the first and second versions of the six concertos taken from *Armonico tributo* is worth while. Muffat cannot always arrange a movement to suit the kind of concerto he admires and so he occasionally substitutes a new one. In the light of north German writing which favoured the *stylus symphoniacus* more than the *stylus phantasticus* except in church music, Muffat's most significant revision is the thorough removal of contrapuntal *grave* sections between the dance movements. Sometimes such sections are merely shortened so that they become introductions instead of pieces in their own right. We see this process in E of Ex. 37, which gives some indication of the transformation from the first sonata to the fifth concerto grosso. The gradation from *p* through *pp* to *ppp* in some of Muffat's concerto movements had been used by others, notably Stradella and Giovanni Valentini.

Not all Muffat's changes please modern ears, for our antiquarian education leads us to relish those characteristic turns of seventeenth-century music that do not survive in the plethora of eighteenth-century *Kapellmeistermusik*. We like Schütz's modal inflexions and the unequal phrasing in Monteverdi which gave way to the smooth sequences of Cavalli, Cesti and Scarlatti. We like points of style which tell Purcell from Handel as much as those which tell him from Lully. We know why Holst did not like what was Italian in Purcell's sonatas though we may not share his taste; and many of us may think that something is lost when Muffat rejects the French saccadé formula and equalizes the notes, or when he scraps the pompous introduction and fugued allegro of a French overture for a piece in the rhythm of an

37.   Muffat. Sonata 1, 1682, revised for Concerto 5, 1701.

1. Grave

Andante

2. Grave

    Allegro

3. Added for Concerto
   Solo

4. Allemande, unchanged.

5. Andante. Halved in length & made to finish on the dominant

6. Gavotte, unchanged.

7. Grave. Omitted from Concerto.

8. Menuet. Rhythm & harmony simplified.

Italian corrente. Sometimes, however, his admiration of Corelli leads him to precede an allegro by a passage of slow, luxuriant counterpoint that almost outshines similar passages by Corelli himself, for the Germans were more skilled contrapuntists than most of the French and Italians. Ex. 38B is a sample of this process.

Benedikt Anton Aufschnaiter was Muffat's colleague and probably his deputy at Passau. The date of his birth is not known, but he succeeded Muffat as musical director of Passau Cathedral in 1704 and died holding the office in 1742. He published much church music for voices with instruments—masses, offertories, vespers, etc. His two main orchestral works correspond exactly with the 1682 and 1701 publications by Muffat. The first is a set of sonatas with concertino sections, the second of concerti grossi. Both have Latin titles:

1695 Nuremberg, *Concors discordia*. (Sonatas for orchestra.)
1703 Augsburg, *Dulcis Fidium Harmonia*. (Concerti grossi.)

Muffat and Aufschnaiter were together at Passau from 1690 and the dates and contents of their corresponding publications suggest Aufschnaiter's open tribute to Muffat. Yet the 1695 work is even more French than the 1682 *Armonico tributo*, and Aufschnaiter's six suites are not called sonatas but serenades. This fact leads us to suppose that Aufschnaiter was influenced by an Augsburg publication earlier in the same year by another Bohemian, J. K. F. Fischer.[1] This was Fischer's Op. 1, entitled *Le Journal du printemps consistant en airs et balets à 5 parties et les trompettes à plaisir*. Fischer and Aufschnaiter concur even as regards the places of change from tutti to concertino, and it is noteworthy

[1] He is often called Ferdinand Fischer to avoid confusion with two other Johann Fischers, one who was Lully's copyist and imitator, the other the oboe player who settled in England. J. K. F. Fischer is known chiefly for his keyboard suites and for the fact that he gave them opus numbers. He is mentioned in books about Bach because his Op. 4 of 1702 is a series of twenty preludes and fugues for organ, using all modern keys except the four acoustically extreme ones. He called this work *Ariadne musica neo-organoedum*, Ariadne's thread having brought Theseus safely through the Cretan labyrinth. Bach used several of the musical ideas in this splendid work which, but for Bach's own *Forty Eight*, ought to be part of every student's library. It seems extraordinary that writers should be unable to make the obvious remark that Bach's is a greater work without disparaging what Bach so highly esteemed. Confronted by some of Fischer's preludes most musicians would be pardonably misled into supposing they were Bach's.

that both of them apply this technique to overtures and chaconnes
but not to minuets, bourrées and gigues. Even the rondeaus,
which naturally suggest echo effects, lack concertino episodes.
The one exception must have been a novelty indeed—the gavotte
in Aufschnaiter's *Serenade No. 6* which uses the concertino as an
echo in every bar!

Aufschnaiter's concerti grossi of 1703 outdo Muffat's in the
number of changes from tutti to concertino. Very rarely does
Aufschnaiter withhold the antitheses long enough to allow a
grandiose opening to spread, as might that in Ex. 39, into a
movement of massive integrity. This extract comes from a concerto entitled *Sonata S. Marci* which was probably composed
simply for Passau's patronal feast; yet it curiously recalls the
canzona concertos of Venice by reverting to a sectionalism that
notably distinguishes it from pieces in Aufschnaiter's usual suite
style.

About a hundred miles to the south-west of Passau is Munich.
Some of Muffat's and Aufschnaiter's contemporaries in the
Bavarian capital should be included in the first school of German
concertists even if their orchestral works were not called concertos or if they rarely applied the concertino-tutti technique.
Luther once wrote to a friend: 'Though they do not love me, I
love your Bavarian dukes because they love music,' and Luther's
compliment would have been deserved by the Electors of Bavaria
of the seventeenth and eighteenth centuries. The facts given in
reference books relating to Kerll, Steffani and Pez show that the
Munich musicians were particularly well treated, even to the
granting of ample leave with expenses for study in Italy. Some
of them were employed as diplomats, yet the patent of nobility
which added 'von' to Kerll's name was purely a recognition of
his musical attainments and repute.

We are concerned chiefly with Johann Christoph Pez (1664–
1716). The composer himself always spelt his name thus. He
belonged to a family of musicians who had been employed either
at St. Peter's or by the court at Munich, and he received his own
good general and musical education partly as one of the cathedral
boys and partly from his father, who was a *Kammermusikus* of
high standing. The most influential and venerated musician in
Munich was Johann Caspar Kerll (1627–93). He is mentioned

here because the main difference between Munich and Passau or any other German city except Vienna was its early and complete musical Italianization. The French characteristics of the Passau composers are no more discernible in the Munich composers than they are in Corelli or Torelli. Kerll did not publish Corellian concertos but he had studied under Carissimi and various teachers in Rome, and he regarded Italy as the supreme teacher and arbiter of musical taste. In 1674 he decided to abandon operatic and secular composition. He left Munich for Vienna where he concentrated his attention upon organ playing, organ teaching and organ composition. He spent a mere ten years before returning to Munich, but upon that ten years his present reputation is based, for his mastery of counterpoint earns him a place given to few organ composers except Bach. Despite our thinking of Kerll chiefly as an organist he was, like Handel, an Italianized Saxon. His thoroughly Italian outlook is less obvious in his organ works than in his operas because, even in the Roman Catholic States, organ technique was more widely and deeply cultivated in Germany than in Italy, and Germany had finer instruments. Italy provides no clear parallels with some types of German organ music.

The imperial court was musically a reflection of Venice; the Bavarian court was a reflection of Bologna. We have already noted Dall'Abaco's employment at Munich. The best-known Italians there were Ercole Bernabei (1620–87), whose two sons left Italy to join their father in the electoral orchestra, and Agostino Steffani (1654–1728). Bernabei is remembered by church musicians for his simple and dignified settings of canticles in *stile osservato*, but Steffani's first publication was a set of orchestral sonate da camera (1683). They might be taken for concertos by Corelli wherein contrasts of concertino and tutti had been replaced by those of *piano* and *forte*. The same comment could be passed upon the Op. 1 sonatas of Pez (1696), which are among the best works for strings by the Munich group. They were first published in Augsburg but they commended themselves both to Roger and to Walsh, who brought out an edition entitled *Sonate da camera, or Chamber Music* in 1707. Other sonatas and concertos by Pez are still dispersed in various libraries and one is printed in Walsh's *Harmonia Mundi*. Some of these manuscript works are said to be concerti grossi but the present writer has seen only the works reprinted in *DTB*, xxvii–xxviii, with a biographical and critical essay by Dr. Bertha Wallner.

Steffani's early sonatas are mentioned because they must have been played by Pez while he was a violinist at St. Peter's or in the royal orchestra. Pez did not publish his own sonatas until he had left Munich to become Kapellmeister to the Archbishop-Elector of Cologne, first at Liège and then at Bonn. In 1705 this employer was exiled by the emperor, Joseph I, and Pez then sought and secured the envied direction of music at Stuttgart, the court of the Duke of Württemberg. During incessant adjustments of the balance of power among the agglomerate of German States in the seventeenth and eighteenth centuries even famous musicians lived precariously if they dared not risk a free-lance career. Migration took them across the political divisions to employment by States allied with the opponents of former employers. One usually stayed where one hoped for advancement to the directorship or to the post next in honour, but the appointment of someone else, still young, could thwart one's ambition and limit one's prospect. Thus despite lavishly generous treatment from the Elector of Bavaria, Steffani left Munich when one of Bernabei's sons succeeded to the Kapellmeistership, and Pez saw many good musicians between himself and Bernabei when he migrated to the Rhine. Steffani became musician and diplomat in Hanover where he was a good friend to Handel and hoped to secure him the Kapellmeister's post; but Handel preferred his independence, and the arrival of the Elector of Hanover as George I could do little to make or mar the fortunes of a musician in England. Though Steffani's election to the Life Presidency of the Academy of Ancient Music in London was 'unanimous', for his famous duets were recommendation enough, Handel may have put forward his name. Among the works he forwarded in acknowledgement of the honour was the magnificent *Stabat Mater*.

Pez's twelve sonatas of 1696 were maniloquently entitled *Duplex genius sive gallo-italus instrumentorum concentus*, and one expects to find them Italianized French suites like Fischer's, Muffat's or Aufschnaiter's. No doubt Pez intended to combine French with Italian features but his music is so utterly Italian as

to make us unaware of the French origins of some of the movements. There are fewer nameable dance measures than in most
of Corelli's church concertos yet Pez certainly intended his sonatas
for concert use. Unlike Kusser, Fischer and Muffat, Pez had not
undertaken the journey to France, and at Munich he would have
heard less French music than in some capitals. French music must
have reached him largely through Italian, and we find no great
range of French galanteries; his French measures are limited to
those used by Corelli. Indeed his greatest debt to French music is
observed in the splendid French overtures to his operas, wherein
also the Neapolitan ritornello technique is so elaborately used in
arias, duets and choruses as to make one wonder how brilliant a
concertist he would have proved if he had come under the influence of Vivaldi. The sonatas were published eighteen years before
Corvelli's concertos (though he probably heard concertos by
Torelli and Dall'Abaco as well as by Corelli) yet they have much
of Corellian suavity and variety. Pez loves to separate his fast
sections with short hymn-like adagio passages in the luxuriant
contrapuntal style of Corelli. The first sonata in the Denkmäler
reprint (No. 4) is fairly typical, and proceeds thus:

(The numbers indicate the bars in each section.)

A. $\frac{4}{4}$ Largo (8) – Presto (8) – Largo (8) – Presto e forte (15).

B. $\frac{4}{4}$ Fuga, allegro (48).

C. $\frac{3}{4}$ Dolce (30) – $\frac{4}{4}$ Adagio (5) – $\frac{3}{8}$ Presto (58).

Nearly all the movements begin with fugued themes. Pez's harmony and counterpoint, like Steffani's, may be said to run on
velvet.

The most striking feature of Pez's music is its frequent
reminder of Handel—not just of the international Italian phraseology but of Handelian turns of harmony and melody. Some of the
snippets quoted at Ex. 40 may bear out this judgement. The third
of them serves as only one of example of Pez's frequent breadth
of melodic thought. The last extract in Ex. 40 is given because of
its anticipation of Bach's fugue in C sharp minor. Possibly Steffani, being a common influence upon Pez and Handel, is the

41.

J.C.Pez. Concerto pastorale.

source of the stylistic similarities just mentioned, for the musical language of Steffani's duets, as Dr. Wallner observes, is frequent in Pez's orchestral work as well as his operas. Pez's fondness for three-strand harmony (other notes added by the keyboard continuo, of course) might also be thought Handelian, and the omission of a fourth strand certainly enables the middle part to be shapely; but whereas in Handel's magnificent three-part textures the violins are massed in unison, Pez likes his violins to be duettists and he makes the viola double the bass. He seeks the same clarity and elegance even when his harmony is of five real strands, as we may observe in the *Concerto pastorale*, the finest of his reprinted instrumental works.

The openings of movements in this concerto, which is on the scale of Bach's longest orchestral suites, are shown at Ex. 41. Although it was composed after Pez had left Munich and is thought by Sandberger to have been for the Stuttgart players, Pez died in 1716 and can hardly have been greatly influenced by the publication of Vivaldi's concertos. The concertante element in the *Concerto pastorale* is made by the antithesis of violins and two flutes. It will be noticed that there are two pastoral movements. Each has the drone-pedal effect (though not without relief), and the minuet not only provides relief from the key of F major but also has a bucolic trio.

We see, then, that before Vivaldi's concertos were disseminated among German musicians the Italian concerto grosso made no revolutionary impact upon Germany. It influenced chiefly the Italian musical colonies of the south. It fertilized works of far greater merit than is yet widely recognized, and it must have given a new incentive to good performance and orchestral discipline; but it did not greatly alter the repertory of German orchestras. Muffat's apostleship affected only the fine composers whom we have grouped with him. When the concertino-tutti idea first reached one or two German orchestras early in the new century as an interesting novelty it involved no radical change in the forms and processes of composition until Vivaldi's concertos arrived. Music on the scale of Corelli's concertos already existed in 'French' overtures which the German aptitude for counterpoint and extended musical thought had made worthy of concert listening. Wind instruments concertized with the strings and composers found the contrasts of timbre as fascinating as those within Corelli's textures. Muffat's or Steffani's chamber works may have influenced Handel, but they had little direct influence upon most musicians who lived outside Bavaria and Austria. The Corellian form of concerto grosso had some popularity in north Germany at a later stage along with English concertos, especially Handel's. By that time the baroque concerto was soon to be ousted by the new symphonies and galant solo concertos.

CHAPTER VIII

The Venetian School

Most concertos by the leading composers of Venice during the first quarter of the eighteenth century justify a new title, such as Scarlatti's *Sinfonie di concerto grosso*, to distinguish them from concertos composed previously in Bologna and Rome or by musicians serving in court or church. Tommaso Albinoni (1671–1750),[1] Antonio Vivaldi (1675–1743), Alessandro Marcello (1684–1750) and Benedetto Marcello (1686–1739) were not forced to live as servant-musicians to princes or to ecclesiastics, nor were they servant-retainers of the Doge, the Senate, the curators of St. Mark's, the Trons, the Mocenigos or any other wealthy owners of an opera theatre.

Albinoni, who described himself on the title-page of his Op. 1 Sonatas (dedicated to Ottoboni) as 'musico di Violino dilettante Veneto', sought experience as an orchestral player and therefore served for a time among the Duke of Mantua's chamber musicians. He inherited the profits from paper-mills but entered into an arrangement whereby a younger brother took over a fine house and management of the main patrimony. Albinoni's passionate devotion to music, his determination to be excellently professional as performer and composer, reminds one of the aristocratic d'Indy who loved to be accepted as an equal by students at

---

[1] Dates given by Albinoni's biographer, Remo Giazotto. Pincherle's book on Vivaldi gives 1671–1741, a correction that seems supported by dates of Albinoni's publications.

the Conservatoire, used as hornist or timpanist at the Théâtre-
Italien or in the Colonne concerts, or as accompanist on the organ
and piano wherever required, and even to be dressed like a poor
musician. It is noteworthy that soon after his father's death
Albinoni usually omitted the 'dilettante' on titles and simply
called himself 'musico di violino'. He had never, as each of the
Marcello brothers, written 'nobile dilettante', and it is possible
that even the 'dilettante' was a concession to the pride of a family
which wondered why a son with great expectations should work
as a *musico di camera*.

The Marcellos were also of high social rank and good education.
Externally Benedetto was less serious than his brother or than
Albinoni. The supposed riotousness of his youth may have been a
rebellion against a father who objected to the time he spent on
violin playing, singing and opera, and who wished him to do well
in his law studies, to cultivate dignified society in Rome and to
secure high government office. In fact he fulfilled his father's
ambitions and his own. Inwardly Benedetto Marcello must have
been as serious as any of this Venetian School. His famous *Fifty
Psalms*[1] (1724–6) excels other Italian church music of the period
and there is savagely serious purpose in his much-quoted satire
Il Teatro alla Moda (1720) which ran quickly to several reprint-
ings. His brother Alessandro's oboe concertos are distinguished by
a tender melancholy which is like Mozart's both in effect and in
at least one point of style, for Alessandro Marcello often secures
a yearning expression by his way of using suspension dissonances.

Though of more humble immediate ancestry, for his father was
a violinist at St. Mark's, Vivaldi would have been distinguished
from other musicians by his priesthood and by his office of musical
director at the Pietà if his genius had not already distinguished
him before his final ordination. By his operas, by the concerts in
which he led performances of his own works, and by accepting as
pupils the nobility of Germany or their chamber musicians,
Vivaldi could have lived in luxury.

It was not directly the social independence of these Venetian

---

[1] Their full title is 'Estro poetico-armonico, parafrasi sopra i primi 50
salmi, poesia di Girolamo Giustiniani'. They are for 1–4 voices with continuo,
some with added 'cello obbligato. They were issued at Venice in two books.
The London edition by Avison and Garth, 1757, took eight volumes.

composers whicn gave their concertos a style and form unlike those we have previously examined, but the fact that they composed operas and loved the theatre. Venice had been the first city to devote her theatres to public opera and to build new opera houses. Until the eighteenth century she was not seriously rivalled even by Naples; she was the most famous city in Europe for musical entertainment and drama, and the styles and forms of movements in the new Venetian concertos of the early eighteenth century reflected the styles and forms of sinfonias, arias and choruses in baroque opera. People rarely refer to concertos by Albinoni, Vivaldi or the Marcellos as concerti grossi, nor is it usual so to designate concertos by Bach and other Germans whose concerto movements were modelled on those of the Venetians.

Undeniable though the debt of these three great Venetians to Corelli and Torelli, no movement in one of their concertos dating from after 1710 could be mistaken for a movement in a concerto of the Bolognese or Roman school. The Venetians in all but very rare exceptions compose concertos of three long movements, the ancestors of the classical symphonies and concertos. The main themes of the outer fast movements are usually incisive, always memorable, and the connective material which prefaces their recurrence in a series of clearly prepared keys is made of sequences, motive development and kinetic recurrences which are as clearly articulated as the themes. There is almost no *Fortspinnung* or feeling of extemporization except in the bravura figuration for solo instruments. The impassioned Venetian slow movements normally begin with a tutti-ritornello, sometimes all'unisono, which may frame a pathetic aria for the solo or concertino and almost suggest the words of an operatic situation. Sometimes the aria-like slow movement is replaced by an equally impressive piece in free chaconne form, with or without episodes. When the outer movements are in a major key, the slow movement is usually in the minor. Ritornello technique is customary in Venetian finales but invariable in first movements.

How much was Albinoni responsible for the form, style and expression of Venetian concertos? Even if later research proves him to have been an outstanding innovator the question will never be fully answered. All we can say is that he had opportunity as a youth to develop his talents in the Ottoboni circle, met Corelli yet was strongly influenced by Torelli and the Bologna musicians, was four years Vivaldi's senior and by many years the first of the great Venetian concertists to see his works in print. He must therefore have strongly influenced Vivaldi. Whole passages in some of the concertos printed by Sala in 1700, which went to press before any chamber music by Vivaldi, could be taken for Vivaldi's. On the other hand Vivaldi was active as performer and composer in Venice long before his Op. 3 concertos were printed. It would be foolish to deny that by his best work Vivaldi proved himself an artist of wider scope and greater emotional intensity than Albinoni, but in a different generation Albinoni would have used the 'dilettante' only humorously or scornfully. Few musicians reveal such professional skill as composers. He wrote |not a single movement which contains careless or even mediocre workmanship, and very few which fail to demonstrate an unusual command of organic form. The quality and originality of all Albinoni's published work must be stressed because he is underestimated even by Bukofzer, and until recently he was almost ignored by historians of music, who apparently accepted some superficial and summary judgements of Albinoni by Fétis.

The reason for a comparative neglect of Albinoni until recently is understandable. He is overshadowed by Vivaldi, and one can hardly complain that Giazotto's book about him, unlike Pincherle's study of Vivaldi, is available only in the original language;[1] rather is one grateful that Pincherle's is translated. If Albinoni had differed from Vivaldi as Bach differed from Handel he would have attracted more attention, but the two Venetians were active in the same fields—as violinists and as composers of opera and of concertos. Albinoni may have been more than anyone else the father of the new type of concerto, but Vivaldi's work, being so very extensive, spans first the history of the concerto from Corelli to Bach and then the whole distance from the high baroque concerto to the symphonies of Sammartini and Stamitz. Otherwise Albinoni himself would be admired as the prolific and versatile composer which he was. It seems sensible, however, to examine the Venetian concerto first from its best known specimens—Vivaldi's Op. 3—and then to compare the concertos of Albinoni and the Marcello brothers with those of Vivaldi.

[1] Remo Giazotto, *Tomaso Albinoni*, Milan, 1945.

The first pieces which Vivaldi sent to be printed in Amsterdam were the twelve concertos called *L'estro armonico*, *Op. 3*. They brought him a fame in northern Europe comparable only with Corelli's fame in England, and Roger probably accepted the sets of violin sonatas which constitute his Op. 1 and Op. 2 because the concertos were commercially successful. In them the composer's personality is much more evident than in the sonatas which, though far from obvious imitations, do show a debt to Corelli's. To prove any debt to Corelli in Vivaldi's concertos would be extremely difficult, for rarely have nearly contemporary artists differed so much in works of the same title. Vivaldi differed from Corelli as much as Bach from Handel, and if any of his concertos reminds us of Corelli the resemblance can be traced to single turns of melody or single musical ideas, not to design or style. Vivaldi's advance in treatment of the solo instruments is by no means the feature which most notably distinguishes him from Corelli.

Within Vivaldi's first and most famous set of twelve concertos only No. 7 in F major contains any strikingly Corellian ideas. If we were strongly determined to find resemblances we could imagine Corelli's influence where Vivaldi employs the solo instruments of Corelli's concertino, but Vivaldi's groups of solo violins are *not* employed as Corelli employed his concertino; instead they become both colleagues and rivals in bravura, first one and then another of them playing as if in a concerto for solo violin and orchestra. Rarely do Vivaldi's groups of three or four violins maintain for long a staid ensemble of continuo harmonies. When No. 7 in F major and No. 10 in B minor are said to be 'for four violins', or when No. 2 in G minor and No. 11 in D minor are said to be 'for two violins', the descriptions are misleading. These four concertos—the only four in the set which have induced any writer to mention Corelli—include within their solo groups an obbligato 'cello. They thus make *available* a contrast between the tutti and a concertino, but the concertino is more accurately called a Vivaldian group of concertizing soloists.

Bukofzer describes two of these concertos as 'of the da chiesa type'. He was careful not to write 'of the *old* da chiesa type' but he is surely too summary. No concerto by Vivaldi easily reminds us of church sonatas. His wonderful violin concerto in C major (No. 14 in Pincherle's catalogue) 'For the Feast of the Assumption' is fortunately recorded, and the listener can hear how Vivaldi wrote dramatic movements upon a religious subject. The preliminary adagio is not that of a church concerto or of a French overture; it is a short gesture such as might silence the audience at the opening of a *sinfonia avanti l'opera*. The chaconne which forms the middle movement is not a display of counterpoint but of dramatic contrasts in the string texture, and the cadenza within the brilliant finale cannot be imagined in a church concerto.

Probably the second, fourth and seventh concertos in Vivaldi's Op. 3 have been labelled 'da chiesa' because they have slow introductory movements; but Vivaldi did not call them church concertos. If we were choosing any of these works for church we should surely choose the Bachian No. 11 for its sheer nobility and seriousness, and this concerto, despite the adagio and fugue with which it opens, seems never to have been called a church concerto. In discussing concertos of the Venetian School it is pointless to maintain any distinction between church and chamber types. They were nearly all for public, semi-public or sometimes court concerts. If by chance they were given in a church, their composer felt under no obligation to imitate the older church style.

Most readers will know Marc Pincherle's *Antonio Vivaldi et la musique instrumentale* or the English translation which contains all the music illustrations but omits the thematic index. One could hardly discuss Vivaldi without either quoting or paraphrasing Pincherle beyond the bounds of decency or else relying upon his researches while stupidly trying to forget his commentary. We can fulfil our present examination of the development of the concerto by dealing with no more than a small fraction of Vivaldi's concertos, of which Pincherle catalogues 447, choosing a few for their historical as well as their aesthetic interest. Then, without quoting too extensively, we can refer to Pincherle's comments which are based on his unique knowledge of Vivaldi's dramatic and instrumental music in the Foà and Giordano bequests to the National Library at Turin, of manuscript copies at Dresden, Paris and elsewhere, and of works by Vivaldi's contemporaries. In a general history of the concerto we are more concerned with any radical change of design than with, say, some fifty concertos which follow a basic general design, and we should particularly notice those concertos which had the most important impact upon composers outside Italy and those which point to the rise of the orchestral symphony. Malipiero's edition of the chamber works for the Vivaldi Institute of Treviso, now reaching completion, does not group the concertos in the order of the composer's original printed collections, which were as follows:

Op. 3. *L'estro armonico*. The title is often translated 'The Harmonic Whim'. It could mean 'Musical Fancy', 'Musical Rapture', 'The Composer's Inspiration' or, in the English style of the period, 'The Divine Afflatus'. These two sets of six concertos were published by Estienne Roger of Amsterdam in 1712. Further editions followed by Le Clerc and Walsh.

Op. 4. *La Stravaganza*. (The meaning is like that of *L'Estro*.) This was a set of twelve concertos published by Roger *c.* 1713. About eight years later Walsh published six of them as 'Vivaldi's Extravaganzas in 6 parts for violins and other Instruments/Being the choicest of that Author's work'.

Op. 6. *VI Concerti a Cinque Stromenti*, published by Roger *c.* 1716.

Op. 7. *Concerti a Cinque Stromenti. . . . Uno è con Oboe.* Twelve concertos published by Roger *c.* 1717.

Op. 8. *Il Cimento dell'Armonia e dell'Inventione, Concerti a 4 e 5.* ('The Contest of Music and Fancy', or 'The Rivalry between Technique and Inspiration'.) The six concertos of the first set have programmatic titles and are printed with descriptive sonnets upon each of the four seasons, a storm at sea, and *Il Piacere*, which defies translation except by such a play-title as 'The Good Natur'd Man'. No. 10 is called 'The Hunt', and Nos. 9 and 12 each bear the information: 'This concerto can be for oboe.' Printed by Roger's successor, Le Cène of Amsterdam, *c.* 1725.

Op. 9. *La Cetra*. (The Lyre.) Twelve concertos of which Nos. 6 and 12 use scordatura. Le Cène, 1728.

Op. 10. *VI Concerti a Flauto Traverso, etc.* Le Cène, *c.* 1730.

Op. 11. *Sei Concerti a Violino Principale, etc.* Le Cène, *c.* 1730.

Op. 12. *Sei Concerti a Violino Principale, etc.* Le Cène, *c.* 1730.

Although the 'Spring' concerto, No. 1 of *The Seasons* in Op. 8 was much in demand, and was a favourite even in France where there was less enthusiasm for concertos than in other countries, and though both this and other programmatic concertos were much imitated by minor composers, Vivaldi's fame was and still is based largely upon his Op. 3 and Op. 4. The scheme of Op. 3 can be quickly understood by scanning the column headed 'Soloists' in the following table. According to the number of solo violins the concertos are grouped in threes; the first in each group uses four solo violins, the second two, and the third one. The table also shows the Bach transcriptions.

VIVALDI, 'L'ESTRO ARMONICO', OP. 3

No. & key	Type & Movements	Soloists	Treatment by Bach and Schmieder No.
1. D major	Allegro Largo e spiccato Allegro	4 vns.	
2. G minor	Adagio e spiccato Allegro Larghetto Allegro	2 vns. with 'cello	
3. G major	Allegro Largo Allegro	1 vn.	Transposed to F major as the seventh concerto for harpsichord solo, 978.
4. E minor	Andante Allegro assai Adagio-allegro	4 vns.	
5. A major	Allegro Largo Allegro	2 vns.	
6. A minor	Allegro Largo Presto	1 vn.	
7. F major	Andante Allegro Adagio-Allegro	4 vns. with 'cello	
8. A minor	Allegro Larghetto e spiritoso Allegro	2 vns.	Third concerto for organ solo, 593.
9. D major	Allegro Larghetto Allegro	1 vn.	First concerto for harpsichord solo, 972.

10.	B minor	Allegro Largo-Larghetto Allegro	4 vns.	Transposed to A minor as the concerto for four harpsichords and string orchestra, 1065.
11.	D minor	Allegro-adagio and allegro (Fugue) Largo e spiccato Allegro	2 vns. with 'cello	Fifth concerto for organ solo, 596.
12.	E major	Allegro Largo Allegro	1 vn.	Transposed to C major as the fifth concerto for harpsichord solo, 976.

A numbered list will make clear the main features which distinguish these and other Venetian concertos from any by older composers. The references are to pages on which each point is discussed in the English version of Pincherle's book.

1. *The establishment of three movements* in the fast-slow-fast order that remained normal for two centuries (p. 143).
2. *Brilliant or impassioned solo parts.* To recognize that Corelli in his fastest movements never required the vivacity or fire of Albinoni's and Vivaldi's allegros is not to disparage Corelli's music. Some musicians may treasure Corelli's and Handel's concertos more than Vivaldi's and Bach's because they are of a rarer type and have no imitators of great genius. As performers the Venetians considerably advanced beyond Corelli's prowess, but the change of style was not determined only by this fact. Though people marvelled at Vivaldi's playing[1] he was not, as a composer, the eighteenth-century counterpart of Paganini. The thread of his expression often inheres in the solo, but it needs a sensitive as well as a clever player. His most characteristic slow movements resemble the pathetic types of aria which require fine musicianship as well as a wonderful voice. Let there be no mistake; the fine technique is essential, and second-rate violinists should not play Vivaldi's concertos publicly, but the masterly display should be of musical perception. To shine brilliantly in Vivaldi one must command faultless intonation and have perfect control of the bow. In the fiery fast movements the parts for the soloists were conceived along with the

[1] The most frequently-quoted testimony to Vivaldi's virtuosity is Uffenbach's journal. . . . 'He placed his fingers but a hair's breadth from the bridge, so that there was hardly room for the bow', etc.

other ideas and textures. Vivaldi did not add the rest of the music to a domineering solo part which, like that of a Paganini concerto, is far more difficult and brilliant than anything required from the ripienists. We do not know if Vivaldi composed or played cadenzas for the concertos in Op. 3, but he composed several for later concertos, and features which we associate with the cadenzas of classical violin concertos appear in the solo developments of Vivaldi's Op. 3.[1] From these works alone his pupils at the Pietà could have compiled a manual of violin playing (p. 88).

3. *The romantic turn of Vivaldi's expression.* If we give 'romantic' the meaning 'combining beauty with strangeness', we must add that some new and strange features of Vivaldi's concertos were not new in the theatre, and that Vivaldi's most romantic movements were his passionate adagios and andantes. 'He glorified a personal feeling, a new lyricism, the vogue for which was as widespread as it was sudden' (Pincherle). It is noteworthy that Vivaldi often seems more romantic in works *without* literary titles than in works like *The Four Seasons*. Eighteenth-century pieces which evoke objects or become onomatopœic—for instance Vivaldi's concertos with bird calls, representations of storms and the beating of hail—seem thereby to become objective and formal to ears which are used to impressionist music (p. 182, *Descriptive Music*).

Writings by ear-witnesses are not enough to tell us how much Vivaldi's performances used level or 'terraced' dynamics, how often all phrases were shaded by the crescendos and diminuendos that became consistent in later practice, what unmarked accentuations, what vagaries of tempo were introduced—in short, what expression was not marked on the parts. Walter Kolneder[2] suggests that, except in echo effects, Vivaldi wanted gradations and not 'terrace' dynamics, but his admirable thesis is not finally proven by his quotation of some twenty

---

[1] Two of these features to which Vivaldi was partial are known by the French names *bariolage* (change of colour) and *brisures* (from *brisé*, broken). The first indicates figures which require rapid changes back and forth between open and stopped strings; the second indicates arpeggio or broken-chord figures, usually with rapid and detached bowings, or a combination of such bowings with a group of notes to the return bow.

[2] *Aufführungspraxis bei Vivaldi*, Leipzig, 1958.

examples of graded directions from fortissimo to pianissimo
(i.e. *ppp*) and the reverse. Locke made clear his desire for
crescendo and diminuendo in his music for *The Tempest* as
early as 1675, writing 'Lowder by degrees' and 'Soft and slow
by degrees', and we have plenty of evidence in the writings of
Veracini, Geminiani and others to make us cautious in accepting literally Burney's tribute to Stamitz and the Mannheimers:
'It was here that the *Crescendo* and *Diminuendo* had birth; and
the *Piano*, which was before used chiefly as an echo, with
which it was generally synonymous, as well as the *Forte*, were
found to be musical *colours* which had their shades, as much
as red or blue in painting.'

Yet Burney, with his wide experience of performances in
different countries, evidently found the expressive range of the
Mannheimers remarkable, and particularly mentions these
gradations. He wrote forcefully of the lack of variety, the continuous forte, at Berlin. Kolneder may have claimed too strongly
that Vivaldi's range of expression fully anticipated that of the
Mannheim symphonists, but Kolneder's work is of unusual
interest because it is based upon manuscript corrections made
by the users of the Vivaldi parts at Turin. Most of these were
collected by Gluck's friend, Count Durazzo, who was Austrian
Ambassador to Venice during 1764–84. He may often have
stayed in Italy for quite long visits before taking up the appointment, and there is no proof that he began to collect Vivaldi's
music only after going into residence as ambassador. The marks
on the music were not made later than the year of Vivaldi's
death (1741), for the public expected music to be performed by
its composer, and Durazzo could secure copies easily when
players no longer wanted them. The corrections and added
directions, sometimes very liberally sprinkled on these pages,
may well have been made either under Vivaldi's own direction
or by those who had heard his performances.

Even if we are unwilling without further evidence to believe
that Venetian concertos were played with all the gradations
and nuances of Mannheim symphonies, we can hardly doubt
that the solo parts and large stretches of the ripieno sections,
especially in movements that showed the influence of opera,
were played with more shading than the 'terrace dynamics' so

dear to historians, and in this matter as in others Pincherle is justified in regarding Vivaldi as romantic (pp. 69–79).

4. *Perspicuity of style, including easily memorable themes.* What induced Bach to make keyboard transcriptions of these concertos, and what did he and other Germans gain (in other forms than the concerto) from Italian music, especially that of the Venetians? A brief and inadequate answer is: 'Simplicity, precision and symmetry, instead of that kind of continuous expression which resembles extempore speaking.' Writing about Vivaldi, Bukofzer speaks of 'the gestic[1] simplicity and precision of his themes . . . the easily-remembered motto of his ritornello'.

Much trivial music is clear in style for it owes its commercial success to easily-remembered ideas. When a single composer produces over four hundred concertos we expect some of them to achieve little more than complaisant catchiness. The eighteenth-century composer-performer rarely remained in demand, private or public, unless he undertook commissions whenever they were offered. Vivaldi, Handel, Telemann and Haydn did not expect that their hasty work would appear with their masterpieces in collected editions; but that fact cannot prevent our recognizing differences of quality among what has been collected. With Vivaldi fair assessment is not always easy.

Let the point be illustrated from those concertos which would be jettisoned from *L'estro armonico* by listeners who believe that the baroque violinist composed not many concertos but the same concerto many times. The opening of No. 5 with a theme consisting chiefly of the tonic sounded all'unisono (Ex. 41) might represent for them the nadir of conventionality, though they could hardly deny its memorability. Their opinion is not discredited merely because the first hearers must have found such a musical idea excitingly modern, nor because

---

[1] During the past twenty years or so the epithets 'plastic' and 'gestic' have come into vogue. The first of them is applied to themes by composers from Beethoven to Berg. As no theme is capable of development unless it is plastic, the word seems too imprecise to be valuable. What 'gestic' means no standard dictionary informs us. Is it derived from *gero*? Has it a connexion with *gestus*, in the sense of stance, posture, bearing, or in the sense of carriage, deportment or motion?

Albinoni's and Vivaldi's strongly metrical themes which emphasized tonic tonality initiated a habit which survived through the classical symphonic period. The succeeding beneficiaries, not the Venetians, must be called conventional. Apart from the fact that 'conventional' used without qualification is not a term of depreciation, these excuses are unsound. If the later composers used Vivaldi's patterns but wrote better themes then we need not treasure Vivaldi's themes.

Valid opposition can come only from those who recognize in the quoted theme not only character in the metaphorical sense but also a personal stamp in the literal sense. The theme quoted at Ex. 41 is as Vivaldian as the opening theme of the Fifth Symphony is Beethovenian, and it should be similarly played with vigorous strokes; whether we regard it as imperious or humorous it is as distinguished as a theme rightly admired by those least fond of Vivaldi, the fugue subject of the D minor concerto. The marvel is not that Vivaldi achieved clarity and memorability but that he achieved it as much in his trivial concertos, such as those for mandolin or piccolo, as in his impressive ones.

Let us consider the other Op. 3 concerto that is most likely to be despised, though it was among those transcribed by Bach. This is the last in the set. So many themes in overtures, concertos and symphonies use the repeated notes and the sequential formulae found in Ex. 43 that the concerto could be carelessly classed with much mass-produced music of the period. Yet if a series of openings from Vivaldi's to Haydn's, chosen for their similarity to this opening theme, were all played in the key of E major, Vivaldi's would probably be voted the most incisive and memorable by any listener who was not prejudiced by acquaintance with one of the others—for instance the Vivaldian opening of Bach's E major violin concerto. In fact this last concerto of Op. 3 is far more personal and original than it seems to be at a first hearing.

Many modern listeners cannot easily overcome impatience with sequential developments depending upon the 'circle of fifths', or upon a chain of chords of the seventh on the strong beats, as in Ex. 43B, or busy but simple materials like Ex. 43C. Two points must be advanced in their defence. The sequences

K   [145]

42.

Vivaldi. Op. 3, No. 5.

43.

Vivaldi. Op. 3, No. 12.

a.

f   p   f

b.

c.

p   f

44. Allegro   Vivaldi. Ripieno concerto (Turin). Pincherle 361. Fanna XI, 21.

(Ground bass)

allowed the performers to delight audiences with changes of style or dynamic, and when the broken chords and repeated short figures followed and offset a powerful main theme they contributed to clarity and memorability.

Some of Vivaldi's memorable themes are not simple but highly organized. Some have the span of Bach's or Handel's; but the command of lengthy ideas, as also of counterpoint and chromatic harmony, can scarcely be judged from Vivaldi's best known works. The slow movements in one or two of his popular concertos, for instance the well-known siciliano of No. 11 in Op. 3, reveal his harmonic resource, but for demonstrations of counterpoint and large paragraphing we go beyond the smaller opus numbers, for instance the works from which the quotations at Ex. 44 are taken. Pincherle surprised many musicians when he first drew their attention to the works quoted on pp. 198–203 of his original and pp. 178–9 of his translated study of Vivaldi.

5. *Ritornello organization*. Before the concertos of Albinoni and Vivaldi, expectant initial tuttis were highly organized only in arias. Vivaldi's and Albinoni's initial tuttis are more elaborate and pregnant than any others before Bach's. From *L'estro armonico* two of the best known concertos, No. 2 in G minor and No. 8 in A minor, provide splendid examples of Vivaldi's ability to devise opening tuttis of contrasted but organically connected ideas which can later be disconnected and then re-joined in a different order; one of them will be used as a ritornello and another (either directly or in a varied form) for treatment by the solo group. The opening allegro of the G minor concerto is outlined at Ex. 45. It is preceded by a stealthy introductory movement.

In many Vivaldi concertos, as in many classical concertos, the solo instruments begin by quoting the most prominent theme that has been heard in the opening tutti. Vivaldi was by no means the first composer of arias who required the singer to begin with a sustained note, a cadential fragment, or a melody which had *not* been heard in the prelude; nor were his concertos the first in which the solo instruments sometimes began with new materials. When the initial tutti does not close in the tonic, the concertino (unless it actually begins the movement) either continues with new ideas or echoes the tutti. When, however, the solo materials are punctuated by ritornelli from the initial tutti, each new solo departure is an advancing and each ritornello a consolidating factor, and the movement begets a series of tensions and relaxations.

45.

Vivaldi. Op.3, No.2.

In the G minor concerto which has just been quoted Vivaldi's two solo violins enter with a small-unit bravura. By silencing the bass instruments Vivaldi puts this bravura into strong contrast with the previous tutti ideas, and again with the same ideas when they follow as ritornelli. The first ritornello is of the section marked B in Ex. 45, the second is of the whole prelude transposed to D minor, and the third is again of B alone, this time in C minor. As far as the end of his expositions and just beyond them Vivaldi established the general first-movement design of the classical concerto; but he did not anticipate J. C. Bach, Vanhall, Wagenseil, Mozart, Viotti, Beethoven and other composers of the pre-classical and classical epoch by introducing new solo themes of strong individuality. Even the attractive arabesques in J. S. Bach's solo groups rarely include themes with the sharp profile of those that are announced within the initial tutti. New lyrical ideas introduced by the solo *after* reaching the key of the dominant (or the relative major key) constitute a feature, notably associated with Mozart, which the classical concerto derived from the classical symphony rather than the baroque concerto.

The final section of this G minor allegro shows that Vivaldi left another point of design to be developed by later composers. (One is tempted to write 'improved by later composers'.) Once Vivaldi's solo violins have again reached the tonic key there is nothing as clearly planned as a classical recapitulatory section, and this is not the only Vivaldi concerto wherein the first movement reaches its conclusion in a brilliant yet somewhat fortuitous manner. After the purposeful organization earlier in the movement, the finish sometimes suggests an improvisatory loss of grip. One should not judge Vivaldi's final sections by Mozart's wonderful recapitulations with their telescoping of ideas from the exposition and their following of the order of the tutti-prelude instead of the solo exposition.

By and large, however, Vivaldi's methods were followed by later concertists, especially after the solo concerto had ousted the concerto grosso. His established procedure should be illustrated from the exposition of a concerto composed later than Op. 3. At Ex. 46 are shown some of the themes from another Vivaldi concerto in G minor, the first in Op. 6. Here the solo materials, some derived from the tutti and some not, are as fine as Bach's, and the four ritornelli (see the letters marking sections of Ex. 46) which punctuate the exposition are organized as in a classical concerto:

1. B and C, *forte*
2. A only, *piano*
3. B only, *forte*
4. A+B+C, i.e. almost the whole prelude, in relative major, *forte*.

6. *Pathetic slow movements.* Though ritornelli were highly organized only in the allegros, they were often used in Albinoni's and Vivaldi's slow movements. It is hard to think of any baroque operas except Scarlatti's and Handel's wherein ritornelli have more impact than in the slow movement of the very first concerto of Op. 3 (Ex. 47). The unison ritornello occurs in several opera and oratorio scores before Vivaldi's, but its relation to a pathetic solo is rarely striking enough to remind us of Beethoven's masterly application of this technique in the slow movement of his fourth piano concerto.

Albinoni brought solo arias into the concerto, yet recollection of the theatre is more frequent in Vivaldi's slow movements which are more impassioned. This does not mean that they are better. Judgement on that point is a matter of taste and temperament which, if likely to cause tendentious evaluations, should be declared. Towards the end of the last century, for reasons so understandable as to make the error excusable, 'conventional' was used by intelligent and sober critics such as Riemann and Parry as if it were summarily pejorative. Those artists who *seemed* most unconventional were lionized. Bach and Beethoven were exalted; Handel and Mozart often abased. If he had been recognized at all, Albinoni would have been thought a very minor artist; but as Vivaldi was almost totally unexplored and badly played, at least he was not exalted to the belittlement of Albinoni. The truth is surely that Beethoven was in many ways wonderfully conservative and conventional, not only in his admiration for Handel and Mozart but in much of his own music. A good case could be made for the proposition that Haydn was a more revolutionary artist than Beethoven.

Vivaldi, too, was in some ways a conservative. He could be highly original in one way while paying tribute to his inheritance in another. A notable instance is the opening of Op. 3, No. 11. Never before had the tonic been asserted so brilliantly— a parallel with the opening of Beethoven's ninth symphony is not far fetched—nor had the turn from tonic harmony been made quite as strikingly as at the 'Adagio Spiccato e Tutti' just before the announcement of the fugue subject.

Some champions of unconventionality do not recognize that lovers of convention and of music wherein convention is vitalized are not necessarily averse to expression like Beethoven's unexpected *quasi recitativo* in a fast movement, or impatient with Bach's *quasi improvisando* in a slow one. The oboe passage in the Fifth Symphony and the slow movement of the Italian Concerto are not made less sublime because they are badly imitated; but it must be insisted that some great artists decline to be unconventional; they are powerful precisely because they require the listener to meet them half-way, to recognize what is expressed through accepted style and with great dignity.

Vivaldi, despite inferior movements, can appeal to both extremes of listener. The highly embellished 'aria' movements in which the tutti may be effaced or reduced to an almost impressionist wash of muted harmony, the adagios with surprising modulations, including the extraordinarily bizarre enharmonic one quoted by Pincherle from Op. 4, No. 7—these

46.

Vivaldi. Op. 6, No. 1.

are peculiar to Vivaldi, despite the fact that Albinoni first printed and probably first composed slow middle movements of the aria type in his Op. 5 concertos of 1707. (Some concertos of that collection merely continue the practice of supplying a short transitional or cadenza-like slow movement as a link and relief.) Yet Vivaldi also writes chaconne slow movements in which the sentiment is not markedly subjective but classically dignified, restrained and stylized. A good example occurs in Op. 4, No. 1, one of the concertos transcribed by Bach. The main key of the work is G major, but the chaconne is in Vivaldi's dignified key of B minor. (The first movement of this concerto is inferior and merely orderly; at his least inspired Albinoni is far better than this. The finale is even poorer than the first movement, and that may be why Bach substituted a gigue from another source.) Albinoni's chaconne slow movements are rarely equalled by Vivaldi's adagio forms, from siciliano or arietta to rondo-like and bithematic conceptions, from the tender or rustic to the intensely tragic.

Vivaldi's finales are varied and free in design, and their orchestral tuttis are usually simple. Even if they are frequently repeated one hesitates to call them ritornelli unless they have been stated as a prelude. When they are brief and melodious or dance-like they remind us of some of the rondo finales in galant and classical keyboard concertos; but the rondo finale is a development which we cannot claim to have been anticipated by Vivaldi, Bach or Handel, despite an occasional rondo in their suites. If it had ever occurred to Vivaldi to invest finales with a complex organization he might have taken a step towards Mozart's rondo finales comparable with his advance of first-movement designs. Instead the tuttis of his final movements are often short, boisterous punctuations, simple echoes or contrasts. Moreover the solo instrument often begins the finale, just as the piano or violin sometimes states the first rondo theme in a classical concerto. In Vivaldi's Op. 3 the seventh concerto provides a finale very similar in mood and style to a galant or classical finale. As will be seen in Ex. 48 its tutti sections can hardly be called ritornelli.

7. *Use of wind instruments.* In scores of the baroque period the antonym of *ad libitum* is *obbligato*, but in concertos we must

[152]

discriminate between obbligato and solo instruments. Vivaldi
sometimes used horns, and in at least one concerto two trumpets. The parts for these instruments are *obbligati*, essential to
the texture. Why does Vivaldi rarely specify wind instruments
in his earlier and famous concertos? Even at Turin there are
few with brass instruments, yet Italians like Torelli who stayed
with German orchestras scored for brass instruments quite
early in the eighteenth century, and Venice had for long been
famous for the wind instruments in church and theatre orchestras. De Brosses, writing of the 1730s, speaks of the horns
playing with the organ to accompany the voices during church
services in Milan and other Italian cities, but Vivaldi's first sets
of concertos were chiefly for his pupils, and though the records
of the Pietà mention young ladies who achieved prowess on
wind instruments, most of these references as well as corrobora-
tive comments by visitors date from after 1730.

Perhaps Vivaldi would not let poor wind players spoil the
intonation and attack of his string ensemble nor add ripieno
parts to upset the balance of a picked band. We have no proof
that composers were satisfied with crude vigour. If Burney
complained of the intonation of oboes at Mannheim he obviously had standards which are not always met today. Burney

rarely fails to notice when singers or players are out of tune. One would suppose exact intonation to be one of the first requirements of first-class performance, yet it is no specially adverse criticism of modern performances that good intonation is not maintained throughout. Vivaldi's standards may have been exacting. His own prestige as a player and his extraordinary interest in sonorities and textures prevent our accepting incautiously the belief that all eighteenth-century composers readily supplied extra parts when they found extra instruments; yet we should briefly note the facts on which that belief is based.

The published parts or scores of eighteenth-century works do not tell us the sizes and constitutions of the orchestras. Accounts of payments to players show that trombones not specified in Walsh's or Arnold's scores were sometimes used in Handel's oratorios, and we can understand that publishers would not incur the cost of unnecessary staves or parts. That is why we may be almost certain that two keyboard instruments were customary when publishers printed two figured bass parts from different plates. One part served in Vivaldi's Op. 3 concertos for 'cello, double bass and harpsichord. Sometimes we lack extra parts when we know that a bassoon or archlute was added to the bass. Unspecified wind instruments were sometimes used in ripieno sections, as we know from the 'strings only' before a slow middle movement; and in some German orchestras all available wind instruments may have joined in concertos which were performed only by strings and continuo in Italy. This *ad libitum* practice required no parts which differed from those supplied to string and continuo players. Mozart added parts to some of his orchestral works on separate sheets without embodying them in the score, and it is possible that several Haydn and Mozart symphonies which appear in the collected editions without trumpets, clarinets or drums were sometimes played with those instruments.

The extent of Vivaldi's composition for wind instruments was not known until his music in the Turin collections had been explored. We need not believe that because he wrote concertos for this or that instrument he had an expert understanding of its character. Special study of the flute, oboe, clarinet or bassoon

[154]

was not necessary before giving it an effective and attractive
solo part. A composer who did not know its working compass,
the 'breaks' in its scale, difficult shakes and notes of uncertain
intonation or poor tone would immediately have been recognized as a badly-trained impostor. The concertos for Dresden,
Darmstadt and Amsterdam, as well as many at Turin, show
that Vivaldi, whose work at the Pietà as well as his experience
in the theatre acquainted him with wind technique, was an
opportunist like other composers of his day when he found good
soloists. For instance, the best known of his bassoon concertos,
which has been admirably recorded several times, is No. 155
in the Foà collection, Pincherle's No. 282 in D minor; but the
same work is found as a 'cello concerto, No. 7 in the Giordano
collection, and the only difference is that a minuet finale has
been replaced by one with a two-four time signature. The 'cello
version is the original, but the work makes an excellent bassoon
concerto.

As far as we know the Marcellos and Albinoni[1] did not compose sets of solo concertos for other wind instruments than oboe
or flute, and in oboe concertos Albinoni may have been the
leader. There are extant eleven Vivaldi concertos for solo oboe
and two for a pair of oboes, the latter strongly resembling
Albinoni's concertos for two oboes. Roger published in 1716 a
set of twelve oboe concertos by one J. M. Müller. Alessandro
Marcello's six concertos of 1708, the set called *La Cetra*, are
for 'Oboe à Travers'. Vivaldi's Op. 10 consists of six concertos
for flute, an instrument much used in the theatre both as an
alternative to oboe in sinfonias and as obbligato in certain types
of pathetic or amorous arias. The flute has exposed sections in
Scarlatti's *Sinfonie di concerto grosso*, begun 1715, but Vivaldi
seems to be the first to give it a set of solo concertos. There exist
eighteen Vivaldi concertos for solo flute, three for solo piccolo,
some for mandolin, but none for harpsichord. The Turin works
include no less than thirty-seven concertos for solo bassoon.

[1] A gramophone record of the London Baroque Ensemble includes a 'Concerto à 5 in D major' by Albinoni with solo or obbligato parts for 'Two oboi
d'amore, bassoon and two horns'. The note on the sleeve, by Karl Haas, tells
us that he 'acquired a manuscript' of the piece and that it was 'written for
an open-air occasion', but does not say where the manuscript was acquired.
The music sounds convincingly like Albinoni's.

Almost all the points which have just been enumerated as distinguishing Venetian from previous concertos apply as much to
Albinoni as to Vivaldi, and may owe more to Albinoni's example
than to Vivaldi's. An exception is 'A romantic turn of expression'.
Although Albinoni's slow movements often match Vivaldi's in
pathos he was in general a more extravert composer. His perspicuity of style consistently exceeds Vivaldi's although his emotional range does not equal Vivaldi's. As his later concertos must
have been affected by some of the many which poured from
Vivaldi he would surely have made articulate the more turgid
and romantic facets of his psyche if while doing so he could have
reached his ideal of workmanship and form. This point may seem
obscure without analogy.

It is a common error to suppose that a man's capacity for
emotional experience (sometimes just called his 'depth') can be
measured by what he manages to express through one of the arts.
It would be as great an error to say that a man lacked brains
because he was a poor public speaker, or fine feelings because he
was a poor actor. From what we know of Mendelssohn, Liszt,
Borodin, Mahler and Busoni, each was a man of rare intelligence
and sensitivity, yet each was more limited as an artist than, say,
Brahms or Verdi. The difficulty facing Liszt or Busoni, each of
whom were profoundly interested in other men's music and in
the classics, was to communicate clearly and powerfully *by music*.
The ideas which they could conceive in music were but parts or
shadows of greater ideas, so that their notation conveyed less than
they wished to convey unless they were writing mere studies or
trifles. As performers they tried to 'play into' the inadequate
musical ideas what they knew to be inarticulate. On the other
hand Borodin, who was intellectually, ethically and musically one
of the greatest men, has little more than a niche in the history of
music because he declined to squeeze or blast from his musical
resources what would not flow easily at the bidding of imagination. By their services to other music and musicians and by the
quality of their own finest work, Mendelssohn and Mahler were
far greater beings than their music represents.

Albinoni strikes one as being an earlier example of the industrious and magnificently equipped musician who did not attempt
such expression as could not be stylized convincingly—shaped in

clear and readily understood ideas and extended into almost perfect forms. After the publication of Vivaldi's first set of concertos a new work by Vivaldi might follow an old path or strike out along an entirely new one. Novelty that seemed extraordinarily daring to the first audience might have occurred in a movement that is now thought disappointing; on the other hand some of the most striking novelties occur in pieces of first quality. With Albinoni there is neither the audacity nor the risk. His last concertos are simply his longest, most highly organized and best, but his styles and structures do not show radical changes. To put the matter in nearly paradoxical form, I consider Albinoni to be Vivaldi's superior in artistry, yet regard Vivaldi as a greater artist, especially when he is so markedly original as to seem crude by comparison with Albinoni.

For reasons which one hopes will be clear later a complete list of Albinoni's published instrumental works is given. He also published some works, including a whole set of sonatas at Amsterdam, without opus numbers.

Op. 1. *Sonate a tre.*	Sala, 1694.
	Roger, *c.* 1695.
Op. 2. *Sinfonie e Concerti a cinque.*	Roger, *c.* 1695.
(Despite the general title, the separate works are called: 'Sonata I, Concerto I, Sonata II, Concerto II, etc.', up to 'Concerto VI'.)	Sala, 1700.
Walsh and Hare published the concertos in this set as 'Albinoni's Concertos in Seven Parts for 3 violins, tenors and a bass violin with a thorough bass for the harpsichord', in 1708. (British Museum, g.671a.)	
Op. 3. *Balletti a tre.*	Sala, 1701 and 1704., Mortier (Amsterdam) 1710.
Op. 4. *Sonate da Chiesa a Violino solo e violoncello o.b.c.*	Roger, 1704. Walsh, *c.* 1712.
Op. 5. *Concerti a cinque.* (A set of twelve.)	Sala, 1707 and 1710 Roger, 1715.
Op. 6. *Trattenimenti Armonici per Camera, divisi in Dodici Sonate, a violino, violone e cembalo.*	Roger, 1711. Walsh, *c.* 1730.

Op. 7. *Concerti a Cinque con Oboi.*	Roger and Le Cène,
Nos. 1, 4, 7, 10, without oboe.	*c.* 1716.
Nos. 3, 6, 9, 12, one oboe.	
Nos. 2, 5, 8, 11, two oboes.	

Op. 8. *Balletti e Sonate a Tre (con le Fughe*   Roger and Le Cène,
     tirate a Canone). Twelve works, of   *c.* 1722.
     which the sonatas take the odd num-
     bers. All the allegro movements of the
     six sonatas are fugues of three parts,
     the upper two of which maintain a
     canon 2 in 1. There is no evidence
     that Bach knew this work, but con-
     clusive evidence that he knew well
     Albinoni's Op. 1 to 6.

Op. 9. *Concerti a Cinque con 1 e 2 oboi.*   Le Cène, *c.* 1722.
     Nos. 1, 4, 7, 10, without oboe.   (British Museum,
     Nos. 2, 5, 8, 11, with one oboe.   g.671d.)
     Nos. 3, 6, 9, 12 ,with 2 oboes.

Op 10. *Concerti a Cinque*   Le Cène, 1737
     (A set of twelve, strings with solo
     violin)

Nearly all these works were also printed by Le Clerc of Paris, and north of Italy Albinoni must have been scarcely less influential than Vivaldi between 1710 and 1725. Bach, who made copies of his works for students, evidently admired the contrapuntal vein appears in Albinoni's church sonatas, but is rarely evident in his concertos after the 1700 set. As late as Op. 7 he composed fast and slow movements in five (sometimes six) real parts which make Lully's five-part work seem merely ponderous. He was also one of the few musicians in all history who could produce long and entirely gay movements as admirable as other men's serious movements. This ability should be valued for its rarity. Unfortunately the mass of listeners cannot do so, any more than the mass of voters can support a truthful and satiric candidate against a solemn liar. Wanting us to value Handel or Haydn, critics nearly always select for special commendation the pathetic or sinister and suggest that it is subjective.

No such pleading for the ridiculously undervalued Albinoni will be made here. To support one's belief in his greatness one first quotes from a light and gay finale. The complete melody of

Albinoni. Op.9, No.9.

the initial tutti is shown at Ex. 49. The first four bars define the tonic with triadic intervals and the complete descending scale. Could they have done so better? Could any music be more suited to a concerto finale and convey the allure of the dance without suggesting the street or barnyard? Within the four bars how well the little climax of melody comes at the high note before the downward scale! There follows a rhythmic subtlety worthy of Haydn or Brahms, produced by kinetic repetition of the pulsating motive which is inverted in the third line quoted. Until this inversion, low tension keeps us expectant and is as rightly placed as the refrain-repetition.

Albinoni's finales are usually of this pulsating yet urbane kind, and the ear alone cannot tell whether the time signature is three-eight, six-eight or twelve-eight. All signatures suggest the same speed, and no finale quite resembles the stylized gigue of Corelli. Three-eight is probably the most frequent time signature of Venetian finales, but Vivaldi's three-eight finales are rarely like Albinoni's; when they are so they are inferior in quality. Many an excellent conerto by Vivaldi concludes with a useful but unremarkable finale, whereas such a finale as that quoted at Ex. 50C would scarcely sound incongruous if it replaced the finale in one of Bach's concertos, for instance the D minor concerto for two violins. The superb rhythmic invention and general workmanship of this last published set of Albinoni's concertos may be judged from the opening movement of the same concerto, Ex. 50A, which may also serve to illustrate Albinoni's application to the concerto of the *Devise* associated with arias of the Neapolitan school. A truncated ritornello from the opening tutti punctuates the first statement by the soloists, who then reiterate before proceeding to new material. The slow movement, of which a portion is quoted at Ex. 50B, seems to show the influence of Vivaldi in its accompanying string texture, but this movement as well as the finale opens with the *Devise*.

If nothing by Vivaldi had survived, Albinoni would be admired as the man who most notably brought the forms and much of the expression of the opera into the concerto. The process began in his first set of *Concerti a Cinque*, Op. 2, which were issued by Sala of Venice in 1700, the year in which the same publisher is said by Torrefranca[1] and Giazotto to have issued the first edition of Vivaldi's Op. 3, though it is unlikely that Vivaldi's concertos were composed before he took up his duties at the Pietà, that is to say before at least 1703.[2] We recognize in some of these pieces by Albinoni incisive and memorable themes (Ex. 51). The concertos from Op. 5 onwards have scarcely less fire and invention than any in *L'estro armonico* except in slow movements. What has been too unkindly called 'archaic stiffness' is not simply

[1] Fausto Torrefranca. Article on Vivaldi in *Enciclopedia Italiana*, Rome, 1937.

[2] Pincherle rejects the opinion that there was a Sala edition of *L'estro armonico* long before the Roger edition, and considers Torrefranca's thesis to be based upon 'une interprétation aventureuse' of the Roger and Le Cène catalogues. It is based upon the serial numbers against works in these catalogues.

Albinoni. Op.9, No. 2.

a) Allegro e non Presto

b) Adagio

c) Allegro

51. Albinoni. Opening themes. 1700.

attributable to their date. Both Albinoni and the Marcellos are
decidedly dignified composers, and even at their finest their
energy glows where Vivaldi's flames. Their solo sections rarely
floreate like Vivaldi's, but they either continue with materials
little differentiated from those of the tutti or offer figuration in
contrast with the broader tutti lines. Albinoni excels in the dignified, free chaconne slow movement, and he is never as jejune
as Vivaldi could be when he lacked time and inspiration.

The comment in Grove and elsewhere that 'Albinoni stands
midway between Corelli and Vivaldi' is utterly misleading unless
we assume that Vivaldi's Op. 3 was known or published c. 1700.
It would be more accurate to place Albinoni's early work midway
between *Torelli's* and *Vivaldi's*. Pincherle considers that Torrefranca's early dating of Vivaldi's Op. 3 concertos 'falsifies their
relationship' to Torelli's and Corelli's, and it certainly makes
difficult the belief that another Venetian then published a volume

in which most of the concertos have more than three movements and retain the intermediary slow sections of the canzona concerto as well as 'continuation' or 'undifferentiated' solo passages like Torelli's. If at this time Albinoni knew Vivaldi's concertos, why do his own pieces of 1700 fail to bring the methods of the opera composer into chamber music, despite the fact that he won laurels in the theatre?

Albinoni's first publications after 1700 are those which make the historian anxious for any evidence that Vivaldi's concertos were in circulation immediately after his work began at the Pietà. Beginning with the Op. 4 sonatas of c. 1703 Albinoni either reflects Vivaldi or appears as his ally in the Venetian desire to bridge theatre and chamber music. The word *patetico* appears over one of the slow movements in these sonatas, and Albinoni's Op. 5 concertos include slow movements of almost the Vivaldian power, sometimes expressed in aria form. With one exception these Op. 5 concertos follow Vivaldi's three-movement plan, and though some of them are of no outstanding merit, none lacks energy and vitality, and none is at all like any earlier concerto.

I have wilfully quoted a good deal from Albinoni because he is badly underestimated by otherwise reliable historians of music, even by Bukofzer. As one hears or only score-reads Albinoni's concerto movements one recognizes a care with the harmony that is not found in Torelli or in other composers of the time and was not necessary for immediate effect if violins and bass were strong and the keyboard continuo filled the chords adequately. Vivaldi was more enterprising in his harmonic colours and often just as sensitive as Albinoni about the detail and spacing of parts, especially when using at the same time a new disposition of instruments; but Albinoni's harmony is consistently careful, as though sensitive part-writing were as natural to him as it was to Handel or Mozart. The passage at Ex. 52 illustrates the point and also shows an early antecedent of the classical minuet and trio. The same quality is evident in a thinner texture at Ex. 53, which comes from the middle of the movement which begins at Ex. 50B. We see also in this connective passage the long sweep of Albinoni's phrasing and his meticulous choice of the notes to include and the notes to omit in a chord of the seventh. Finally we may well note the same virtue in one of his finest movements,

52. Allegro — Albinoni. Op. 9, No. 6. Finale.

which bears the direction *Senza cembalo e il violone pizzicato*, thereby preventing the continuo from remedying any weakness in the harmony. Two extracts are shown in Ex. 54A and B.

Alessandro Marcello (1684–1750) and Benedetto Marcello (1686–1739) published far less than Albinoni and Vivaldi, and what has survived of their music suggests that they were able, like Schubert, to be greatly indebted and yet original.

Outside Italy, Benedetto was the more famous of the brothers, probably because of the *Teatro*, but also because he composed so many sonatas, copies of which are well dispersed among the German and other north-European libraries. Moreover his Op. 1 concertos appeared as early as 1708 and reached even Stockholm in manuscript copies. Knowing by name only Marcello of the satire and the 'Psalms', people sometimes attributed Alessandro's work to Benedetto; but in Italy itself, especially in Venice where Alessandro remained as head of the family and long outlived his brother, he was held in great esteem as a mathematician, philosopher and composer. He was a member of the Arcadian Academy and used his arcadian name, 'Eterio Stinfalico', on title-pages of works which were played at meetings of the academy held in his own house. If his concertos were ever played except at these and other private concerts, I have not seen or heard evidence of the fact.

Despite an account of Benedetto which is valuable as far as it goes,[2] a bibliography of the two Marcellos, telling us where originals are preserved and how different publishers' and musicographers' opus numbers can be conflated or put in chronological order, is still lacking and seems to be a difficult task. It cannot be done by sending for microfilms, and even if I could afford the journeys to attempt what has defeated better researchers I should not wish to delay publication of this book merely to give a more satisfactory account of two concertists who, for all their great merits, are less important than Albinoni and Vivaldi. Eitner (*Q–L*, vol. vi, p. 310) gives details of Alessandro's 'Concerti di Eterio' and mentions copies at Schwerin and Augsburg—they were published in Augsburg by G. Chr. Leopold *c.* 1735—and of the famous oboe concerto in the second book of a collection of concertos by many composers issued by Jeanne Roger and Le Cène at Amsterdam *c.* 1716. In the *Quellen-Lexicon* Eitner simply writes 'Instrumentalwerke' against Benedetto Marcello, evidently because he was baffled by the bibliographical problem at the time of publication; but he wrote an article[2] on this composer which may be regarded not only as supplementary to the *Q-L*

---

[1] Andrea d'Angeli, *Benedetto Marcello, Vita e opere*, Milan, 1940.
[2] Robert Eitner, 'Benedetto Marcello', *Monatshefte für Musikgeschichte*, vol. xxiii, 1891.

entry but also as the only reliable published matter from which to continue inquiry.

The title-page of the only set of (six) concertos by Alessandro which has survived is magnificently embellished by a classical prospect of a grove with the muses and graces holding instruments. At the top is a medallion bearing the words *Si placet iste labor mihimet non displicet alter*, and at the bottom a larger shield-shaped tablet with this inscription:

LA CETRA
CONCERTI
DI ETERIO STINFALICO
Academico Arcade
PARTE PRIMA.
Oboe Primo o Traversiere
col. Violino Principale.
Publicati
DA GIOVANNI CHRISTIANO LEOPOLD
IN AUGUSTA
Cum Gratia et Privilegio Sacrae Caesar. Majestatis.

Within, there is a prefatory address, first in Italian and then in German, pointing out that the orchestra should consist of two oboes or flutes, six violins, two violas, two 'cellos, double bass, bassoon and harpsichord, but that if two violins replace the oboes or flutes there should not be less than six violins altogether. The concertos have been printed exactly as they should be played, and should not be 'added to'. (Does this mean no embellishments?) The *piano* and *forte* directions are to be well observed.

This publication is not dated. It may have been issued at any time between 1730 and 1740 and the concertos may have been composed long before they went to the printer. The title 'La Cetra' was used by other composers and was not necessarily suggested by Vivaldi's Op. 9. Indeed in the six concertos of this set Alessandro Marcello seems deliberately to have avoided imitation of any models by other composers. They are concertos for a select audience of connoisseurs, and most of them include movements which evoke dark moods and turbulent emotions, sometimes including abrupt and stormy contrasts. Four are in minor keys, and

[167]

there are frequent transitions to the minor key during the course of movements beginning in the major, as well as sharp dissonances and chromatic harmonies. Alessandro Marcello was decidedly a romantic, and these concertos could have been called 'L'estro armonico' or 'La Stravaganza' even more aptly than Vivaldi's.

It is true that all are cast in three movements, but none in three movements that can be described as 'typically Venetian'— e.g. (i) Allegro with initial closed tutti later forming ritornelli between solo sections, (ii) Adagio in aria or chaconne form, (iii) Vivace in triple time with rondo-like recurrence of a tutti strophe. Nor can any of these works be called an oboe concerto, a violin concerto, a concerto for two oboes or two violins, a concerto for violin and oboe, or a ripieno concerto. To explain these points one would have to quote more extensively than is possible and even then the quotations would reveal little but the nervous energy, the large number of ideas, and suggest that the movements as wholes were diffuse—which is certainly not true, despite the fact that Alessandro Marcello shows an extreme contrast with the economical, precise and clear-cut Albinoni. Though technical description makes for arid reading, I ask indulgence for briefly saying what happens in just one of these concertos, perhaps the finest.

Concerto No. 3 in B minor. (i) Andante larghetto (3/4). A movement which occupies three-quarters of the time taken to play the whole concerto. The two uppermost moods are of sombre, even sinister solemnity (from a texture of even, repeated bow strokes beginning 'pianissimo') and of angry interruptions marked 'forte'. This movement gives no indication that a solo instrument or instruments will be used. It is like a long entre-acte in the middle of a tragedy. It could have been used by Gluck without seeming anachronistic. So could the next movement. (ii) Adagio 4/4. Here, despite the change to the relative major, is plenty of reference to the pathos of the minor key; but the scoring would lead one who had not heard the piece to suggest Rameau's authorship. The movement is *senza cembalo* and the strings are pizzicato, accompanying a dialogue aria for solo violin and solo oboe; at the end they play *arco* a dignified passage that seems like a final ritornello. After the first movement with no solo work, we have what would normally belong to a concerto for two

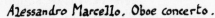

soloists. (iii) Presto 3/4. Though it returns to B minor, this is not a tragic movement, for the saccadé rhythm persists, the opening idea being recurrent between solo episodes—but these are for two oboes, not the oboe and violin of the second movement!

As we pass on to the fourth concerto, in E minor, we again find solo parts differently distributed in different movements. The first movement is that of a solo violin concerto of Vivaldian type, though moderato, not allegro. The second movement, largo appoggiato, is not for soloists; it sounds like the full orchestral version of a grandiose Handelian bel canto aria in G major. The finale goes back to E minor but not to become the finale of a violin concerto, nor to the triple measure usually favoured in Venetian finales. It is in steady, gentle 4/4, and the solo episodes are duets for oboe and violin. The last concerto of the set, being in G major, bids fair to be less stormy than some of its predecessors; but its placid opening allegro is a ternary movement, allegro-lento-allegro, the slow middle section giving much rein to two solo violins, which are not featured in succeeding movements.

Despite the fascination with which these romantic concertos must have held their privileged first audiences (and will certainly hold other audiences when they are revived) there is one concerto by Alessandro Marcello which so remarkably combines romantic pathos with classical integrity and elegance that many must regard it, as Bach evidently did, as one of the supremely beautiful works of the Venetian School. This oboe concerto in D minor, wrongly attributed to Benedetto Marcello and transcribed by Bach for harpsichord, is usually played in C minor from an edition which slightly amplifies some of the harmonies. Bach's version retains the original key and makes scarcely more than the minimum changes necessary for keyboard performance; but it includes embellishments which, belonging so closely to the period of composition, remain a safe guide to the oboe soloist in a concert performance.

As Eitner first reported, this work appeared in a collection of concertos published in two books *c.* 1716–17 by Jeanne Roger. Each book was entitled *Concerti a cinque con violini, oboi, violetta, violoncello e basso continuo, dei Signori G. Valentini, A. Vivaldi, T. Albinoni, F. M. Veracini, G. St. Martini, A. Marcello, G.*

[170]

Rampin (not mentioned in reference books), *A. Predieri*. (The last of these, 1688–1767, was maestro di capella at St. Petronio; later he became kapellmeister at Vienna until succeeded by Reutter. He was chiefly an opera composer.) The British Museum possesses a full set of the parts of this collection and the Bodleian has an incomplete set. Bach's unusual reticence in his keyboard treatment of Marcello's concerto is surely a tribute to its appeal as it stands. Those who are familiar only with the usual C minor version may wonder if the sevenths and other romantic harmonies are original. Almost all of them are. No movement in the concertos of 'La Cetra' contains the restrained yearning effect of the passage quoted at Ex. 54A. It is undoubtedly an earlier work than any concerto in 'La Cetra'. Those who value unconventionality and experiment, the kind of expression which makes one say 'This *is* fine music' rather than, at the end of a movement, 'That *was* fine music', must greatly prefer 'La Cetra'. As I do not believe it possible to give a purely objective account of musical history, nor worth while to write history without judgement or evaluation, I have thought it only honest (especially in the chapters on Handel, Bonporti and Leclair) to declare my prejudice for formality and symmetry, my love of style and convention, hoping that the reader is as well served by disagreement as by agreement with me. Plainly, however, the most magnificently formal expression would be arid if its artist could not take advantage of such advances beyond contemporary convention as Marcello was making in 'La Cetra'.

I have embarked upon this discussion of classical and romantic ideals because in this earlier D minor concerto Alessandro Marcello was clearly beholden to the experiments made by Albinoni and Vivaldi—chiefly to Albinoni's own concertos for solo oboe. The elegiac beauty of the first movement, the noble pathos of the second, and the clean strength of the finale could have been matched by Bach himself but for the fact that the style is so thoroughly Italian. We notice at the very opening a skilful application of the *Devise*, a gambit of which only Albinoni among the Venetian concertists was markedly fond, as he was of the upward-moving chains of anticipatory notes found in the first movement (there are some just before the passage quoted in Ex. 54A) and also in the second movement; as for the finale (Ex. 54B),

[171]

an expert could be excused for supposing it to be by Albinoni, who was surely among those who attended some of Alessandro Marcello's academies.

We have probably lost many fine concertos by Alessandro Marcello which existed only in manuscript and were used at his own concerts or those held in the music rooms of Arcadians. We may have lost even more by Benedetto, despite the fact that he died when only middle aged—not in Venice; he moved to Brescia for nearly the whole of the last decade of his life because his health was said to have been ruined either by the climate of the Venetian lagoons or by that of Pola, on the eastern Adriatic, of which province he had been made governor. It is known that Benedetto had lessons in composition from Lotti and on the violin from Tartini.

The only printed set of Benedetto's concertos so far known is that printed by Sala at Venice in 1708, the date being on the title-page, and also 'Opera Prima'. (D.Angeli has added his own opus numbering of Benedetto's works to two other conflicting orders.) The title of this set of six is *Concerti a cinque, con violino solo, e violoncello obligato, di Benedetto Marcello, Nobile Veneto Dilettante di Contrapunto*.[1] It would, of course, be unfair to compare them with Alessandro's 'La Cetra' of much later date and then call them old-fashioned or unadventurous, which they certainly are not. The passionate blood of the Marcellos shows even in works which begin with the slow introduction and fugued allegro of the church concerto. As we see in Ex. 55, the composer of the 'Psalms', the 'Dilettante di Contrapunto', can charge the formalities of counterpoint with fire.

Fortunately for the student, a string concerto by Benedetto Marcello of later date than the 1708 set is printed in Eulenburg Miniature Scores (No. 1209). This is also a 'Concerto a cinque'— the four string parts with a 'violino concertino' added. The work is edited by Dr. Richard Engländer from a set of manuscript parts in the University Library at Uppsala which bear the signature of J. D. Gudenschwager, violinist of the Stockholm court orchestra and secretary of the musical director, J. H. Roman. It is in the Vivaldi-Tartini virtuoso style at its most brilliant—a ritornello-style allegro in D major with strong unisons (sometimes with

[1] N.B.—Not 'di violino' or 'di musica'.

THE VENETIAN SCHOOL

massed tremolo bowing) to offset brilliant passage work, an impassioned adagio in B minor for the solo violin, punctuated by a
short heavy unison figure (as in Vivaldi's first concerto with the
same key scheme), and an incisive presto from which Ex. 56
comes. [The score costs little and therefore further quotation is
pointless.]

Like the violin concertos of Bonporti or Leclair—or for that
matter those of J. S. Bach—the concertos of the two Marcellos
founded no new school; they are precious luxuries, music for connoisseurs like their first hearers. So are many of the most unusual
Vivaldi concertos now being garnered, those outside the famous
'sets'. If we were concerned only with the historical importance
of concertos, and if the savouring of music and of individual expression meant little to us, we should think of the Venetian
School simply in terms of the sets of three-movement concertos by
Vivaldi which made him the figurehead of Venice in northern
countries. In his work both the classical concerto and the classical symphony are latent, and I for one accept Pincherle's opinion
that with him they exist in all but the vocabulary and syntax we
call musical style. Unquestionably in some countries Vivaldi
represented all the Venetian musicans, conservative and radical;
but the concertos of the great *dilettanti* show that in Venice itself
Vivaldi was a peak in a group of mountains.

CHAPTER IX

Concerto and Concert

N owadays we distinguish recitals from concerts, and we
speak of serious music, light music, background music,
dance music and so on. The seventeenth and eighteenth
centuries classified music according to the places in which it
sounded, and they recognized only three kinds—church music,
theatre music and chamber music. The last classification could
include an overture or a concerto played to a large assembly in a
palatial hall for the honour of state visitors, and it could also
include a sonata for two or three instruments played to or with a
few members of a noble family, to London citizens in a tavern,
auction room or dancing school, or among members of a college
or university. Chamber music was defined by J. G. Walther as
'that which is customarily performed in the apartments of the
upper nobility'.[1]

Before Burney's time even the most musical among the nobility
lacked any considerable *historical* culture of music. Until at least
1750 the phrase 'a musical culture' could have meant only training as a performer and composer. 'The literature of music', if
such a phrase was ever used, must have meant writings about
music by theorists and ancient philosophers. When private and
public concerts had become regular and widespread listeners
began to compare styles, contemporary and near-contemporary.
The name of the composer was less important than connoisseurship of the French, the Italian, the English and the 'old fashioned'

[1] J. G. Walther, *Musikalisches Lexicon*, Leipzig, 1732.

[174]

styles, the last meaning the styles of motets, madrigals, canzonas and string fantasias. The 'academies of ancient music' did take note of composers—Carissimi, even Purcell—but they belong chiefly to Burney's generation, which acclaimed the first historians of music and also welcomed a commentary upon the state of music in different European countries.

If anyone qualifies as an 'absolute' listener Burney does, though he lived after the period of the concerto grosso and cannot be held to represent the average listener. To know how novel was 'absolute' listening in the earlier years of his century let us turn to another keen music lover. Reading that sonatas and concertos 'lacked moral and laudable purpose'[1] we might take the writer for a puritan expanding St. Paul's 'sounding brass and tinkling cymbal' and illustrating the vanity of faith without charity; but Mattheson was an apostle of music as well as morals. His difficulty was actually produced by his education. His 'musical culture' taught him to sing, play and be a coxcomb. Germans of the next generation, such as Spiess in his *Tractatus musicus* of 1746, speak highly of sonatas and concertos, but Mattheson's first crop of writings dates from 1712 to 1728 and it reflects French rationalism and the aesthetic of Boileau. Musical souls were no less musical in the Age of Reason than in the Age of Sensibility, but whereas the verbiage of the Age of Sensibility makes us wonder how much was heard with the natural ear and how much with the ear of imagination, the verbiage of the Age of Reason makes us wonder if ears were used at all in forming judgements. The intelligent Scheibe, a good musician who became composer and Kapellmeister at Copenhagen and elsewhere, goes down to history as the man who supposedly failed to understand J. S. Bach,[2] and who was gulled by that worthy as the donkey-eared Midas in *Phoebus and Pan*. Scheibe was a product of Leipzig University which at that time was as francophile as the petty German courts, for it was dominated by the redoubtable J. C. Gottsched, a Prussian who had formerly been professor at Frankfort and was determined to spread French ideas in Germany.

[1] Mattheson, *Der musikalisches Patriot*, 1728.
[2] Several writers treat Scheibe as if he were a clown or a Beckmesser. Almost every remark he passed about Bach was true, and what he liked in Bach's work he praised generously. He failed to like music that belonged to a generation before his own. Is that an unusual failing?

How could Gottsched ridicule opera during his apostrophizings of Reason, Clarity and Naturalness while Mattheson, extolling the same virtues and attacking cantor's counterpoint, thought all good music theatrical and set himself to imbue the Lutheran cantata with operatic expression? How could Mattheson regard the French overture as the best of music yet despise the concerto grosso of nearly similar design? Apparently a church concerto had a purpose which it lacked when it was played at a concert. An operatic sinfonia 'explained' something. Did a sonata merely tickle the ears and allow people to gape at the performers? One can be glad that Mattheson wrote so much, but one cannot agree with those who praise him as forward-looking, as if the forward-looker were more intelligent than the backward-looker or the looker-around. One doubts the progressiveness of a man who finds no laudable purpose in absolute music yet praises an overture played at a concert because it 'explains the different dance movements'. One prefers Schering's opinion that 'the concerto represented modern music, the art of the younger generation'.

It would be wrong to blame France for the Matthesons, and hasty to say that she was the nation least prepared to hear the new Italian works and listen absolutely. The historian can gain few statistics about music in France except those bearing upon one central establishment theoretically controlled by the king. The title of Couperin's trio sonata *Le Parnasse, ou l'Apothéose de Corelli* tells us something about the judgement of professional musicians in France. That work dates from 1725, in which year Philidor inaugurated the *Concert Spirituel*, the first adequate and regular public concerts like those of London, Vienna, Amsterdam, Hamburg and other big cities. Concertos had a hearing at Philidor's concerts but they do not seem to have produced a harvest of French concertos to compare with the German or English ones. Yet before we rashly imagine that French listeners could not listen to absolute music or that they were deficient in musical culture we should remember that nothing had influenced standards of ensemble playing, and therefore of listening, during the second half of the seventeenth century as had French orchestral discipline under Lully. It took an Italian to make French connoisseurs of the lyric stage into an audience for instrumental music. Himself from Italy, Lully was aware of all developments

5. 'Concert in a Convent' by Guardi

in Italian music. Music from the French theatre, from Lully's ballets and tragedies, and from the overtures, airs and dances by Campra and Destouches, formed the first considerable repertory of orchestral music. When it left France it left the theatre to become chamber music for princely establishments in Germany and for public concerts in England. French overtures, chaconnes, entrées, dances, symphonies and marches remained in the repertory of German court concerts throughout the period of the concerto grosso and were imitated by Germans. The concerto might absorb them but it did not oust them, and if it had not given scope to the great violinists or other solo performers it would not have rivalled them.

England has the credit for providing musical evenings and public concerts long before they were established in France or Germany; but we should not assert that English audiences in general were very much more familiar with first-rate music, or that they enjoyed a first-class musical culture *long* before plebeian audiences in Vienna, Hamburg, Venice or even Paris. The indisputable facts in the history of the public concert are misleading unless the following points are set against them:

1. Though there was fine music in London theatres before the Commonwealth and a unique development of English chamber music from before the Commonwealth until after the Restoration, the first public concerts of reasonably high standard in England were Banister's.

2. Banister's concerts began in 1672. Those of the Vienna Music Society (*Tonkünstlersocietat*) began in the same year. Buxtehude's evening concerts (*Abendmusiken*) at Lübeck began in the following year. Thereafter we hear of public concerts in Berne, Leipzig, Hamburg and other European cities. England led by only a few years in providing the type of concert we can regard as the forerunner of those which are sought by most music-lovers today. Moreover some of the continental concerts, such as those at Vienna and Lübeck, were surely finer than Banister's. The Vienna concerts must have been particularly fine, for Vienna was musically an Italian colony. Some of the Hapsburg emperors of the seventeenth century had been performers and composers of music, and the imperial opera outshone the Italian ones in splendour.

M [177]

3. Against the English advance in providing public concerts must be set London's failure to establish permanent opera. Passing to the third class of music, that for the church, we must admit that England was peculiar and has remained so. At the Restoration only the Chapel Royal seems to have used the string ensemble, and this was in imitation of the French royal chapel. English church music and Chapel Royal music cannot be compared with that of the greater Italian and Lutheran churches. All largish city churches in Italy and Germany used other instruments than organs.

4. Some of the London concerts, though not Banister's and Britton's, were little better than variety entertainments.

5. Purcell composed sonatas in admiration of Italian ones; he composed no concerti grossi although he lived till 1695 and proved by his overtures that he could have outshone any Italians in concertos. If England had been ahead in taste the concerto and the orchestral sonata of the type found in Muffat's first *Armonico Tributo* (1682) would have appeared in England before it appeared in Germany.

Though it is not proposed once more to tell the whole history of early concert-giving in England we should notice one or two evidences that music was sometimes more than convivial pastime before Banister's enterprise. H. A. Scott[1] quotes a pamphlet by Theophilus Cibber which, though undated, refers to London theatres at some time during Ben Jonson's great days. Jonson himself was annoyed because music, dancing and adjuncts to the drama seemed to attract people more than the plays; but Cibber tells of a man who 'would take a place in the pit to hear the First and Second Music, which latter used to be some select piece, but prudently retired, taking his money again at the doors before the Third Music, and by that means kept out a spectator who would have been glad to enjoy the whole entertainment, though he paid for it'.

Evidently the man was within the law in playing this trick on the management. Perhaps the theatres put the idea into his head by advertising that they would return money to dissatisfied patrons. Plainly he could claim his money if he did not stay for the play.

---

[1] 'London's Earliest Public Concerts' by Hugh Arthur Scott. Article in *The Musical Quarterly*, November, 1936.

Suppose this music to have been well performed and ambitious. Suppose that Dent does not exaggerate in saying that 'the play was habitually preceded by a concert'[1]—The First Music, Second Music and Curtain Tune or Overture—and that there was more music between the acts. Suppose this was much better music than continental theatres offered except in operas. It still does not give the Londoner a musical advantage over the Venetian commoner. Nobody in Venice was prevented from hearing the grand concerted pieces of Gabrieli's school. Who, when the Tron family opened the San Cassiano opera, and when other public opera houses were established in the same city, was refused admission on the grounds of social rank? The Londoner had to wait for Davenant's ventures before comparable music came his way, though anyone might have heard Locke's music for the royal sackbuts and cornetts when Charles II made his progress through the city on the day before his coronation.

When Parliament ordered the closing of the theatres in 1642 there dawned the heyday of those taverns which were called music houses. The state of music in England under the Commonwealth is fully documented by P. A. Scholes,[2] two of whose entries may serve to represent many. After telling us how music houses were quick to employ string players, oboists and other former theatre musicians, and to buy at ridiculous prices the organs pulled from the churches, Scholes observes that some of the tavern concerts must have included good music well performed. Chilmead, formerly minor canon of Christ Church Cathedral, Oxford, ran a weekly music meeting in London at a Fleet Street tavern; his friend Ellis, formerly organist at one of the Oxford colleges, remained as a private teacher in Oxford and ran concerts there. A further witness to the fact that not all tavern music was mere pastime to accompany eating, drinking and gossiping is Ned Ward of *The London Spy*. He was not musical, and 'would rather hear an old barber ring Whittington's Bells upon an old cittern than all the music the houses afforded', thus suggesting that tavern music needed a more cultivated ear than his. River travel being popular in London during the seventeenth century, several famous music houses which had *built* music rooms quite separate

---

[1] E. J. Dent, *The Foundations of English Opera*, Cambridge, 1928.
[2] P. A. Scholes, *The Puritans and Music*, London, 1934.

from the other reception rooms were by the waterside. Ward heard 'fiddles and hautboys together with a humdrum organ' (continuo?) as he approached the 'Mitre' at Wapping. He paid not to hear the 'ravishing concert of caterwauling' but to inspect the sumptuous music room. Despite 'the many pretty whimsical pictures on the walls' it reminded him of a church, for the 'musitians box' was like a railed chancel and the organ was in a fine gallery.

Scholes redressed an unbalanced view of the state of music in England under the Commonwealth but he could not whitewash the Government itself. During the last few years of its tyranny the spirits of English musicians must have been low. The one great asset to be set against the suppression of church, theatre and popular holiday music was the unique and splendid cultivation of domestic consort music in families that were not infected with an ungodly and unorthodox unwillingness to delight the senses. But what was the status of professional musicians who had not gone abroad? A law of 1657 enacted that any persons 'taken fiddling, playing or making music, in any inn, alehouse, or tavern' were to be punished as criminals. Though public opinion seems to have prevented the wholesale enforcement of this nastiness, since the music houses persisted to the Restoration, a glut of applicants formerly employed by church and theatre must have made musicians' wages poor.

The re-opening of the theatres and the beginning of public concerts may actually have caused a decline in the quality of other music. Tavern rooms were often hired by a club or a private promoter of music, and from various entries in Pepys's diary we gather that they sometimes provided the equivalent of modern seaside music and the maudlin favourites of vulgar eating places. Under an entry for 21st August 1663, we are told that only 'paltry' music could be had at the 'King's Head' in Greenwich until 'along came the master organist, whom by discourse I knew, having employed him for my Lord Sandwich, to prick out something (his name Arundell) and he did give me a fine voluntary or two'. Another entry is of great interest:

'Called up this morning by Lieut. Lambert, who is now Captain of the *Norwich*, and he and I went down by water to Greenwich. There we went and eat and drank and heard Musique at the "Globe", and saw the simple motion that is there of a woman with a rod in her hand keeping time to the musique while it plays.'

The material from Roger North's *Memoires of Music,* 1728, which describes the tavern-like arrangement of Banister's concerts, has been so often quoted that we may omit everything except 'Banister was able to procure the best hands (i.e. players) in towne', and 'Banister himself (inter alia) did wonders upon a flageolett to a thro' Base, and the severall masters had their solos'. This suggests that despite the constant changing of the venue of Banister's concerts, no doubt because they increased their audiences, the attention of audiences was largely taken with the appraisal of single players, not with listening to a sonata-like ensemble.

When Britton took over Banister's audience, at first securing Banister himself as a player, the smallness of his loft must still have favoured soloists and small groups, yet there was a change between the atmosphere of Banister's concerts and Britton's. A fondness for serious music which went with Britton's fondness for other arts and for the collecting of old books may have been based on a sounder musical culture than Banister's. Banister arranged his room 'rounded with small tables, alehouse fashion' during what was not, as still seems widely supposed, his first venture in giving concerts 'alehouse fashion'. On 21st January 1660, that is to say before Banister had been singled out for special honour in the royal band, Pepys went to the 'Mitre' in Fleet Street and took a drink of wine because there was no music, 'the house being in fitting for Banister to come thither from Paget's', which we take to be another music house. Let anyone who has invited friends to his home for serious music ask what happens once food and drink is brought in or talking is allowed. Admittedly Banister's Whitefriars concerts were at fixed times and the charge was for the concert, not for general hospitality including music. . . . 'One shilling was the price and call for what you will.' We lack proof that talking or orders for refreshment continued during the musical items, but North's words suggest sitting-easy to French-style airs and dances mixed with songs. One of Banister's advertisements[1] of 'a rare concert of four Trumpets Marine, never

---

[1] *The London Gazette,* 4 February 1676.

heard before in England' seems to cater for variety lovers. The notice that 'every concert shall continue one hour, and so begin again', may refer only to the silly novelty. If Banister turned out his audience after an hour's concert on other days, and then had a second and third house, he must have done very well from the shillings he took. Perhaps he paid the musicians well. No wonder that he was able to procure 'the best hands in town'.

Probably Banister's more serious concerts reached high standards of performance, for he was a good player himself on the flute and the violin. He had been sent to study Lully's training of the *Petits violons* so that he could imitate it with a small band of the best players in the English royal service. According to Wood[1] he returned full of conceit and was deprived of this new honour for 'saucy words spoken to his maj.', and he had been guilty of embezzling the musicians' pay. Pepys, entry for 20th February 1667, says that Banister stayed in the royal service, which seems to show that his talents were valued. He had to attend rehearsals called by the detested Louis Grabu who followed Nicholas Lanier as director of the royal music. He soon left the room at Whitefriars, and he moved more than once subsequently for greater accommodation, for his concerts were successful. Britton was not the man to have taken over Banister's audience unless many of its members had appreciated fine chamber music.

The phrase 'mere virtuoso' ought to be nonsensical, and one shrinks from using it; yet good players sometimes confine their listening almost entirely to other players' performances of a few pieces. It is conceivable that interest in 'the masters' and 'their solos' was paramount with Banister's auditors but that as they passed to Britton they took more interest in the music itself and its different national styles, for Britton had no wish to gain private money if the audiences enabled him to buy music and pay the musicians. Lest, however, this comparison does less than justice to Banister, another of his advertisements must be mentioned. In it Dr. Scholes[2] notes 'a capital synonym for "concerted music" —a *Parley of Instruments*', which implies a listener's interest in

---

[1] Powys's one-volume condensation of Clark's *The Life and Times of Anthony à Wood* (orig. 5 vols., Oxford, 1891–1900), Oxford, 1932.
[2] P. A. Scholes, *The Oxford Companion to Music*, 1938.

the contrast and interplay of such sounds as were later organized
in concertos.

Britton's long, narrow loft over his charcoal store in Clerken-
well was approached from a passage and some wooden stairs
outside his house, but during no less than thirty-six years of
weekly concerts Britton attracted a galaxy of titled patrons who
were willing to sit with commoners and endure the heat and
discomfort of the loft. In the words of Ward, 'anybody that is
willing to take a hearty Sweat may have the Pleasure of hearing
many notable performers in the charming Science of Musick'.
The titled patrons came to include the Earls of Oxford, of Pembroke and of Winchelsea, famous book collectors, for Britton himself was a bibliophile and they liked his conversation. He acquired
a fine collection of books on scientific subjects and on occultism.
All the contents of the Somers Collection in the Harleian Library
were once in his possession. The 'notable performers' were to
include Handel and Pepusch, both of whom were frequent players
on his fine Ruckers harpsichord and on a small chamber organ
which he installed in his loft.

Britton is one of the most admirable of music lovers. By day he
peddled his charcoal in London streets from the sack carried on
his back and he also sold cups of coffee to his audiences; but
these earnings were for music, books and improvements to the
premises. At first he made no charge for admission. If his hospitality had been only an advertising gesture why did he not
make an admission charge immediately after the few inaugural
concerts and why, having decided to ask patrons for a yearly subscription, did he make it only ten shillings? He treated his
audience as guests or as members of a club and he actually did
form a sort of club, not to perform before audiences but to practise music.

Banister and Britton had competitors. We know of at least one
successful series from Roger North, who adversely criticizes some
of their programmes:

'Now a consort, then a lutinist, then a violin solo, then flutes,
then a song, and so peice after peice, the time sliding away, while
the masters blundered and swore in shifting places.'

The origin of this series was the Gentlemen's Meeting. Unlike
gatherings of amateurs in Pepys's time this society did not sing

the catches in Playford's collection and rest at intervals to hear a few professional soloists. The Gentlemen's Meeting was formed specifically to practise concerted instrumental music. Members soon began to give open concerts at a tavern in Fleet Street. They stiffened their ranks with professionals and incurred the frequent consequence—the better the performance the more the audience recognizes and demands professional standards. At least the land-lord of the tavern made a handsome profit by taking over the concerts when the amateurs had withdrawn and by charging half a crown for admission. His success led the professional players themselves to build a concert room in Villiers Street,[1] sometimes called the Adelphi or the York Buildings Music Room. 'York Buildings' was a name used as we now use 'Barbican'; it did not refer to a tenement or series of houses but to the whole area once occupied by York House and its grounds. Villiers Street, now a narrow duct from Hungerford Bridge to the Strand, was then the grandest street in the grand district of York Buildings. During the period when Corelli's concertos were becoming famous in Italy the more important London concerts took place in the Villiers Street Music Room. The name of another popular concert hall, 'The Vendu' in Covent Garden, is not found in announcements after 1700. ('Vendu' = saleroom or auction-room.)

During the second and third decades of the eighteenth century the Villiers Street Hall was often called 'Sir Richard Steele's Great Room'. Steele was not very musical but he had either bought the property as part of his residence or he wanted it for his 'Censorium', a series of entertainments which combined speeches and music with the representation of classical scenes. This room was still used for concerts until about 1730, but from 1700 onwards concert promoters favoured dancing schools, which naturally required largish rooms with platforms for musicians. They were still named after the dancing masters—Hickford's, Clarke's and Barker's. Hickford's dancing and auction room in Panton Street, Haymarket, eclipsed the others in popularity as a concert hall, and in 1738 Hickford took or built larger premises in

---

[1] In *Musick's Monument*, London, 1676, Thomas Mace deplores the fashion-able concerts which breed a love of loud instruments in ensemble, yet he advocated the construction, at public expense, of a splendid concert room, elaborately planned for acoustic excellence.

Brewer Street, Golden Square, which the present writer was shown in process of demolition during 1934.[1]

Books about Handel remind us of the London taverns which were still used for concerts late in the eighteenth century. These, the dancing schools and the various 'Long Rooms' or 'Great Rooms' were not large enough for many of the London concerts in Handel's time, and either the Stationers' Hall or various theatres were requisitioned especially when voices and orchestra were combined. One of them, the Haymarket, is still with us though it was built in 1721 as 'The New Theatre in the Haymarket'—not 'The King's Theatre in the Haymarket' which was the favourite for operas and oratorios. Most of the important concerts, advertised as 'vocal and instrumental' in the *Daily Courant*, the *Daily Post* and other newspapers during the years between 1715 and 1740, were in theatres. They included concertos between the vocal 'Parts' of oratorios.

Two matters concerning the state of music in England during the ascendance of the concerto grosso are particularly striking: (1) the number of concerts and concert rooms in London, (2) the high prices that could be charged despite the competition and the small size of London. For an oratorio most seats cost half a guinea; for a 'Concert of instrumental music by the best masters, with some Italian songs, etc.' tickets were rarely less than five shillings. If public concerts alone—chamber music without opera or church music—were the sole criterion, then London would have to be reckoned by far the most musical city in Europe, not excepting Venice.[2] Late in the century Burney found no regular concerts in Hamburg except those given in churches, and no public concerts at all in Berlin. (Had Weckmann's *Collegium Musicum* in Hamburg declined?) He reported regular concerts in Amsterdam, including both private and public ones given by Locatelli, and he mentioned the fact that an important venue of big concerts was lost when a theatre was burnt down. He referred

[1] Even large halls look small when exposed to the sky, as one remembers who showed young musicians the wrecked Queens Hall, wherein orchestras from twenty to a hundred-and-twenty players sounded better than in any halls used since. Hickford's 'Great Room' looked small and of course shabby, so that one dropped no tear at the destruction of a place where Mozart played.

[2] Mattheson wrote in *Das neu-eröffnete Orchester*, 1713: 'He who . . . wants to make a profit by his music goes to England.'

[185]

to 'frequent concerts among the students' at Leyden. In most parts of Germany the university or other *Collegium* was the only orchestral concert given outside a private residence until late in the century.

Sonatas and concertos were what chiefly constituted 'the Italian style' at concerts. Overtures, chaconnes, rondeaus, gavottes, airs and other items from the theatre which had preceded sonatas and concertos were called 'the French style'. It is generally held that Vitali was the best of the Italians whose style was studied by Purcell, who by 1685 could hardly have seen printed copies of Corelli's sonatas; it is highly likely that he knew some of them before he died, for they spread north of Italy at an unprecedented speed. Whether Purcell himself wished to write a preface to his *Sonatas of Three Parts* or whether it was suggested by Playford, men thought it was expedient to commend a new publication of 1683 by a childish affectation to despise the 'levity' of French music and by a declaration that the composer 'faithfully endeavour'd a just imitation of the most fam'd Italian Masters; principally to bring the seriousness and gravity of that sort of music into vogue, and reputation among our Countrymen'. English and Italian musicians imported much manuscript music, and wealthy amateurs brought it back with them from their visits to the Continent. Purcell witnessed the great popularity of Draghi and Matteis and he praised the latter's airs for violin in the 1694 edition of Playford's *Introduction to the Skill of Music*.

North calls Purcell's sonatas 'noble' but adds that they are 'clog'd with somewhat of an English Vein, for which they are unworthily despised'.[1] Today the sonatas are valued less for the suave Corellian passages than for Purcell's insular and idiomatic turns of melody, harmony and counterpoint. Whittaker called the figured basses 'the despair of the continuo player'.[2] Purcell's precaution in issuing the preface, together with North's report of critics who did not think its promise to have been fulfilled by the composer, tells us that in the city most favoured by public concerts an admiration of Italian music was not merely the affectation of

[1] Roger North, *An Essay of Musicall Ayre* (British Museum).
[2] W. Gillies Whittaker, 'Some Observations on Purcell's Harmony' in *Collected Essays*, London, 1940.

ears which could not recognize it. In 1695, the year of Purcell's death, John Ravenscroft published in Rome a set of sonatas which so closely imitate Corelli that they might almost be passed off as his. They were evidently used at Britton's concerts for they are mentioned by Hawkins in his list of the items that were sold from Britton's library after his death in 1714.

It is interesting to note that Gustav Holst did not share his friend Whittaker's enthusiasm for Purcell's last compositions. He held an opinion which has persisted in much English musicography, that Purcell was the first prominent English composer to 'deny his birthright', to 'capitulate'. Holst sincerely reflects the prejudice of creative artists during a phase of the romantic movement which sought a 'combination of strangeness with beauty' in national and supposedly national idiosyncrasy, but neither Purcell's nor Holst's genius is fairly assessed by taste or distaste for the particular catalyst which stimulated its invention. It is ridiculous to blame Handel for the lack of outstanding English composers during the eighteenth century unless we deny that Handel was a genius because he resigned his German birthright and capitulated to the Italians. The English who received with delight first Corelli's sonatas and then his concertos, who welcomed Handel and the Italian opera, who forgot Purcell's fantasias and sonatas but who made Boyce's sonatas 'longer and more generally purchased, performed and admired, than any productions of the kind in this kingdom, except those of Corelli',[1] were as intelligent as the English of Holst's generation who highly valued the insular features of our music.

It could be strongly argued that, though England has not been granted another native musical genius of Purcell's stature, English music lovers have shown both a liking for absolute music and also a willingness to hear foreign music that are less evident in other countries. From the eve of the concerto grosso until now a core of English listeners has taken interest in music from abroad, partly because it has preferred instrumental music to vocal. If we really loved singing we should demand better standards. (Too many English singers seem to imagine that one can sing dispassionately with the vocal chords and resonators instead of with the

---

[1] Burney, *A General History of Music*, vol. iii.

whole being—body, mind and soul.) A nation of concert-goers must like music for its own unaided expression, and the bulk of its listeners soon become bored unless they cultivate an interest in the forms and processes of composition. A love of concerts shows no greater sensibility than a love of opera, but it does make the intelligent listener highly critical of the composer as a musician, not as creator or collaborator in a *Gesamtkunstwerk*, and that may be why, despite Germany's lead by many years in musicology and the history of music, English musicographers from Burney onwards have included some of the clearest and shrewdest critics of the works they most admire.

Few English listeners at the beginning of Burney's century may have been able to name the technical processes which commended the Italian sonata and concerto. They were content to speak of 'grace', 'smoothness', 'pleasing harmony' and so on; but they had already embraced the high baroque ideal of musical form—an expansive and balanced structure, not a patchwork like the seventeenth-century canzona or fantasia. Within the grand structure were larger and smaller antitheses. On the largest scale was a balance of paragraphs, each with a main tonality, each the continuation of a musical main idea or association of ideas; within the paragraph that was neatly finished by a cadence lay the balancings on the smallest scale—of sequences, rhythmic imitations and densities of harmony, especially in concertos; between the two lay the balances of tension, the advancing passage or the ritornello, the statement of new material or the episode. This ideal persisted into the classical concerto and symphony, wherein the play of balances became more complicated, the romantics especially delighting in upsetting balance, for instance by an abrupt modulation.

No writings suggest that the English associated Corelli's sonatas and concertos with the church or the palace. They simply regarded their dignity and suavity as Italian characteristics[1] which showed an advance in taste. In his dedication of the sonatas to the Duke of Somerset, Purcell wrote:

[1] Frenchmen did not always share this opinion unless they treated some Italian composers as exceptions. According to the Abbé Raguenet's *Comparison between the French and Italian Music and Opera*, 1709, the Italians 'venture the boldest Cadences, and the most irregular Dissonance; and their Airs are so out of the way that they resemble the Compositions of no other Nations'.

'Being farther from the Sun, we are of later growth than our Neighbour Countries, and must be content to shake off our Barbarity by degrees. The present Age seems already dispos'd to be refin'd, and to distinguish betwixt wild Fancy, and a just, numerous Composition.'

Modern equivalents of 'numerous' are 'smooth', 'regular', 'integral', 'well proportioned'. Mathematics being regarded as an exact science, numbers were symbols of regularity; so Dryden and others called a poem numerous if they admired its rhythm. We see in such commendation and in the admiration for Corelli an early idealization of *le grand simple*, gratification of which was one reason for Handel's popularity.

Balance and grandeur had already found expression in architecture, and the newly increasing audiences must have thought that even the most impressively unified of older pieces, such as certain choruses in Carissimi's oratorios or Lully's tragedies, were rather short-breathed, shifting between tonic and dominant or between minor and major for variety rather than in the course of a grand plan. Dissatisfaction with short movements and patches of diverse texture did not easily assail those who followed the words of songs (in France the book of the entertainment was either bought at the theatre or well studied beforehand) or who, as spectators of operas and ballets, judged the poet and choreographer more than the composer.

It is not suggested that the only lovers of absolute music lived in Italy, England, Holland, Denmark and Sweden. Some satirical lines by La Fontaine in 1667 remind us that concerts in Louis XIV's time were sometimes on a grand scale, although the royal Sunday concerts were not public in the same way as London concerts.

> 'Grand en tout, il veut mettre en tout de la grandeur;
> La guerre fait sa joie et sa plus forte ardeur;
> Ses divertissements ressentent tous la guerre;
> Ses concerts d'instruments ont le bruit de tonnerre
> Et ses concerts de voix resemblent aux éclats
> Qu'en un jour de combat font les cris des soldats.'[1]

The trouble with French rationalist aesthetic of the period was not simply that it required a meaning or purpose in art, for by

---

[1] *Epttre à M. de Niert sur l'opéra.*

definition art that expresses nothing, art for art's sake, is insig-
nificant. Error came from expecting what was expressed by one
art to be fully expressed by another, and from thus failing to
recognize that music has a realm of expression which other arts
can envy but not share. Music was valued when what it meant
could be conveyed or at least partly explained in words. Although
it would be equally erroneous to assert that music is less valuable
(as in a pastoral symphony or Christmas concerto) when some of
its meaning is explicit, it is certain that when music is *wholly*
explicit in words or gesture the music is either adipose or ancillary, as when it serves merely to prolong words or action. If
French music of the seventeenth century lost significance when
it lost the theatre then people who thought so much have been
baffled by music which did not even ask them to imagine the
theatre. Apparently such music held no mirror up to Nature—
one of the rationalist watchwords. If it illuminated nothing in
Nature, human or otherwise, yet accompanied no explanatory
poetry, then it was unnatural because undirected. Exercises during the training of a composer were directed towards the appraisal
of forms and processes, and served Nature only indirectly, but the
important part of training was the rational classification of musical
symbols. To be a composer of taste one should learn the proper
rhythms, harmonies, figurations, textures and formulae which
convention associated with different ideas and emotions. Absolute
music was artifice that had not become art because it was unfinished. Explicit purpose was necessary to its completion.

For the influence of Corelli and Vivaldi upon French styles we
examine sonatas. First we note the development of Couperin's
from the end of the last decade of the seventeenth century (N.B.
long after Biber's or Purcell's)[1] until the *Apothéose de Lulli* and
Les Nations of 1725–6. We pass to what are perhaps the finest
French sonatas of the high baroque, those of the elder Leclair,
which date from 1723 to 1738, and those of Mondonville, 1733.
The instrumental music most representative of France in the

[1] C. M. Girdlestone in his *Rameau* (London, 1957), p. 39, quotes a passage
from Lecerf's dialogues which admirably reveals the attitude of some Frenchmen to the Italian fashion elsewhere. 'Les Anglais on fait des sonates plus
sonates, plus difficiles et plus bizarres que celles du cinquième opus de Corelli.'
We should not go far wrong if we interpreted 'plus sonates' as 'more absolute'
or 'more meaningless except as an arrangement of sounds for their own sake'.

early eighteenth century is found in Couperin's *Concerts Royaux*. They were published in two volumes, 1722 and 1725, and are best described as suites intended for a small ensemble but effective with a larger one. Though they show Couperin's familiarity with Italian music their forms are distinctively French and uniquely personal. Their issue on two staves like harpsichord suites and the ease with which they can be treated as keyboard suites show them to be unlike Italian concertos. Louis had a genuine taste for music, though it was limited and conservative. The *Concerts* were performed, to soothe the king's malaise, by Duval (violin), Alarius (viola), Philidor (oboe), Dubois (bassoon) and Couperin himself (clavecin). The royal ear was served with slow movements during which both string and wind players took solos by turns, but they cannot be said to have concertized.

Regarded by other countries as a creator of fashions, France has rarely been quick to accept novelty herself. Mace's conservatism, which must have made English musicians regard him as a fogey, was widespread in France during the grand epoch and after it. Ensembles of violins, used in Lully's works only for overtures and dances, not for accompaniment, were associated with dances and divertissements, and several critics in Paris regarded them rather as a modern concert-goer regards dance bands. Even when violins were employed in the royal chapel the Italian sonata for two violins was called *strident* and *furieux*, and its performance at social gatherings seems at first to have had an effect like the introduction of saxophone choruses at Mayfair musical evenings before the 1920s; but where the sonata was accepted the concerto could follow, and Pincherle notes that the Lyons *Académie des Beaux-Arts* inscribed Vivaldi's concertos in its repertory not later than 1718 and probably in 1713. Both forms of music were fully accepted in Paris and the rest of France by about 1725, but the concerto does not seem to have attracted many French composers, and as far as I know the only *sets* of French concertos published during the first half of the eighteenth century are those by Boismortier, Aubert 'le vieux' and Leclair. Later, especially between 1760 and 1780, Paris became the leading centre for violin concertos. Leclair was followed by Gaviniès ('the French Tartini') who published at least seventeen concertos. Then came the enormously popular Giornovichi, or Jarnovik, and then Viotti.

In strong contrast with its tardy reception in Paris, the conquest of greater Germany by the Italian concerto was early and complete, the infiltration being only slightly resisted in those courts, cities and universities where French ideas and taste were venerated. It penetrated even the domain of the Lutheran cantor. England and Holland also took quickly to Italian music because the citizens of London and Amsterdam could have what they liked and paid for at public concerts. Their programmes were not the prerogative of a princeling who wanted Italian music chiefly in an opera theatre for the building and maintenance of which he cruelly bled an already hard-taxed burgessy and peasantry. Though Burney wrote of the state of music in different German principalities fifty years after the time which here concerns us, the interval made little difference in social conditions. Here are his comments upon Stuttgart, the Duke of Würtemberg's capital:

'The most shining parts of a German court are usually its *military*, its *music*, and its *hunt*. In this last article the expence is generally enormous; immense forests and parks, set apart for a prince's amusement, and the expence of agriculture, commerce, and indeed, the necessaries of life, keep vast tracts of land uncultivated, and his subjects in beggary.

'The soldiery of this prince's present capital are so numerous . . . that nothing like a gentleman can be seen in the streets, except officers. The soldiers seem disciplined into clock-work. I never saw such mechanical exactness in animated beings. One would suppose that the author of "Man a Machine" had taken his idea from these men: their appearance is formidable; black whiskers, white peruques, with curls at the sides, six deep; blue coats patched and mended with great ingenuity and diligence.'

Here is his report upon a 'free' city:

'I stayed but a short time at Augsburg; for, to say truth, I was somewhat tired of going to imperial cities after music; as I seldom found anything but the organist worth attending to. . . . These cities are not rich, and therefore have not the folly to support their theatres at a great expence. . . . Whoever seeks music in Germany, should do it at the several courts, not in the free imperial cities, which are generally inhabited by poor industrious people, whose genius is chilled and repressed by penury; who can

6. THE HOLYWELL MUSIC ROOM, OXFORD

(By courtesy of *The Oxford Mail*)

bestow nothing on vain pomp or luxury; but think themselves happy in the possession of necessaries. . . .'

As he travelled through Bavaria he was shocked at the almost 'barbaric state of those not in royal employ'. He mentions magnificent orchestral playing before spoken plays which he saw in Austrian theatres, particularly two at Vienna. He even put a footnote suggesting that he enjoyed orchestral pieces best when he heard them singly. . . .

'The symphonies of Mannheim, excellent as they are, have been observed . . . to be *Manierées,* and tiresome to such as continue there any time, being almost all of one cast. . . .'

He considered that when frequent wars impoverished people it was well that the costly open-air imperial operas were stopped. . . . 'this expensive custom would be now "More honoured in the breach, than the observance", for though I love music well, yet I love humanity better. . . . I frequently heard soldiers upon guard and sentinels, as well as common people sing in parts. The music school at the Jesuits' College in every town accounts in some measure for this faculty. There is scarce a church or convent in Vienna which has not every morning its mass in music . . . with 3 or 4 violins, a tenor and base, besides the organ (as well as voices singing in parts) . . . and as the churches here are daily crowded, this music, though not of the most exquisite kind, must, in some degree, form the ear of the inhabitants . . . which may account for the taste of the common people in Italy, where indeed the language is more musical than in any other country of Europe . . . but the excellent performances that are every day heard for nothing in the churches, by the common people, more contribute to refine and fix the national taste for good music than any other thing that I can at present suggest.'

Muffat introduced the concerto grosso to Germany in 1701, and the following years saw the rapid growth of German writing about music. English musicians are generally acquainted with the part of this musicography which appeared in book form, for instance the publications of the indefatigable Mattheson; but Mattheson and others founded periodicals devoted to music and the arts, and they also contributed to political and cultural journals. We are familiar with some of these articles in Scheibe's magazine *Der kritische Musikus* because they pass opinions on works by

N   [193]

J. S. Bach. It is noteworthy that there is little mention of concertos and almost no discussion of the Corellian concerto grosso. Moreover the Denkmäler collections suggest that very few German composers cultivated this type of work. They were not inclined to restrict themselves to strings and keyboard continuo when most of their court and opera orchestras had fine wind players and when the cities could benefit from their guilds of *Stadtpfeifer*. The Vivaldian and the solo types of concerto were also more popular in Germany than the Corellian type because the Corellian texture was less acceptable to solo performers, who wanted to display their attainment in order to secure engagements or advancement in the establishments to which they belonged.

Yet there is a considerable harvest of German concertos in the generation before J. S. Bach's, and we need further explanations of the few references to them in critical writings. One point worth considering is that the periodicals and treatises came from musicians in the free cities rather than the princely orchestras. Schering also suggests, both in his history of the concerto[1] and in one of his prefaces to a music collection,[2] that the church concerto grosso was preferred to the solo and Vivaldian concerto in Lutheran churches. We may presume that it was immediately welcome in those districts of Germany, especially Rhineland and the south, which had remained under the Roman obedience. Walther Krüger gives another reason for the paucity of German concertos of the Corellian type.[3] He quotes an article in *Der kritische Musikus* (an issue of 1758, but the late date does not affect the argument) in which Scheibe says that much more time and consideration must be given to the composition of a concerto with several strands in its concertino than to a concerto between solo and tutti. Even if we look beyond German-speaking countries we must admit that there are very few concertos after Corelli's wherein there is plenty of antithesis between a string concertino and the tutti. Many such concertos are from free-lance composers like Geminiani and Avison who were not required to finish them by a given time, but it took Handel to outshine Corelli. As Scheibe points out, the heavily-worked composer of a ducal establishment would not

---

[1] Arnold Schering, *Geschichte des Instrumentalkonzerts*, Leipzig, 1927.
[2] *DDT*, vols. xxix–xxx.
[3] Walther Krüger, *Das Concerto grosso in Deutschland*, Wolfenbüttel, 1932.

commit himself to this labour if a suite, a 'sonata-concerto' (Scheibe), or solo concerto would be just as acceptable or more so. Krüger also draws our attention to the frequent mention in German eighteenth-century writings of an ideal '*vermischten Geschmack*' or '*vermischten Gout*' (the gallicism being in favour)—a combination of French and Italian taste which explains the frequent inclusion of passages for concertino or solo in works of the later period, for instance in overtures by J. J. Fux.

Germany's good fortune in securing from her composers a 'happy mixture of French and Italian' styles is discussed at length in the *Tractatus musicus* of M. Spiess, 1746, but the better-known earlier books by Mattheson and Heinichen as well as articles by Telemann, Mizler and Scheibe are full of the French aesthetic taught by Gottsched at the Leipzig which Goethe called later 'a little Paris'. The main crop of German concertos came after the second decade of the century. It favoured the Vivaldian scheme of three movements (fast–slow–fast) and the incorporation of wind instruments into the tutti begun by Vivaldi. Not by accident did the decisive growth of the classical symphony come from German-speaking musicians.

At the time of writing (1959) the student of music is provided with more and clearer information about Italian music for concerted instruments between 1600 and 1750 than about similar German music. Giovanni Gabrieli and Monteverdi draw one's attention to Italy at the beginning of the period as do the violin virtuosi at the end of it, and copies of their works are accessible. One is inclined to think of German music of the same period with one's mind focused first upon Praetorius, Schütz, Schein, Scheidt and the music of the high Lutheran liturgy, reminding oneself that there were many ducal musical establishments and that their owners, if intelligent and artistic, liked Italian opera and French orchestral music. The English musician is pardonably vague as to exactly what music was played by ducal or public orchestras before the days of C. P. E. Bach and the pre-classical symphonists, for documents are lacking where private concerts were not advertised in newspapers as London concerts were. Most non-Germans can become acquainted with solo concertos and symphonies played in Berlin, Dresden, Mannheim, Vienna and other centres after 1750, but a vast quantity of early German instrumental music, not easily accessible to non-Germans, has yet to be examined before we can amplify our general impression of the effect of Venetian and other Italian music upon German music of the seventeenth century. The Denkmäler and other collections, such as *Das Erbe Deutscher Musik*, give us a tantalizing indication of its extent and quality.

The French overture and suite tended to eliminate the concertino of strings but to favour sections and phrases for oboes or flutes. Gabrieli and Monteverdi had affected German church music, whereas the secular French styles affected the court orchestras and the keyboard players. The arrival of Vivaldi's concertos, however, inclined the Germans to a new application of concertante principles in secular music. Considering the huge number of orchestras and musicians in German-speaking Europe, and those of Poland, Denmark and Sweden where the older canzona-type of concerted music had been most assiduously cultivated, we cannot but notice that the new concerto fascinated Germany for a very short period, roughly 1715 to 1745, before it was supplanted by the galant solo concerto and the pre-classical symphony. Yet the influence of the Vivaldian form even on works which were not called concertos was almost all-pervading. It is no exaggeration to declare that after 1715 any German piece of music that was not a fugue or a chorale prelude, or of simple organization (e.g. a short song or dance) was to some extent in concerto form. Thus most of Bach's longer choruses and arias are elaborate concertos, and that is why he could so easily adapt an accompanied chorus to make an instrumental concerto or use a concerto movement to make an aria or chorus. Often what is miscalled a fugue is basically a concerto. An example is the first chorus in the *Mass in B minor*. Its shape, with the first outcry replacing the slow introduction, is not unlike that of the opening movement in a church concerto. This chorus is certainly not a fugue, as that term is normally applied to Bach's music; it is thematically and tonally sectional and symmetrical, one of its ideas being the memorable fugal exposition and another the long ritornello. The big difference between such a chorus and an instrumental concerto movement is the effect of the most weighty sections, those for full chorus and orchestra. They replace concertino sections while the orchestral tutti, the heavy part of

[196]

the instrumental concerto, becomes the light part of the choral concerto.

A Kapellmeister who could not compose enough concertos to display his own prowess, that of the best local string or wind players, above all the performance of an exalted employer or members of his household, risked the commissioning of an outside composer with orders for sets of six or a dozen, or even the promotion of someone else to directorship. The great difference between the solo and ripieno parts in technical difficulty is said by some writers to indicate the participation of the composer's pupils, especially members of the household, and such servants as footmen and huntsmen who could offer a certain musical attainment to commend their application for employment. It is certainly true that the ripieno parts in many German concertos—for instance most of those in the Brandenburg Concertos—lie within the ability of average student players, but there are plenty of purely artistic reasons why they should often do so. Trumpet and arpeggio intervals linked by conjunct notes in bold square rhythms, the simple brilliance of scales played tutti—these not only made ritornello themes memorable but provided an effective contrast with the florid writing for the solo instruments.

The parts for wind instruments are on the whole decidedly more advanced in north German concertos than in Italian and English ones, and this applies even to concertos known to have been composed for the *collegia musica* (musical societies) that were formed in university cities at the beginning of the eighteenth century. A *collegium* was not always a circle of amateurs, students and subscribers, like the Telemann Society at Leipzig which welcomed Bach's presiding at the harpsichord—a parallel to the London 'Gentlemen's Meeting' of earlier years. It was sometimes a series of commercially organized concerts run by an enterprising manager.

With the Italian conservatories of orphans and other pupils hugely expanding as training grounds for singers and players, with Naples as the Hollywood of the international opera industry and with Italian as the universal language of opera, advance in purely orchestral playing and performance passed to Germany which, being an agglomerate of principalities, employed a vast number of players. Even without the composers associated with

Mannheim and Vienna the classical symphony would have given Germany a fame for concerted instrumental music which France might have enjoyed if she had employed fifty Lullian orchestras instead of one. The number of Germans who were employed as *Kammermusiki* may be judged from the list of orchestras which Carse[1] compiled from statistics given by Marpurg, Dittersdorf, Forkel and others. More than one member of some royal families maintained a kapelle. For instance while the King of Prussia employed some twenty-eight regular players in 1712 and had increased their number to thirty-six by 1754, Prince Carl and Prince Henry of Prussia had each a band of about fifteen. Most of them were string players, but Bach's concertos form a notable testimony to the virtuosity of the wind players that were occasionally if not always available in the small court at Cöthen, certainly in the Margrave of Brandenburg's establishment and, judging from church cantatas, in St. Thomas's Kantorei.

One or two pictures dating from the early eighteenth century show large numbers of players. There is, for instance, Guardi's *Concert in a Convent* which may faithfully represent the conditions in which concerts were given at the Pietà under Vivaldi's direction. We should not judge this to be the normal size of a concert room any more than we should suppose that concerts in Handel's London were normally accommodated as spaciously as in the big chapel of the Foundling Hospital where the annual *Messiah* was given by Handel with concertos between the 'parts'.[2] Theatres were requisitioned both for oratorios and for large-scale concerts. When we look at the Holywell Music Room in Oxford we may reflect that the eighteenth century thought it to be splendidly commodious. More is lost than gained when performers treat the Brandenburg Concertos, or even the piano concertos with which Mozart first made his reputation in Vienna, as though they had been composed for a large modern hall or for a post-Wagnerian orchestra from which some of the wind players are temporarily withdrawn. Sometimes by using small orchestras and avoiding large halls conductors offer us 'baroque' conditions

---

[1] A. Carse, *The Orchestra in the Eighteenth Century*, Cambridge, 1940. See also the statistics given in the next chapter.

[2] The only sacred building used by Handel for an oratorio and the only oratorio not always given in a theatre.

which are almost a greater travesty than the music would receive from a large orchestra. The arrangement of the players markedly affects the balance of a concerto, and when the disposition of the performers and the style of the playing are similar to those used for the splendid string pieces of nineteenth-century composers the older music is made to sound less splendid. Merely to deplete the numbers, show the audience a harpsichord, and then let the violinists use the same slurs and the same type of bowing as were conceived for a large string orchestra by Tchaikovsky, Dvorak or Elgar is as foolish as to put the harpsichord at the back or to one side and to admire the continuo player the more his part gives a faint shower of ornamental silver-dust on the silken sheen of romantic string effects, the more he indulges in fanciful embroideries (though they may have a place in certain movements) and the less he maintains a firm tread of chords.

Like nineteenth- and twentieth-century audiences, those of the eighteenth century enjoyed the colours and varieties of concerted sound; otherwise there would have been no concerto grosso; but theirs were the primary colours and the broad varieties. The modern listener who would relish them must become like the gourmet who discovers the excellence of well-cooked farmhouse fare. He must learn to enjoy its quality and contrast though it lacks the *kind* of elaboration to which he has been accustomed. To know the splendour and variety of the first concerti grossi we should not give them a splendour and variety which does not belong to them, or we should merely make the *substantia* seem unworthy of the *accidentia*. We must listen as though we were the first listeners, judge as though we knew no other musical language and rhetoric. At every point in history musical souls have been granted the experience expressed in Wordsworth's lines about the French revolution:

> *Bliss was it in that dawn to be alive,*
> *But to be young was very heaven.*

It was very heaven for young Muffat as he heard Corelli's orchestra or for young Pisendel as he heard Vivaldi's. Portraits and pictures from the Age of Reason mislead us into supposing that those solid and bewigged creatures were never moved to intense ecstasy. We speak of a later generation as witnessing 'The

Enlightenment', and though one cannot supply a better short name for a well-documented phenomenon, one wishes that it were possible to suggest the dawn and radiance of a new mental and aesthetic horizon without implying that those who did not live to know it never knew the flush of dawn and were content to live and walk by a more limited radiance. We can safely talk about the Enlightenment and the Romantic Era if we do not forget that our musical imagination can hope for no greater enlightenment than was vouchsafed to Handel and Bach, and that, in Stendhal's aphorism, 'All art is romantic in its own day.' For rightly tuned ears a second, third or tenth hearing of Handel's Op. 6 still opens the very heaven that was Handel's because he knew the bliss of being alive in Corelli's Rome.

CHAPTER X

The Main German School—I
The Saxons and Berliners

Concertos by Vivaldi and Albinoni led a Venetian mission to the German orchestras quite distinct from the first Italian mission to Bavaria and Austria. Even where Corelli's concertos were known, the new Venetian concertos cannot have seemed modifications of the old ones. They penetrated to many middle and northern States of Germany where Corelli was yet known only by sonatas. In the south Muffat's school had extolled and imitated Torelli's and Corelli's concertos long before most of them were printed, for as regards availability in print we should not speak of Corelli's and Vivaldi's concertos as the old and the new.

German concertos on Venetian models were not superseded by other concertos but by symphonies. Vivaldi's Op. 3 arrived in Saxony, Prussia, Hanover, Hesse-Darmstadt, Brunswick, Poland and elsewhere along with Italian operas and singers, for the concertos themselves were vehicles of operatic expression. The Corellian concerto disappeared entirely as the symphony and the galant solo concerto emerged, but both of these were already implicit in Venetian concertos, and Pincherle asserts that the pre-classical symphony was completely achieved by Vivaldi in ripieno concertos and sinfonias. It is true that Handel's concertos, which pay one of the noblest tributes to Corelli that one composer has ever received from a greater, were popular in Germany during the middle

[201]

years of the century, and so were other English concertos and symphonies; but this music did not come from Italy, and the German musicians who admired it had already absorbed the designs of Vivaldi's movements into their own concertos for orchestras which included wind instruments. Reverting to older designs and silencing the wind instruments when they played concerti grossi by Handel, Geminiani and English composers (they may not always have silenced the wind instruments) the German orchestras paradoxically enjoyed novelty. When Muffat imitated Corelli the novelty lay simply in the contrasts between concertino and tutti and the method of performance upon which Muffat was so insistent; but the Venetian concerto was new in style as well as expression.

The Germans had notably enjoyed the beginning of that process by which theatre music became chamber music, for the main repertory of northern as well as southern orchestras had been of French overtures and suites. The Venetian concerto completed the introduction into the concert room of almost the whole range of operatic expression. Schering's declaration[1] that the concerto grosso and ripieno concerto were preferred to the solo concerto in Lutheran churches has not been verified, but we may note that the three German composers whom Schering regards as more Corellian than Vivaldian—Telemann, Graupner and Molter—wrote for ducal establishments and collegia musica whether their concertos were used in churches or not. Moreover these composers, like Handel himself, often showed points of Vivaldian style and structure, and the general shape of their movements cannot be called particularly Corellian. Corelli's concertos were not known in most parts of Germany until manuscript and printed parts of Vivaldi's Op. 3–7 arrived.

Vivaldi had no outstanding champion like Muffat. He needed no champions, for he was admired by dozens of grandees and professional musicians whose visits to Italy were usually lengthy sojourns in Venice while the Red Priest was its brightest musical star. 'Dozens' is not hyperbole but meiosis. Venice was *the* pleasure city of Europe during the whole of the eighteenth century. Its more censorious moralists would have us believe that the delights sought there by most visitors were directly sensual rather

---

[1] Preface to *DDT*, vols. xxix–xxx.

than artistic. Towards the end of the century and even when Burney was there Venice lacked notable genius in most of the arts, and the music at her operas, concerts and churches was not as fine as elsewhere. At the beginning of the century, however, she could claim undisputed excellence. Margraves and princes like those of Dresden and Darmstadt who were dedicatees of Vivaldi's works, orchestral leaders like Pisendel who were his direct pupils, and almost every German aristocrat of musical tastes and every Kapellmeister or Konzertmeister who achieved fame between 1700 and 1750 visited Venice. For present purposes we disregard only those who were drawn exclusively to opera (with Vivaldi still a leading composer) or who were in Italy chiefly to engage artists for the fine new court theatres in the German capitals or residences.

Vivaldi was sometimes his own publicist in Germany. He seems to have been a valetudinarian, yet he travelled farther and more frequently than Corelli. Not all his absences from the Pietà are known or explained, and although the belief that he stayed in Darmstadt is now discredited, he could not have reached Amsterdam in a few days, and there were musical honours during the outward and the return journeys. One of his letters declares that he visited 'several European cities'. In Vienna, where he was later to die, he was very cordially received, and it was said that the emperor talked more with the Red Priest during a few weeks than with ministers of state during as many months. The first districts in which Germans imitated his concertos were not those known to have been visited by him but those ruled by his admirers. The most notable of these districts was Saxony—not just Dresden but other cities of the principality or just outside its boundaries, including courts and towns associated with Bach, such as Weimar, Cöthen and Leipzig. A surprisingly large number of the German concertists of Bach's generation were boys at St. Thomas's School during Kuhnau's cantorate and proceeded to Leipzig University, ostensibly to study law but actually to prove their talents in a collegium musicum or in one of the churches. By composing German or Italian-style German operas for the fairs at Naumburg or Leipzig they often attracted the notice of patrons who appointed them to court orchestras and opera theatres and gave them the opportunity to visit Venice.

GEORG JOHANN PISENDEL (1687–1755) is the central figure
of the Saxon group, for no German except a prince could have
been more lucky in his contacts with the Italian concertists.
Pisendel came from Bavaria. He had been a remarkable boy
singer and violinist at Ansbach when Torelli was there. He went
to the university at Leipzig and he knew Bach at Weimar. At the
end of his university years the first patron he secured was the
King of Poland who made him his Konzertmeister at Dresden, but
there he was favoured by the music-loving Augustus of Saxony
in whose entourage he visited Berlin, Paris, Italy and Vienna.
His years in Italy were spent chiefly in Venice where he was
Vivaldi's pupil. A batch of Vivaldi manuscripts at Dresden which
includes six concertos is dedicated in autograph 'Fatto per il Sigr.
Pisendel', and Albinoni also dedicated works to him. He had more
influence than other musicians upon the Saxon Court Orchestra
from 1720 until his death, but he was not its titular head while
the great French violinist, Volumier, was still living. When Hasse
arrived, Pisendel and his royal master became chiefly interested
in the new theatre which was one of the grandest in Europe. The
high standard of playing at Dresden during the years 1720–40
seems largely due to Pisendel's efforts. He was one of the finest
violinists of the whole century, trusted by Vivaldi to grace his
adagios with impeccable taste.

Closely associated with Pisendel was JOHANN DAVID HEINI-
CHEN (1683–1729). He was educated at Leipzig and employed at
Dresden. He must have studied jurisprudence seriously, for he
actually returned to his native Weissenfels to practise as an
advocate; but after two years some operas which he wrote for
the fairs brought him an appointment at Zeitz, a court in the
Bach country of Thuringia and no larger than, say, Celle. He
published his famous *Anweisung* at Hamburg in 1711.[1] Soon
afterwards he undertook the Italian journey and stayed for six
years, being almost the first German to see his operas mounted
in Venice.[2] There the Elector of Saxony asked him to become his
Kapellmeister at Dresden. As we are made aware in biographies

---

[1] *Neu-erfundene und gründliche Anweisung, wie ein Musikliebender könne zu
vollkommener Erlernung des Generalbasses gelangen.* The revised edition of 1728
is simply *Der Generalbass in der Komposition.*

[2] He was not the very first to have this honour, for Handel's *Agrippina* was
staged in Venice on 26 December 1709.

[204]

of Bach, Frederick Augustus of Saxony was a Roman Catholic.
Evidently Heinichen was of the same persuasion for he composed
many masses and other church music for Dresden, and his concertos and symphonies were probably used both as church and as
chamber music. Before Hasse's arrival he must have collaborated
with Pisendel in the theatre. In his quarrel with Senesino and the
Italian company the elector seems to have taken his side, for the
Italians were dismissed. Afterwards Heinichen devoted himself
chiefly to church music. The large collection of his works at
Dresden includes over sixty cantatas, but sixteen of his concertos are to be found either in the Dresden or the Darmstadt
archives.

Heinichen's closest friend at school and university was CRIS-
TOPH GRAUPNER (1683–1760). After a few years as harpsichordist
under Keiser at the Hamburg opera, Graupner settled as musical
director to the Margrave Ernst Ludwig of Hesse-Darmstadt,
Vivaldi's admirer, and stayed at Darmstadt even when Leipzig
elected him Cantor in 1722 after the death of Kuhnau. He tells
us drily in Mattheson's *Ehrenpforte* that 'so much came between'
the election and his acceptance of the post 'that it could not be
brought about'. He means that his prince bought him off with a
large sum and by settling pensions upon him and his children;
so Bach went to Leipzig. For Darmstadt Graupner wrote many
operas, edited a *Darmstadtisches Chorälbuch* (1728) and brought
the standard of orchestral performance to a level that invited
comparison with that of the Dresdeners. He and Heinichen remained good friends all their lives. Their works are found in the
libraries of Dresden and Darmstadt, but they would probably
have been copied for the use of two such eminent establishments
even if the personal friendship had not speeded the exchange.
Graupner is known to have composed some fifty concertos for
various solo instruments and over a hundred symphonies. The
Denkmäler volumes reprint only his cantatas, but eighteen of his
concertos composed between 1727 and 1744 are preserved at
Darmstadt.

Graupner's Konzertmeister or leader at Darmstadt was a native
of that district, JOHANN ADAM BIRKENSTOCK (1687–1733) a
superb violinist who had made his reputation in Amsterdam.
Some of Birkenstock's sonatas have appeared in modern editions,

but one has inquired in vain about the twelve concertos which Eitner mentions as using a concertino of four violins. It is not known if they were written at Darmstadt or at Eisenach where Birkenstock became Kapellmeister in 1730.

Another boy from Weissenfels who was first a Thomaner and then a student at Leipzig University, JOHANN FRIEDRICH FASCH (1688–1758) was also admired by Bach, against whom he was invited to compete for the Cantorate, for he had composed operas for the Leipzig and Naumburg fairs. Bach copied five of his orchestral suites, and it has been suggested that Fasch returned Bach's esteem and declined the St. Thomas appointment out of respect for him. He was strongly influenced by Telemann at Leipzig. German musicologists regard the collegium musicum founded by Fasch, not the Telemann Society, as the ancestor of the regular public concerts which later found their venue at the Gewandhaus. Fasch did not settle in Saxony but held several appointments as civil servant and musician, notably to Count Morzin in Bohemia. No less than thirty-six of his concertos are to be found at Dresden or at Darmstadt.

The last well-known Saxon concertist of Bach's generation was GOTTFRIED HEINRICH STÖLZEL (1690–1749). Being seven years younger than Heinichen and Graupner he was at Leipzig University when Telemann's Music Society was flourishing, and he took a prominent part in its performances. Like the others he wrote his first operas or Singspiele for the Naumburg fair seasons. In 1713 he undertook the Italian tour and is known thereafter to have taught music and composed operas for Breslau, Prague and Bayreuth. In 1719 he settled for the rest of his life as Kapellmeister to the Duke of Gotha.

The Saxon School is not complete, however, without the inclusion of JOHANN DISMAS ZELENKA (1679–1745) the son of a schoolmaster-musician in Count Morzin's district of Bohemia. Zelenka was well educated musically and otherwise by his father and at the Jesuit College in Prague. After lessons in counterpoint and composition from Fux he was engaged as a double bass player at Dresden under Heinichen and Pisendel, though his many manuscripts at Dresden show that he was most active as a composer of masses, motets, oratorios and psalms, as well as the instrumental pieces required for church and chamber use. He succeeded Heinichen as director of the church music with the title Hofkomponist in 1729.

Though a Saxon, Telemann was a free-lance musician like his friend Handel. We shall regard Telemann as a school to himself—prolific, versatile and unregional. Following Schering, Krüger places him with Graupner and Molter among the German concertists most influenced by Corelli, and he contrasts them with Pisendel, Fasch, Heinichen, Zelenka, Quantz and the Grauns who, like Bach, were Vivaldians. Without questioning this classification for the moment we shall deal with the German concertists by regional schools beginning with the most important, that of Saxony. It includes Pisendel, Heinichen and Zelenka at Dresden itself, Fasch in Bohemia, Stölzel in Gotha and Graupner in Darmstadt. Next in importance comes the Berlin School. Very few of its leading musicians were Berliners or even natives of the northern States—Brandenburg, Prussia, Silesia and Poland. We may take as its central figure JOHANN JOACHIM QUANTZ (1697–1773). Once more Saxony was the training ground—first Pirna, then Dresden.

Quantz was not favoured with a university education. He was the son of a blacksmith in a village near Göttingen where he played the double bass from the age of eight and quickly grasped the essentials of harmony and figured bass. His father died while he was a boy and he came under the care of uncles who were Stadpfeiffer or Stadtmusici, though he studied keyboard playing under Kieserwetter. He came to know Heine, one of the city musicians of Dresden, and went to lodge with him in 1716. He not only heard Pisendel, Veracini, Zelenka, the flautist Buffardin and other fine artists but he also undertook a thorough study of Vivaldi's concertos, and he somehow earned or secured the means to go to Vienna for lessons in counterpoint and composition. These were from Zelenka, not Fux, though he must have known Fux and have heard the imperial orchestra. On his return in 1718 he secured an appointment as oboist with the 'King of Poland's Orchestra' at Dresden (formerly the Saxon Court Orchestra) and he took lessons on the flute from Buffardin.

Quantz played in Fux's *Costanza e fortezza* at Prague in 1723 when that opera was given in honour of the coronation of Charles VI. Soon afterwards he stayed in Italy for three years and came to know Scarlatti, Vivaldi, Hasse and Leo. He returned through France where he was greatly admired, and he visited London at the peak of Handel's operatic career. Perhaps he lived frugally or had the gift of incurring hospitality; perhaps his royal employer fully financed his tour. By 1727 he was back in Dresden. In the following year during a visit to Berlin he attracted the notice of the crown prince, later Frederick the Great, who arranged that he should come twice a year to instruct him in flute playing. When Frederick succeeded to the throne in 1740 he offered Quantz unusually high remuneration to induce him to become Kammermusicus and Hofkomponist at Berlin. Above the annual salary of two thousand thaler he received extra payment for each concerto or other orchestral composition and for each new flute that he supplied for use at Potsdam—a clause that needs explanation. As Quantz tells us in his *Versuch*,[1] he had added the second key to his instrument while on his tour abroad, and he had also invented the telescoping top which is still employed to adjust the tuning.

For the king's use Quantz composed some three hundred flute concertos. A well-known picture and some much-quoted comments by the harpsichordist at Potsdam, C. P. E. Bach, enable us to imagine the punctilio of the royal rehearsal and evening concert with the tutor's discreet bravos for the exalted soloist. We know from Bach how difficult formal release was to obtain. Why did not the more vital musicians of the Berlin establishment flee in disguise after a few years of the unchanged repertory and the musical equivalent of the morning parade? Because they were considered fortunate. Even as late as the 1780s Leopold Mozart could see in his son's precarious finances the consequence of not living in the security of servitude, not seeking a post as Kapellmeister or Konzertmeister.

Quantz's book is one of the most quoted of treatises, for only a small portion of it concerns flute technique. It was often reprinted in Germany and translated into French and Dutch. What purported to be an English version, called *Easy and Fundamental Instructions*, was concerned chiefly with embellishments. At the time of the original publication, 1752, Quantz shared the taste of

---

[1] *Versuch einer Anweisung die Flöte travierse zu spielen*, first published 1752 in Berlin, dedicated to Frederick, and containing twenty-four plates.

C. P. E. Bach rather than of conservatives like Agricola who pleased Frederick, and we therefore refer to him in discussions of the *galant* and *empfindsamer* styles—a distinction which means little if we are determined to classify compositions of the period, but which gives us insight into the minds of vital musicians. Some interesting sections of the book are translated in Strunk's *Source Readings in Music History*[1] under the heading 'How a performer and a piece of music ought to be judged', and they include the following remarks on the composition of a concerto:

'There should be a magnificent ritornello with all the parts well elaborated. . . . There should be regular imitations (sequences). The best ideas of the ritornello should be broken up and used for relief *within* or *between* the solos. The ritornello should consist of at least two main sections. The second of these, since it is to be repeated at the end of the movement, must be clothed with the finest ideas. Insofar as the opening idea is neither singing nor wholly suitable for solo use, the composer must introduce a new idea, directly contrasted with the first, but so joined to it that it is not seen whether it is introduced from necessity or after deliberation. The solo section must be in part singing (i.e. lyrical), while the ingratiating should be in part relieved by brilliant passages suited to the instrument, and also, to maintain the fire to the end, by short and lively tutti sections. . . . The accompaniment must be alternately of many parts and few, so that the principal part may now and then have room to come to the fore. . . . Light and shade must be maintained throughout. . . . It is effective that the accompanying parts should introduce something familiar from the ritornello.'

The concerto by Hasse[2] from which excerpts are given at Ex. 57 well illustrates Quantz's points concerning the first movement. Here is Quantz, the student of Vivaldi, writing about the slow movement:

'For arousing and subsequent stilling of the passions the Adagio offers greater opportunity than the Allegro. In former times it was written in a plain dry style, more harmonic than melodic. The composers left to the performers . . . to make the melody

---

[1] Faber and Faber, London, 1952.
[2] Printed in *DDT*, vol. xxix (Schering).

57.

Hasse, Flute concerto.

singable, but this could not be well accomplished without considerable additional embellishments . . . and since the performance was seldom as the author wished, there has come of this evil some good, namely, that composers have for some time past begun to make their Adagios more singing. But since the Adagio does not usually find as many admirers as the Allegro, the composer must endeavour to make it pleasing even to those listeners without musical experience. . . . The melody must be just as touching and expressive as though there were words below it. From time to time something from the ritornello must be introduced. . . . The accompaniment beneath the solo must be rather more plain than figural, in order that the principal part may not be prevented from making ornaments. . . . The composer must endeavour to characterize the Adagio with some epithet clearly expressing the passion contained therein, in order that the required tempo may be readily determined.'

Quantz is here describing what he calls a concerto da camera, a designation which he seems to regard as synonymous with 'solo concerto'; he distinguishes this type of concerto from the 'concerto grosso' which he then proceeds to describe in a way which shows that he would not have regarded any of Bach's concertos as concerti grossi, but that he would so have regarded some of Telemann's.

JOHANN GOTTLIEB GRAUN (1703–71), born near Dresden, became a pupil of Pisendel, travelled to Italy, had lessons from Tartini, joined the Saxon Court Orchestra as a violinist, left it to become Kapellmeister at Merseburg, where W. F. Bach was his pupil, and in 1732 entered the service of the Crown Prince of Prussia at Rheinsberg, moving to Berlin as leader of the orchestra in 1740 after his master succeeded to the throne as Frederick II. His duties included the rehearsing of the band. Burney regarded him as responsible for its excellent performance during the middle years of the century. There are fourteen of his concertos in the State Library at Berlin.

His brother KARL HEINRICH GRAUN (1704–59) is better known. He first attracted notice as a tenor singer worthy to perform with the Italian company at Dresden. He studied Keiser's German operas and those of Caspar Schürmann, Kapellmeister at Brunswick, to which court Graun was attached for some years and for which he composed several operas, including one for the wedding of the Princess of Brunswick to the Crown Prince of Prussia in 1733. Within two years the bridegroom had made him Kapellmeister at Rheinsberg, from which he followed to Berlin in the same office at Frederick's accession. He thus had his brother for Konzertmeister at both places. The new King of Prussia wanted to build an opera theatre and engage a magnificent Italian company. Graun was sent to Italy. He then composed sixteen operas (*Montezuma* occupies *DDT*, vol. vi) and shared with Hasse alone his monarch's favour as an opera composer for Berlin. He is best known for the sacred works of his later years, especially the *Te Deum* for Frederick's victory at Prague and *Der Tod Jesu*, a cantata often loosely called 'Graun's Passion', being almost as popular in Germany as *Messiah* is in England. His concertos

[211]

include some for the fortepiano. Krüger says they are much inferior to the concertos of his Berlin colleague C. P. E. Bach but they are composed in similar styles to his.

Though not a Berliner, JOHANN MELCHIOR MOLTER is an important concertist of this northern group. The date of his birth has not been decided but we know that in 1719 he was a chamber musician employed by the Margrave of Baden at Durlach, from which place and in which year he was sent to Italy. The Durlach Kapellmeister, J. P. Käfer, died during Molter's absence and he was succeeded by Molter when he returned. Among hundreds of Molter's manuscripts at Carlsruhe are many concertos, including some for clarinet. He lived until 1765. Before he went to Venice he called his concertos *Sonatae Grossae*. Some of the movements are headed *Tempo di minuetto* and *Tempo di gavotta*, and this inheritance from the French suite together with the Corellian design of many movements suggests that Molter was well acquainted with works of Muffat's school. A closeness of style to Corelli's church concertos can be seen in the openings of movements given at Ex. 58 and 59. The instruments for the *Sonata Grossa* in G minor are not specified but they were presumably strings. The D major work seems to show exactly what one can imagine Corelli to have supplied if asked to contribute to the repertory of trumpet sonatas at St. Petronio.

Because Telemann's works are the most reprinted and illustrate procedures common to the others we shall deal with him last. We should now examine the constitution of the orchestras for which these men composed. Using statistics from Carse's *The Orchestra in the Eighteenth Century*,[1] which were compiled from pay books, and counting sets of parts in various libraries, we first trace the growth of one particular orchestral establishment, that maintained by the King of Poland at his residence near Dresden. Carse's figures for most of the first half of the century are taken from C. Mennicke's *Hasse und die Brüder Graun als Symphoniker*,[2] but some of them were verified by counting the players in pictures of the period—for instance one of the plates in Rousseau's *Dictionnaire de Musique*.[3] We have to remember that trumpets and drums were available wherever the employer was in

[1] Cambridge, 1940.
[2] Leipzig, 1906.   [3] Paris, 1756; Amsterdam, 1768.

command of militia, and that where there was no militia the trumpeters could usually be obtained on application to the guild. Stadtpfeiffer and other city players such as those who served in the churches could also augment an established orchestra, and some of the servants in almost any German residence during the eighteenth century were engaged to assist in the chase, one of their qualifications as applicants being that they were good horn players.

KING OF POLAND'S ORCHESTRA (Dresden-Warsaw)

	Strings	Wood	Other mentioned Instruments
1697	6 violins, other strings not specified	6 oboes 3 bassoons	Theorbo, three trumpets and drums.
1709	4 – 2 – 4 – 1	2 flutes 4 oboes 2 bassoons	Two theorbos. Viols: Haute-contre and taille.
1719	7 – 5 – 5 – 5	2 flutes 5 oboes 3 bassoons 2 horns	

[213]

	Strings	Wood	Other mentioned Instruments
1731	6 – 3 – 4 – 2	3 flutes 4 oboes 3 bassoons 2 horns	Two harpsichords.
1734	12 – 4 – 5 – 2	3 flutes 3 oboes 3 bassoons 2 horns	
1754	15 – 4 – 3 – 3	2 flutes 5 oboes 5 bassoons 2 horns	

The next sets of figures have been selected:

(a) to compare the size of the Imperial Establishment at Vienna with that of smaller (but not the smallest) court orchestras,

(b) to show the size of orchestra requisitioned for important *public* concerts in London and Leipzig at about the middle of the century.

Vienna (Imperial Court Orchestra, 1730).

32 strings, 5 oboes, 5 bassoons, 13 trumpets, 4 trombones. The trumpets probably only for imperial ceremonies, since only two are specified in the Imperial *opera* orchestra. It is noteworthy that Jahn mentions far fewer strings in the opera orchestra, c. 1780, but 2 flutes, 2 oboes, 2 clarinets, 2 bassoons and 4 horns.

Stuttgart (Duke of Würtemberg, 1757).

21 strings, 3 flutes, 3 oboes, 2 bassoons, 4 horns. (Players used for concerts and opera, but some specified as *Kammermusiki* and some as *Hofmusiki*.) Trumpets and drums not mentioned; supplied by militia as required.

Brunswick (Court Orchestra, 1731).

12 strings, 5 flute-oboe, 3 bassoons, 2 horns, 7 trumpeters if wanted.

Gotha (Court Orchestra, 1754).

10 strings, 2 oboes, 1 bassoon, 2 horns.

London (Handel's Foundling Hospital Orchestra, 1759).

20 strings, 4 oboes, 4 bassoons, 2 horns, 2 trumpets, drums.

[214]

Leipzig (Concert Society, 1746).	16 strings, 3 flute-oboe, 3 bassoons. (Trumpets evidently on application to the guild, the militia or the Stadtpfeiffer.) By 1765 this orchestra was considerably larger, and there were two each of the wind instruments, but without clarinets.

These lists include the largest and most famous orchestras of the concerto grosso period, which almost finished before the notable ascendance of the Elector Karl Theodor's orchestra at Mannheim. Orchestras as large as most of those just mentioned were rare, and the very large orchestras brought together for such occasions as the Handel Commemoration of 1784 in London or two years later under Hiller in Berlin were rarer than coronation ceremonies. We must not even suppose that the number of strings entered on Carse's lists were normally heard at concerts or in the places and at the times mentioned. All 32 members of the imperial establishment at Vienna may have played together on a rare occasion. If they often did so, surely it is strange that no traveller recorded the fact. These, like the 21 mentioned on the Würtemberg establishment, are the total for chamber and opera; some of the players may have served in both. The period of the concerto grosso is not that of Burney's travels when Mannheim was at its zenith. We may safely assume that before 1750 a court chamber concert with more than a dozen strings was considered to be a large one. As late as 1812 Beethoven writes to the Archduke Rudolf hoping that there shall be not less than four first and four second violins for his *seventh* symphony!

When the Venetian concerto was imported and imitated in the years from 1710 onwards the 'King of Poland's Orchestra' at Dresden[1] was regarded as the finest in Germany. The repertory was still largely French or in the French style, and Dresden had the advantage of training under the first-class discipline and example of Jean Baptiste Volumier, who is known to have visited Cremona to buy violins for Dresden from Stradivarius. When Volumier died in 1728 Pisendel crowned his work through his own gifts and his experience with Vivaldi. Quantz served in this orchestra from 1728 until he left it for Potsdam in 1741, and he should have

[1] Really the Saxon Court Orchestra, given the grander name when the Elector, Frederick Augustus of Saxony, became King of Poland in 1734.

thought highly of the orchestra maintained by his royal pupil; yet he declared in Marpurg's *Beyträge*[1] that in all his journeys he had never heard finer playing than that of the Dresdeners under Pisendel. Rousseau's dictionary corroborates Quantz's opinion. Hasse's arrival at Dresden and his collaboration with Pisendel brought Dresden to the height of its fame. Despite frequent absences, usually without his Faustina who remained the *diva* of the Dresden opera, Hasse was titular Kapellmeister. Pisendel, like Volumier, was called Konzertmeister but the office was not necessarily a subordinate one, for it could carry with it the chief responsibilities of training, leading or directing, and maybe all three. Thus neither Quantz nor C. P. E. Bach was Kapellmeister at Potsdam, and surely they were not considered inferior to either of the Grauns.

Dresden in the period of the concerto grosso was what Mannheim became in the period of the ascendant symphony, but the glory largely departed from Dresden and from Saxony with the ravages of the Seven Years War. After Frederick of Prussia entered the city on 7th October 1745 Hasse was required to superintend nightly performances for the conqueror;[2] and though he and the other musicians were handsomely rewarded he later lost much property and manuscript music in the Siege of Dresden (1760) after which he left for Venice. Burney who was in Dresden in 1772 wrote: 'It was from the dispersion of this celebrated band, at the beginning of the last war, that almost every great city in Europe, and London amongst the rest, acquired several exquisite and favourite performers.'

Meanwhile from 1740, the year of Frederick the Great's accession, the Berlin orchestra entered its finest period. Burney was referring to the year 1752 when he wrote: 'At this time the whole band of vocal and instrumental performers was the most splendid in Europe.' If he had been speaking only of orchestral ensemble he might have allowed Dresden the pre-eminence. The orchestra of Quantz, C. P. E. Bach, the Grauns and the Bendas must have been a fine one. It lost its high repute soon after the middle of the century because the king's taste was only for the music of composers he liked as a youth, especially Quantz, Hasse, Graun and

[1] F. W. Marpurg, *Historisch-Kritische Beyträge zur Aufname der Musik*, Berlin, 1757.   [2] Mennicke.

Agricola, and this taste was imposed despotically upon the repertory. He had no ear for the music of C. P. E. Bach who had
escaped to Hamburg when Burney visited Potsdam in 1772 and
recorded his disappointment in the performance. Orchestras in
other parts of Europe, Burney declared, had 'discovered and
adopted certain refinements, in the manner of executing even old
music, which are not yet received in the Berlin school, where
pianos and *fortes* are but little attended to, and where each performer seems trying to surpass his neighbour, in nothing so much
as loudness'. That was when Agricola was Kapellmeister. He died
in 1774 and Frederick had some difficulty in securing a successor
who would consent to maintain the established repertory. When
Frederick himself died in 1786 Kapellmeister Reichart, who had
shown himself a vital trainer even under the tyranny, brought
the Berlin orchestra to a standard that made Dittersdorf praise
it with unusual warmth in his autobiography.[1]

Probably the next finest orchestra after Dresden during the
concerto grosso period was the Duke of Würtemberg's at Stuttgart, for many of its members were Italians. It reached its zenith
just after the middle of the century when Berlin began to decline,
for Jommelli became its director in 1753 and stayed for fifteen
years. Evidently his standards were not maintained after his
death, for Burney wrote: 'though the operas, and the musical
establishment of this prince, used, during the seven years' direction of Jommelli, to be the best and most splendid in Germany,
they are now but the shadow of what they were.' Schubart[2]
speaks of the Stuttgart orchestra as 'one of the best in the world'
during the Jommelli regime, and as Schubart died in Stuttgart
where he was a theatre manager and had previously lived at
Mannheim he should have been a good judge.

It is noteworthy that travellers tell us little about the chamber
performances of the imperial court orchestra at Vienna. We know

[1] Karl Ditters von Dittersdorf, *Lebensbeschreibung*, ed. Schmitz, Ratisbon,
1944. English translation: *The Autobiography of Karl Ditters von Dittersdorf*, by
A. D. Coleridge, London, 1896.

[2] C. F. D. Schubart, remembered as the versifier of 'Die Forelle', 'An
mein Clavier' and other Schubert songs, was himself a minor composer and
organist, who wrote a book on musical aesthetics, *Ideen zu einer Aesthetik der
Tonkunst* in the mid-1780s. It was published posthumously in Vienna in 1806
by his son but was fortunately reprinted in Leipzig in 1924.

that many of the grandees living in and around the city had their
own orchestras and that the most famous composers, singers and
players were ambitious to shine in the opera, church and chamber
music of Vienna. Haydn's biographers cannot be blamed for telling us less than we should like to know about the playing at
Esterház during the earlier part of his stay there, and Dittersdorf's autobiography merely gives us an amusing account of his
determination to improve the playing of the Hildburghausen
Kapelle . . . ('Gentlemen this will not do; there are too many
wrong notes') . . . and of his prince's pleasure in this apparently
bold rehearsal criticism. But what of the private orchestras belonging to the Lobkowitz, Liechtenstein, Kinsky and other Austrian
houses which are mentioned in books about Haydn and Beethoven? We hear far more about opera and church music than
about concerts in Vienna during the first part of the century, and
in the later part Burney sampled only the theatres. In the 'German Theatre the orchestra has a very numerous band, and the
pieces which were played for an overture and act-tunes were very
well performed, and had an admirable effect; they were composed
by Haydn, Hoffmann and Vanhall'. He found the orchestral
pieces in the French Theatre just as admirable and well played.
We know, however, that Fux and Caldara were Kapellmeisters,
but that when Reutter took charge in 1751 the orchestra shrank
in numbers to about twenty. Since at this time the control of the
opera was handed over to the municipality, it seems likely that
the large numbers quoted by Carse for 1730 comprise musicians
for opera and concerts, and that only about half of them normally
played in the imperial concert room. The orchestra grew large
again during Mozart's lifetime when Salieri was Kapellmeister.

A very welcome contribution to our shelves would be a compilation of the numbers employed during various periods between
1700 and 1800 in *public* operas and concerts, such as those at
Hamburg and Leipzig, in churches and in the many court and
private establishments of Germany—Bonn, Brunswick, Cassel,
Coblenz, Darmstadt, Gotha, Mainz, Mannheim, Munich and so
on. The researcher's work is complicated by the fluctuations
caused by war and political unrest; but the important matter for
us to notice is the enormous *number* of orchestras throughout
German-speaking States, Bohemia, Hungary, Poland and as far

north as Stockholm where Johan Helmich Roman (1694–1758), only a decade younger than Bach and Handel, composed works which cover the history of orchestral music from the French-style repertory of the seventeenth century to the style of the Mannheim symphonists and of Haydn. He is chiefly represented today by the symphonies which, come last. If we wished to illustrate the history of the baroque and rococo orchestral repertory by pieces chosen for their distinction we should more often quote music by Roman than by most of the Saxons and Berliners with whom this chapter is concerned.

Not many concertos stand out to shame our negligence of the worthy *Kapellmeistermusik* of Pisendel, Heinichen, Fasch, Graupner, Molter, Graun and the rest. Schering's *Concertos by German Masters* (*DDT*, xxix–xxx) was presumably a selection of the most impressive, and Schering was a very good judge of musical vitality. Of the intrinsic worth of concertos after Vivaldi's (except those by Bach and Handel) we can form some idea by reflecting that Telemann provides most that are likely to be heard again. This is not because the Germans wrote poor music or poor concertos, but because at no time in the history of music, not even the third quarter of the sixteenth or of the nineteenth century were musicians and their patrons more unanimous and settled in their taste—what sort of expression music should provide and in what forms—as they were between about 1715 and 1745. Mattheson, Spiess, Heinichen and the others praised a mixed, catholic style.[1] They were not merely showing satisfaction in the achievement of music which combined the elegance of French dance rhythms, Italian string textures, operatic expression and good German craftsmanship in harmony and counterpoint; they were reflecting the thought and feeling of an age which, through Dr. Johnson's pen, considered that 'civilisation has arrived'. Frederick of Prussia was but an extreme example of a conservatism that was more widespread and strongly entrenched towards the middle of the eighteenth century than in any other epoch.

It is precisely when forms and style have reached full maturity, precisely when thousands of composers are fluently imitative and when the filling of moulds and the maintenance of length presents

---

[1] 'Gusto' is often better translated by 'style' than by 'taste' in writings of the concerto grosso period.

few technical problems—nothing to forge and little to devise—
that individual genius must be outstanding to be recognizable at
all. Unless Bach and Handel had been supremely great artists
they would have been at a disadvantage, as regarded by posterity,
by comparison with Monteverdi, Purcell or Schütz. That is probably why today we hear a concerto by Muffat with more interest
than one by Pisendel or Telemann even if the latter is scored for
trumpets and wood-wind; and that is probably why the most
striking concerto in Schering's selection is not among the many
composed by the outstanding Germans we have mentioned but
one by an Amsterdam organist, CONRAD FRIEDRICH HURLE-
BUSCH (1696–1765), who was the son of a distinguished Brunswick organist. He is included in *Ehrenpforte*, and recent research[1]
amplifies Schering's description of him as having only 'local
importance'. He made the Italian journey, and stayed in Hamburg, Munich and Stockholm. His best movements show his
command of counterpoint: others make their impact by memorable simplicity. It is counterpoint or such part-writing as
reveals the composer's contrapuntal training that marks the few
German concertos worth retrieving after the first flame of inspiration from Italy had become only a gentle glow and the fire
of concerto composition was large but dying. Stölzel, like Hurlebusch, is worth resurrection largely because of his contrapuntal
vigour. Bach used the main theme of the finale of Stölzel's concerto grosso for four chori (probably reprinted by Schering because
it is so unusual and imposing, but musically inferior to other
concertos by the composer) in his *Clavierbüchlein* for Wilhelm
Friedmann—the G minor bourree. Two subjects from Stölzel's
concerto in E minor are shown in Ex. 60. The concertino in this
work is variously chosen from two flutes, two oboes and two
bassoons; the violins are *all'unisono*.

The well-trained contrapuntist is so well revealed in Hurlebusch's concerto that the music could be mistaken for Bach's. The
Vivaldian opening tutti (Ex. 61) does not close in the tonic but
proceeds to the relative major and in that key the solo violin
is first heard in very Bachian figuration. The movement is of full
length but does not reach a close; instead it is followed by two

[1] See the lengthy article on Hurlebusch by Liselotte Bense in *Die Musik in
Geschichte und Gegenwart*.

bars of 3/2 marked *adagio*, after which the second violins announce the fugue subject of the second movement, *alla breve*. These connecting bars can hardly be interpreted as are those in the third Brandenburg concerto, that is to say as the musical expression of *attacca* or *segue* after a slow movement for the harpsichord or perhaps for solo violin and harpsichord, for they are carefully scored and include parts for oboes and bassoons. The fugue is followed by a slow movement in 6/8 for string quartet. This is in binary form. The solo violin replaces the ripieno violins and is given a florid and pathetic part which embroiders a basic siciliano rather like Vivaldi's best-known siciliano slow movement, especially where Hurlebusch indulges in chromatic harmony. The triple-measure finale is also strongly reminiscent of Bach.

It is difficult not to judge the German concertists by Bach and Handel, or by Vivaldi before them and Bach's sons after them. We value personality highly and are more willing to hear inferior works in which it is recognizable—say Bach's F minor harpsichord concerto or the first of Handel's 'oboe' concertos—than the best efforts of the Pisendels and Grauns. To be fair in judging concertos by men whose most inventive music cannot be regarded as approaching the best of Bach and Handel we must try to imagine the value we should put upon them if the giants had composed no concertos, and admit that to know thoroughly the music of any two of them, say Pisendel and Fasch, is also to recognize some individual turns of expression within a limited vocabulary. The samples from concertos, one by Pisendel and one by Graupner, which are given in Ex. 62 and 63 were not chosen to support the last statement, but simply because they could be copied from Schering's selection. If they reveal nothing that is recognized as personal they at least show the diversity of design and style that was possible between two contemporary German concertists (working in almost neighbouring capitals) who had much in common as well as the spending of their formative years in Leipzig.

Both of these concertos need oboes and bassoons, and in the Graupner two flutes echo passages for two oboes. Pisendel is the more Vivaldian but both composers write an interesting part for the solo violin. Did these concertos strike their first hearers as original, or at least novel, or did they seem no more than honourable *Gebrauchsmusik*?[1] Whether most of the hundreds of concertos by German chamber musicians are little more than pedestrian for all their sound workmanship, or whether the best fifty are unduly neglected during a wholesale revival of Italian concertos, some of which are thin enough in all conscience, the Germans are certainly not represented by the few concertos that have been issued in pocket scores for their appeal to solo performers, including some flute concertos by Quantz and Telemann which most nearly deserve to be regarded as fillings of moulds. A surprising number of the German concertos which have not been reprinted illustrate the fact that German *Individualismus*

[1] Since Hindemith made this term popular it has been translated 'workaday music'. A better equivalent is 'repertory music' or 'practical music' lest it become a term of reproach to describe the idle thoughts of busy fellows. *Gebrauchsmusik* does not plumb the depths of pathos or give us intimations of immortality, but if it means inferior music then we must regard most of Haydn's symphonies as inferior music.

62.

Pisendel. Violin concerto. [Dresden.CX,700]

Vivace

Ob.

f Bass doubling at 8ve.

for 31 bars, ending :—

Adagio

p

più p

for 10 bars. The vivace is repeated to close in tonic. Then :—

Solo

p

Cembalo only

+ 8ve.

2nd. mov. Andante

Strings only. Middle parts omitted

3rd. mov. Allegro

Tutti *f*

[Used as full ritornello in A, B minor and G]

Solo

[223]

.63.

Graupner, Ripieno concerto. [Schering]

found expression in the very period which critics rightly regard as one of the most conventional in the history of western music.

We see in Ex. 62, for instance, that Pisendel inserts ten bars for string trio, with a change of time signature and the direction adagio, at a place in his opening allegro that seems to have been chosen by no other concertist or symphonist. This concerto as a whole is no work of supreme genius, yet the feature to which attention has been drawn is almost as striking and beautiful as Mozart's insertion of a minor-key minuet into a major-key rondo in duple tempo. Taken as a body of work, the concertos by Bach's inferiors genuinely advanced the genre in form and design.

For instance we noticed that in first movements Vivaldi and some of the early concertists gave the impression that after they had taken their ideas to the key of the dominant—after what corresponds with the end of the expository section of a classical first movement—they left modulations and other procedures largely to the inspiration of the moment. Sometimes they sound as if they are improvising; sometimes there seems to be too much music in the tonic, a lack of reference to themes, a parade of conventional figuration and busyness, or a finish that comes too quickly. The methodical German concertists obviously planned their designs as thoroughly as their harmony and instrumentation. Their progression of keys advances towards that of the classical symphony and sonata, even to the use of incidental or digressive modulations. Having reached the first section in the dominant they complete a cycle of tonalities, including at least one section in the minor key if the movement is in the major, and passing to the subdominant side of the main tonality before finally establishing it. Is there a single German concerto composed after about 1720 in which the general design of a movement seems careless or unbalanced, or in which a long movement lacks an adequate final section?

If only some ten of the best 'Kapellmeister concertos' could be regularly heard we should add intrinsically attractive (not merely worthy) pieces to the repertory and recognize more clearly what is unique and what is not in the concertos of J. S. Bach. For thousands of musical folk they alone represent the German concerto, just as Bach's overtures and suites alone represent the chief German chamber music of the late seventeenth and early eighteenth century. Bach's concertos and suites came to us in the course of the Bach revival, not of a general historical revival of chamber music. For most musicians, as for the present writer until very recently, they were compared with other music by the same composer, not with any other works of the same genre except Handel's and a few of Telemann's, which would also be more fairly appreciated if a wider repertory enabled us to recognize the very quality which they are unjustly denied—originality.

CHAPTER XI

The Main German School—II
Bach and Telemann

The variety within the Brandenburg concertos is a monument of *Individualismus* simply because it is concentrated within six works by one man who may have composed it within a few weeks or months; but if we were to spread the period of time and choose from a number of smaller composers we could secure a similar variety. From Fasch we could take one of his concertos in which the treatment of horns and oboes is so similar to Bach's in the first Brandenburg Concerto as to make us suppose that Bach's instrumentation was an open expression of his admiration of Fasch. We could choose Molter's *Concerto con l'Echo* (Carlsruhe, No. 354) in which a Corellian trio-concertino echoes the string tutti. From Graupner we could take one of his concertos with chalumeaux and viola d'amore, from Heinichen a concerto wherein transverse flutes are contrasted with flutes of the recorder type; and from many composers we could select a concerto which uses the clarino register of one or two trumpets in more exacting parts than were required by any Italian concertist. (One has seen no trumpet part quite as exacting as that of the second Brandenburg Concerto.) None of these choices would be of an extraordinary piece like Stölzel's *Concerto Grosso a Quattro Chori* (*Gotha*, p. 99d, no. 3). The four bands required are:

   i. Three trumpets and drums.
   ii. Three trumpets and drums.
   iii. Flute, three oboes and bassoon.
   iv. Four violins, viola, 'cello, bass.

Instrumentation alone puts the German concertos into the main stream from Vivaldi to the classical symphonists and concertists. Many German concertos are so carefully scored that they cannot be played by strings alone or by that free choice of few or many instruments which printers of the period welcomed, and which some writers would have us believe was a matter of indifference to composers before Haydn and Mozart. Bach's fourth Brandenburg Concerto is only one of many violin concertos of the period which would be spoilt if harpsichord or strings were substituted for wind instruments. The Brandenburg Concertos must not be regarded as novel *because* of their exposed sections for wind instruments or *because* Bach experimented with the concertino grouping. Some of Bach's groupings are treated in an original and distinctive way, but such groupings were far from unusual in a Germany whose minor composers suited their design to their instrumentation, or rather made design and instrumentation one conception, as effectively at their own levels of inspiration as Bach did at his. Telemann used most of the concertino groups found in Bach's concertos, as this table shows:

BACH	TELEMANN
1st Brandenburg Concerto 2 horns, 3 oboes, violino piccolo, strings and continuo.	With one oboe less: Concerto in D major, Dresden, CX.181, no. 6 and Concerto in F major (Bach's key), CX.187, no. 12. Several Telemann concertos are for 2 horns with 2 oboes or 2 flutes.
2nd Brandenburg Concerto Trumpet, flute, oboe, violin, strings and continuo.	*Musique de Table*, part 2, no. 1 is a suite in D major for solo trumpet, oboe and strings. Telemann's Concerto in D major, Rostock, XVIII, 18, 45 is for 2 trumpets and 2 violins with strings.
4th Brandenburg Concerto Solo violin, two flutes, strings and continuo.	Concerto in E minor, Darmstadt, 6063, no. 13 and Concerto in D major, no. 15. Several Telemann concertos in Bach's key of G use 2 solo flutes without solo violin, e.g. Dresden, CX.893 and 896.

BACH	TELEMANN
Concerto for 2 violins with strings and continuo.	Concertos in G major, D major, E minor and other keys in Darmstadt, 6053. Other concertos for 2 violins at Dresden, but orchestra in these always includes wind.

Büttner's book on Telemann's orchestral suites,[1] many of which are as much concertos as the Brandenburg Concertos or Bach's Suite in B minor, informs us of many wind or string-and-wind concertino groups.

What sort of works would Bach have produced if he had not wilfully forsaken the court career which led to wider fame and greater prestige than a cantorate? Is there not an answer within the corpus of his non-chamber music? He never wrote a nobler concerto movement than the prelude to the great B minor organ fugue, and then there are the great choruses designed like the first movements of concertos. The celebrated feat of composing a concerto for a two-manual harpsichord in the *Italian Concerto* had been achieved often before, for instance in the prelude to the fourth English suite. We may be certain that if Bach's dream for the Leipzig churches had been fulfilled there would have been a wealth of instrumental concertos as well as the already existing *Kirchenkonzerte*.

There seems to be considerable popular misunderstanding about Bach's status, fame and treatment, and his original aim in going to Leipzig. If we say that he was poorly paid and undervalued we must add 'by comparison with a music director to a nobleman'. There is a similar contrast between the income and fame of a modern conductor and the income and fame of a cathedral organist, or a teacher who may be a good orchestral player, conductor and routine composer, but bears no envy because he knows that he lacks precisely the qualities which have secured the conductor's advancement. Bach was irritable but is not known to have envied court musicians. He left the court for a cantorate at one of the most famous centres of Lutheran orthodoxy, the post being by standards of the day well paid and highly esteemed. Yet his activities and compositions during his first Leipzig years and his

[1] Horst Büttner, *Das Konzert in den Orchestersuiten Georg Philipp Telemanns*, Wolfenbüttel, 1935.

subsequent increasing absorption with the ideal conceptions which he printed suggest that he planned a glory which the Leipzig city council, clergy and school officers could not envisage. Bach hoped in Leipzig to bring about Luther's ideal of a liturgical music embracing the resources of princely chamber music yet achieving greater splendour.

The influence of his concertos and pieces in the forms of concerto movements was not noticeable while he lived, nor was it acknowledged for many years after his death. Is it acknowledged fully yet? One has never yet read or heard the recognition that the most popular and satisfying form, the concerto for solo keyboard instrument and orchestra, originated in the fifth Brandenburg Concerto, in the arrangements for solo harpsichord or two harpsichords of Italian and other concertos, and in Bach's original works for the instruments. How were they influential—with the Telemann Collegium Musicum at the university? Perhaps, but rather with Bach's own sons, who heard them and played them at home as they also played the many concerto movements in what are now called the six trio sonatas for organ. C. P. E. Bach and J. C. Bach are often regarded as the fathers of the harpsichord and piano concerto, but the ancestry should be carried back to their father. If he was not the inventor of this genre, who was?

Little will be said here about most of Bach's concertos, not because one regards them as less wonderful or attractive than his other works but because they are analysed in popular accounts of concertos, or in books of programme notes, whereas Handel's concertos are comparatively disregarded or treated as a lump of similar consistency, apparently because the Great Twelve are all for strings and continuo. We lack no appreciation of Bach's concertos, but it is worth our while to ask why they did not create a furore in their own day. Are they not strikingly unlike the kind of music which Scheibe and others deplored? Scheibe himself wrote to the effect that if only Bach would compose more in his chamber style he would earn as a composer the international fame which he already deserved for his prowess as a player and his command of the materials of music; but Scheibe complained after Bach had forsaken the career of chamber musician. This chapter is less about the kapellmeister-concerto than about two independent spirits.

[229]

Bach's surviving and available concertos, as distinct from his arrangements of other men's work and his solo pieces in concerto style or form, are as follows:

Six Brandenburg Concertos, dedicated 1721.
Two violin concertos in A minor and E major ⎫ Composed
Concerto for two violins in D minor ⎭ 1717–23
Seven concertos for solo harpsichord and orchestra, composed 1729–36.

  (a) Those not extant in other versions:
     D minor, E major, F minor, A major.
  (b) D major. Version of the violin concerto in E major.
     F major. Version of Brandenburg Concerto No. 4 in G.
     G minor. Version of the violin concerto in A minor.

Two concertos for two harpsichords in C major and C minor, and a third in C minor arranged from the D minor concerto for two violins.
Two concertos for three harpsichords in C major and D minor, *c.* 1733.
Concerto for violin, flute and harpsichord in A minor, *c.* 1730.
To these should be added the 'Ouvertures' or French Suites:

  C major, for woodwind and strings.
  B minor, for solo flute and strings.
  Two in D major for trumpets, drums, oboes, bassoons and strings.

The Brandenburg Concertos were composed when Bach was aged thirty-six and the dedicatee some eight years older. We are assured that Christian Ludwig of Brandenburg was an enthusiastic music-lover with a fine orchestra, but it is not supposed that he greatly valued Bach's concertos. The dedication tells us that two years previously the Margrave 'took pleasure' in Bach's playing and asked for 'some pieces of my composition'. (If Bach wrote the dedication without help he commanded elegant French.) The Margrave may have heard Bach at Meiningen, and like most other musical people he valued him as a performer rather than as a composer. He did not specially want specimens of Bach's art but more concertos for a collection which ultimately amounted to 177, for that was the number recorded by Spitta from an inventory in the Berlin Royal Library. Bach's unusually neat and careful manuscript was secured by his pupil Kirnberger and has found its way back to the Berlin archives through a Prussian princess who was Kirnberger's pupil.

We have no evidence as to whether the Brandenburg Concertos (or for that matter other Bach concertos) were performed often or only once. We do not know if some of them were performed at all. They may have circulated in manuscript parts to several orchestras, yet Bach himself seems to have given them little thought after settling at Leipzig. Why were they not widely popular? Why are English concertos, above all Handel's, but not Bach's, found in many German libraries? Because none of Bach's was printed except the *Concerto in the Italian Style* for solo harpsichord in Part 2 of the *Clavierübung*? That is not sufficient explanation, for many of the English concertos in Germany are manuscript. Handel's reputation was international, and one can understand the popularity of his concertos where his friends Telemann, Graupner, Steffani and others were influential, but the question is still not answered.

It is hard to understand why unprejudiced ears should have thought some of Bach's concertos old fashioned or some of their movements less elegant than Telemann's, Pisendel's, Graupner's or Handel's. Why, for instance, was not the concerto for two violins, with a slow movement so limpidly lyrical and other movements so Italianate that Corelli and Handel would have loved it, a popular favourite throughout Germany? Why, when flute concertos were as fashionable as concertos for solo violin, did not the fourth Brandenburg Concerto commend itself as a work which featured both of the solo instruments in a series of the neatest and happiest movements ever composed? Why were not a score of courts charmed by the novelty of the fifth concerto with its harpsichord cadenzas, its affecting slow movement, its gigue which should have satisfied the champions of French as well as of Italian styles?

These questions are baffling precisely because one can quite understand why Scheibe wished Bach's keyboard works had been less contrapuntal. Indeed one almost sympathizes with Bach's adverse critics when not even baroque organs can make some of the five-part textures with crossing parts sound less than thick, or when one finds Bach inclined to write what looks well on paper but sounds congested; but we do not need the evidence that Bach admired Albinoni and Vivaldi to tell us that if he had decided to stay with a court kapelle he could have become in his own day the most famous German composer of chamber music, and have enjoyed in harpsichord concertos the kind of admiration which Handel enjoyed when London crowded to the King's Theatre in the Haymarket less to hear the oratorios than Handel's interspersed organ concertos. Surely we have found that answer—'if he had stayed'. The point to notice is that Handel was present to play his concertos. Vivaldi's concertos were popular while Vivaldi played them; then they were neglected. Bach's concertos were neglected because Bach ceased to be a chamber or concert musician, however much he was admired on Thursday nights at the Telemann Society.

The phrase 'he summed up' has often been misused by historians of music and is now happily out of fashion; but it is validly applicable to much of Bach's work, including some aspects of his orchestral music. Though the Brandenburg Concertos are unique, and though one has already asked if any previous concerto used the harpsichord as the *cembalo concertato* is used in No. 5, it is doubtful if the choice of concertino groups caused any astonishment if these works were performed soon after they were despatched. As we have seen from Telemann and from minor German composers whose works are not in the repertory, concertini as heterogeneous as Bach's were common.

What we notice in Bach, however, is the *desire* to sum up. The mind which later set itself to demonstrate all known ways of treating a chorale, to compile chorale treatments for the complete Lutheran Kalendar, to show progressively all the known artifice of fugal composition, to illustrate canon at all intervals in a series of variations—this mind also set itself without explicit didacticism to demonstrate in six concertos not merely six types of concertino (for in that case it could be said that Nos. 3 and 6 were similar conceptions) but six different relationships of tutti to solo materials. Bach would cover systematically as widely as he could in six concertos all that he knew of concerto technique, just as later he covered systematically the techniques of chorale treatment, canon and fugue. The average listener might suppose him most original in concertos like the first two, which include brass instruments. That is not so. In them he was 'summing up' what had been done in other German suites and concertos. He was most exploratory and ingenious—indeed unique even in scoring— when he came to each of the two concertos for strings and continuo only, and it is not proposed to discuss separately any others than these two.

The third Brandenburg Concerto is one of the few works which one ought to see in score at a first listening. The map is not the landscape nor the score the music, and we do not listen properly until we take our nose out of a score; but we may sometimes miss beauty when no map or guide has warned us, and we may miss several clues to thread of this concerto if we have not seen a score. Bach exploits the broadening or sharpening of focus as applied to the sound of strings. Their ensemble may be spread, opposed, balanced or concentrated. At one extreme is the sound of nine strands and at the other a powerful unison; in one bar a chain of chords by the three violins, in the next a contrasting chain in the richer alto register of the three violas, or the full fathom of the three 'cellos and basso continuo. Bach surely intended the work for exactly eleven instruments, but the designation of each instrument in the singular does not prove this. The singular form is used in the other concertos and on most Bach scores. We imagine the three 'cellos behind the flat side of the harpsichord, the violone player standing behind the harpsichordist and following his figured bass; flanking this central group we see the three violins on the right and the three violas on the left. The opening tutti goes from solid three-strand harmony reinforced by continuo to heavy unison. Where the solo usually begins, the three violins are heard alone, and are answered by the three violas which pass the thread on to the three 'cellos. Concertino and tutti, as well as all subsidiary patterns in the design, are produced by the same players in different groupings; the concertino makes its own tutti or vice versa, an arrangement which remains the greatest but least advertised stroke of originality in any concerto grosso. (This does not mean that one considers the work to be the best of the Brandenburg Concertos.)

Yet the other string concerto, No. 6, is also unique in its outlay of instruments. It also was surely intended only for the six instruments specified, plus the continuo, and should be played as a chamber work in the later meaning of the term. It is not at all like the ripieno concertos of Vivaldi; rather does it anticipate the rococo sinfonia concertante in which all participants except the continuo bass make individual contributions to a discourse. Violins are excluded, yet there is a gigue finale and a lively first movement of a kind associated with violins, so that the concerto has a strange but most attractive sound once a solution has been found to its particular difficulty for modern performance. The two viole da braccio are simply violas, but violas vary greatly in size and sonority, and for a good performance these upper instruments need careful selection. Then, unless the concerto is to sound unclear and unbalanced, the great problem is to secure either players of the two violas da gamba which support the middle strands of the texture or to find a tolerable substitute. The present writer has never heard one. Finally one needs a very clear, reedy bass rather than a loud one, and it is well to ensure that the harpsichordist maintains the bass line with octave stops drawn.

The chief stylistic distinction of Bach's concertos is one which would make for boredom in a smaller artist and can be tedious when Bach himself is not at his best in certain of his less familiar harpsichord concertos. The elaboration of line, which he could not entirely forgo in genial chamber music, despite his admiration of the Venetians, is a personal and marvellous Bachian quality that is not fully explained by 'Bach wrote out all his ornaments' or 'Bach's line reveals the improvising of the organist-cantor'. Nobody in the whole history of music provides us with such a wonderful and elaborate line as Bach does in such familiar instances as the second movement of the Italian Concerto or the ritornello to *Laudamus te*. Handel would have needed a completely new and more limited experience from the age of about sixteen to have written passages like those shown at Ex. 64, or even to have wished to write them. They are by no means the simple consequence of contrapuntal training, for nothing like them is found in the treatises or music of other famous contrapuntists. Bach's maintenance of small and large patterns produces discords which are not classified in contrapuntal theory. Undoubtedly much keyboard practice, including improvisation, and much practice in the invention of two contrapuntal parts or of

64.

Bach. Brandenburg Concerto No. 1.

Partita No. 2.

65.

Larghetto affettuoso   Handel. Op. 6, No. 4.

66. Allegro   Bach. Clavier concerto in F minor

invertible counterpoint—shapely, purposeful and continuously patterned lines, not *Fortspinnung*—made such music spring readily to Bach's command whatever his medium, instrumental or vocal. The nearest approach in Handel's concertos to this Bachian melodic elaboration is at the opening of the A minor concerto, Op. 6, No. 4 (Ex. 65) but let us notice that this movement is only twenty-four bars long and that it forms a prelude to the fugal allegro. Moreover the piece is in clear sections, punctuated by cadences after which all but the first violins have long rests. If Bach had begun this movement the patterning would not have been thus punctuated; it would have been 'endless' and not restricted to the upper line, for there would have been counter melodies or imitations in at least one or two of the other voices and probably in the bass itself.

We cannot imagine from any other composer a concerto beginning with the sort of melody quoted at Ex. 66, and we do not disparage Bach by saying that without his particular genius to hold our interest on the elaborate melodic thread such materials make dull concertos; for they preclude broad contrasts, the high lighting of main themes and a series of climaxes and relaxations of tension. In short, such concertos least resemble the classical symphony. To Bach's contemporaries concertos in this style were not in the Italian or the French style; they were in parish cantor style, a preludizing and improvising style—*phantasticus* not *symphoniacus*. Even to our more tolerant ears Bach's most satisfying concertos are those wherein an arresting rather than an elaborate main theme, such as the opening of the E major violin concerto, shows the influence of Vivaldi by being well differentiated from the subsidiary development of patterns and figurations.

When composing in the French style, Bach and Handel can sometimes be very similar. Which of them wrote the melody quoted at Ex. 67, strongly reminiscent of Purcell?[1] In which Bach concerto does the fugato of Ex. 68 occur?[2] Very few passages in orchestral dance movements by Handel and Bach might have been composed by either of them, and no dance in Bach's keyboard suites could be mistaken for one by Handel; but in the concertos of the two giants the greatest contrast is within the movements that do not derive from the French suite, and the contrast is not explained by 'Bach favours Vivaldi and Handel favours Corelli'. Though German musicographers should be honoured for outstripping others as historians of the baroque concerto and suite one cannot accept their general division of concertists into Vivaldians and Corellians. The chief Corellian feature of concertos by Telemann and his friend Handel is not of design but simply of

[1] Handel. Op. 6, no. 8.
[2] In none. It comes in Handel's Op. 6, no. 10.

general style, and it can be observed in most of their music, not just that for strings. Similarly it is fanciful to recognize notable Vivaldian features in the Brandenburg Concertos or in any of Bach's concertos and suites except those for solo violin or violins. (Notable, that is to say obviously recognizable features as distinct from the general influence of Vivaldi upon Bach which one does not try to minimize.)

67. *Allegro*

68. *Allegro*

Georg Philipp Telemann (1681–1767), so far from fitting into a niche labelled 'Corellian', represents the whole history of the concerto and other forms of French and Italian concert music as reflected in German composers from Muffat until after Quantz, for in his last years Telemann composed almost like Stamitz. This most prolific and versatile of all the German concertists seems to have been a man of charm, energy and wisdom; otherwise he would not have maintained the life-long friendship of Handel and apparently incurred no uncomfortable relationship with Bach, despite the fact that he was in the very post at Leipzig which could have ranged him with the Bach baiters. He left three accounts of his useful and happy life,[1] the fullest being his contribution to Mattheson's *Ehrenpforte*. His laconic comments upon

[1] All three are found in Willi Kahl's *Selbst-Biographien Musiker*, Cologne, 1948—a little compilation so valuable that one regrets its claim to be among the most disgustingly-produced books worth a place on every musician's shelves. The quality of paper and printing is rivalled only by those French copies of music or musicography which are more insulting to the reader than untidy manuscript.

his musical tastes and activities reveal, both in style and content, something of his character.

He was the son of a Lutheran pastor at Magdeburg. When he went to Leipzig he read languages and natural science, and he must have been strongly influenced by the francophile thought and culture of the university. (To lament the death of his wife he composed a poem in French which we should not consider insincere; the choice of language was a way of honouring her memory.) Telemann could hardly have become a performing and composing lackey to a prince or a town council. He was regarded as a man of wide general culture who published articles in the Leipzig *Musikalische Bibliothek*, edited by Mizler, wrote several of his own librettos and was himself responsible for the first musical periodical that included whole musical compositions. This was *Der getreue Musikmeister* which he first edited at Hamburg in 1728. Most of the pieces were in the non-contrapuntal French style which he championed, but the catholicity of his taste is shown by the fact that one of them is a canon 4-in-1 by Bach. Though one can accuse him today of slipping into the democratic fallacy—that a work of art is meritorious in direct ratio to the wideness of its appeal—it was a generous and liberal nature that wished the public to share the musical pleasure and culture of the privileged, and naturally that culture had to be French. Telemann advised the young musician to avoid what 'was not melodious', and to disregard the teaching of old men who 'write compositions for fifteen or twenty voices in which not even Diogenes with his lantern could discover a drop of melody'.

This passage occurs in the account of his early studies which Telemann contributed to Mattheson's *Grosser Generalbassschule* (1731). In the same context he writes:

'Because it was a happy change I also began concertos. Yet I must say of them that at heart I did not care for them although I have written a great many . . . but it is not true that they smell of France. Although it may be that Nature did not give me the right faculties we cannot expect everybody to achieve everything, and that may be one of the reasons why in most concertos. . . . I have found difficulties and crooked roads but little harmony and less melody . . . they have lacked the qualities to which my ear was accustomed in French music.'

This is strange from a composer who not only wrote a great many concertos (at least 170) but included within the many a comparatively small number for solo violin or flute. No composer seems to have explored more varieties of concertino for two, three and four instruments, and to have done so in *Musique de Table* and hundreds of other suites as well as in concertos.

Several of Telemann's *obiter scripta* have been taken from their contexts and used to support harsh judgements of the man and his music. The example just quoted should warn us to be careful. Silly heresies have been defended by isolated quotations from translated Scripture, and silly judgements of artists have been based upon their words instead of their works. The supremely great composer is rarely made the victim of his own attack; people are willing to enjoy *Die Meistersinger* or *Tristan* without recalling Wagner's opinion that music should be the servant of the drama; but they are ready to find most of J. C. Bach's music trivial and most of C. P. E. Bach's profound because they have heard a remark attributed to the former—'My brother lives to compose; I compose to live.' Many a piece could have been composed by the one brother or the other, but C. P. E. has the advantage of being catalogued as serious and as emotionally turbulent in expression; indeed he has been admired for the very works in which he loses his thread and dissipates his invention; but Telemann has the disadvantage of being like J. C. Bach—excellently formal and usually cheerful. If he had murdered or been murdered, composed muddled or despairing music in the intervals of carousing and philandering, told as many lies as Berlioz about the circumstances in which he composed, or merely been a rather eccentric priest with ginger hair, or an emaciated and provoked controversialist like the Rameau he admired, Telemann might have been thought a subtle artist whose profundity is not revealed to dullards.

To set up Telemann as profound (somebody will, sooner or later, for he often composed in the minor mode and used chromatic chords) is not more stupid than to depict him as among the most shallow contemporaries of the two giants of the eighteenth century, for the giants themselves were better judges than we are. Bach copied several of Telemann's cantatas; Handel declared that Telemann could write in eight parts as easily as most people could

69.

Grave — Telemann. Concerto for 4 violins soli.

write a letter; and no decently-trained musician can examine
music by Telemann without thinking Handel's tribute to be
a reliable testimonial. Telemann's feeling for the materials of
music is almost comparable with Mozart's. At one extreme is the
eight-part texture admired by Handel; at the other the sonatas for
two flutes or two violins without bass, which are the most effective
works of their kind before Mozart's duets for violin and viola.

Telemann had the rare feeling for medium which qualifies him
as an admirable concertist, and no contemporary of Bach except
Handel and Rameau had Telemann's sense of the character of
instruments, singly and in groups. At Ex. 69 he deals with what
many would regard as a challenge—a concerto for four solo violins
—and meets it with unimpeachable workmanship and apparent
facility, changing the idea and texture at just the right moment
to hold the attention of listeners as well as players.

Why or for whom did he compose a concerto for four violins or, to mention an unusual mixture, two concertos in B minor for two flutes (or two violins), two dessus,[1] chalcedon or bassoon, viola and bass?[2] The answer is: 'Either for one of the amateur or semi-professional societies which he ran himself (for Telemann's infectious enthusiasm gathered student and other players round him wherever he went) or for someone who commissioned them.' The task of determining the places and players for which all of Telemann's works were originally composed has not yet been accomplished.[3] It may be impossible, for most of Telemann's instrumental music is either at Dresden or at Darmstadt, in neither of which he held any appointment; yet there is none at Leipzig where he was active and influential. Despite their great number, Telemann's concertos are but a small fraction of his total output, and we shall not use many pages in tracing the life and movements of a composer who was as much a free lance as Handel. The appointments and migrations which are briefly recorded here made Telemann enormously influential, and partly explain the developments in his style and aesthetic:

b. 1681 and schooled at Magdeburg, then Hildesheim.

1700 Leipzig University.

1704 Organist of the New Church.
Forming of his collegium musicum.
Composition for the fairs and for the theatre in Leipzig.
Kapellmeister to Prince Promnitz at Sorau.

1709 Succeeds P. Hebenstreit as Kapellmeister and 'Secretary' at Eisenach, and holds directorship of music at St. Catherine's.

1712 Undertakes direction of the Frauenstein Collegium Musicum at Frankfort-on-Main and, in his own phrase, 'Kapellmeistership' at the Barfüsserkirche, and evidently to the Prince of Bayreuth. (Frauenstein was a small court and town near Frankfort.)

---

[1] *Dessus.* 'Fr. noun=top. A bowed string instrument of the violin family, used in the seventeenth century and now obsolete, with the lowest string tuned to e'—*Grove*, 1954.

[2] Holographs: Darmstadt Ca. 36, nos. 27 and 28.

[3] It has been well attempted in Hans Gräser's dissertation, *Zur Geschichte von Telemanns Instrumental-Kammermusik*, Munich, 1924.

Telemann seems to have been free to travel or appoint deputies, being regarded as a 'secretary' by his noble patrons.

1721 Cantor of the Johanneum (municipal school) and music director of the five chief Hamburg churches. At Hamburg he directed a public concert each Monday and Thursday, composed for the opera and continued to send works to Eisenach, Frankfurt and Bayreuth.

Did he hold offices in plurality or was he paid for engagement as director for a concert and for the pieces delivered? He was unable to enumerate the operas, suites, etc., he had composed, but he mentioned: 'About forty to fifty operas, thirty-two works for the installation of pastors, over six hundred suites, thirty-three pieces of Captain's Music,'[1] etc.

Within the scores which poured from Telemann's pen from youth to a healthy old age, and during a life of apparently happy domesticity, much is unremarkable though expertly fashioned because it manifestly caused little expenditure of creative imagination as distinct from that technical care and self-criticism which is sometimes called invention. One does not ask for a fresh assessment of Telemann in order to place him in the second or even the third class of creative genius, but in order to show that a huge majority of Germans who thought him the best living composer were not stupid. He thoroughly deserved the continuous requests made to him because his standard of work in fulfilment of the request was more reliable than anybody's. To the question: 'Why is Telemann not as great an artist as Vivaldi or Rameau?' no answer could be more untrue than: 'Because he composed so many inferior works and so few good ones.' When people are asked *which* of Telemann's works are among the least inspired they never have a ready answer. Unlike Handel he is not the kind of artist who leaves so-much work of supreme creative genius, so-much music that is almost as wonderful, a good deal of worthy music with some fine passages, a certain amount of music that is inferior and some which is utterly sterile. The remarkable fact about Telemann is that so prolific a composer seemed able to

---

[1] *Capitäns-Musik* consisted of a sonata and a cantata or oratorio performed when someone in the Hamburg merchant navy was given command of a ship.

maintain a small flame of imagination throughout his work. He never lacked the ability to invent melody, harmony, rhythm and texture of sufficient character to hold attention—not to thrill, rarely even to excite.

If this were not true, musicians could not have remained happy in the belief that many of the ideas which Handel is now known to have borrowed from Telemann were entirely Handel's,[1] nor would it be possible to deceive audiences by slipping dance movements from Telemann into ballets, the *Fireworks Music*, the *Water Music* or the more suite-like concertos of Handel. Telemann's melodic invention was certainly not of a much lower order than Handel's second best. A proof that Telemann's music cannot accurately be likened to water from an ever-flowing tap lies in its change of style through works of his early, middle and late production—periods as valid in their less distinguished and less significant way as those of great artists like Beethoven. Fortunately the development can be seen in his concertos.

To represent his earliest concertos we should probably choose from works for strings, or for strings with only oboes or flutes. The concertos for two violins include works originally needed for the collegium musicum in Leipzig, Telemann himself playing one of the solo violins. We shall see later that the patronage of amateur or semi-amateur societies, corresponding with the German collegia musica, accounts for the persistence of Corellian designs in England, and for the brisk printing of orchestral parts by such composers as Geminiani and Avison whose technical demands upon string ripienists were not very much greater than Corelli's. It is the concertos most like those of Geminiani which seem to have led some historians to call Telemann a Corellian concertist. The concerto in E minor, from which beginnings of movements are quoted at Ex. 70, will serve to illustrate this facet of Telemann's work. It seems to be an early work.

Telemann tells us that while he was still a schoolboy he made frequent visits to hear the orchestras at Hanover and Brunswick, where he 'had the best of France's science', but that he studied Corelli and Caldara, and could at that early age distinguish the

---

[1] Handel's extensive borrowings from Telemann are examined in Seiffert's introduction to his edition of 'Musique de Table', *DDT*, 61–2. Reprinted as a booklet, *G. Ph. Telemann*, Leipzig, 1927.

70.

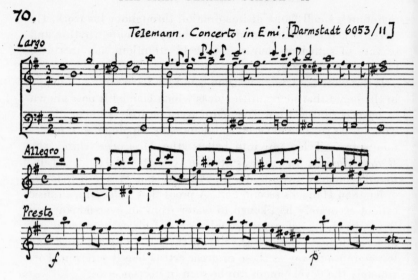

French from the Italian style. Whether many of the extant concertos for two violins were used at Leipzig one cannot tell, but
they were almost certainly used at Sorau and Eisenach and for the
second of his collegia musica. He seems to have visited Panteleon
Hebenstreit at Eisenach or to have played with him at Sorau
before he succeeded him in office, for he writes: 'I remember this
Herr Hebenstreit's prowess as a violinist . . . if we were to play
together in a concerto I had to confine myself for a couple of days
with the violin in my hand, so that I could do something against
his power.' It is therefore unsafe to assume that all of the easier
violin and two-violin concertos date from Telemann's Leipzig
days. We turn, however, to a fine concerto that cannot be called
Corellian at all. The oboe concerto in F minor (excerpts at Ex. 71)
is cast entirely in the Venetian design as developed by German
court composers, and if this work and many like it were suddenly
reprinted in a set of six and said to be by Fasch or Graupner there
would surely be critics ready to make amends for previous neglect.
How much more clearly would Telemann's merits and short-
comings be recognized if our legacy from him had been of two
sets of six concertos arranged in a scheme like that of the Brandenburg Concertos, instead of over 170 single concertos for whatever
instruments or whatever patron required them!

[244]

The oboe concerto just quoted is available in a Eulenburg pocket score and the editor, Felix Schroeder, thinks it belongs to Telemann's Frankfort period because the Frauenstein Collegium Musicum consisted of strings and oboes. Although one fails to recognize much of a galant style, as Schroeder does, it has certain forward-looking tendencies. They form a parallel with Vivaldi's advances which are less evident in Bach and Handel. They therefore serve to illustrate a fact which needs much assertion—that the greatest artists are those who make the greatest advances in expression, not in style, not in the mere chronology of taste. We note in this concerto that the bass and continuo rest frequently in all movements, although the solid baroque tread of harmony still underlies Telemann's musical thought. The rests and the sometimes independent or melodic basses lighten the texture. Telemann constantly spoke of melody, and even in such a first movement as this he sought melodic ideas which must be offset by passage work and then restated; in his last period, to secure an even more ingratiating melody, he ensured that the harmonic rhythm and bass no longer formed a regular tread. Like Vivaldi, Telemann advanced towards the ideals of the Mannheim symphony and the galant concerto, but the driving influence was that of French music and French melody. Since Telemann's was the music most widely performed in Germany, how much was he responsible for the drift of style towards that of the pre-classical symphony and concerto? We can assert that Telemann was the musical hero of young and forward-looking composers and connoisseurs of music.

The direction of Telemann's stylistic progress is wonderfully shown by the violin concerto in F which represents him in Schering's collection (Ex. 72). If this fine work were not cast in the form of a French suite of seven movements, parts of it might remind us of symphonies by J. C. Bach, though much of the scoring seems to come straight from Rameau. It is scored for trumpets, horns, flutes, oboes, bassoons and strings like a classical symphony, and it must have been used at Telemann's concerts in Hamburg. There is a cadenza for the soloist in the first movement and again in the fourth, which has a drone bass. The rhythmic ingenuity of the *corsicana* is masterly, and so is the thrumming pizzicato of the accompanying strings during the brilliant solo

[246]

Presto (Opening tutti)   Telemann. Concerto in F. [Schering]

Fl.

Str.

2nd. idea

3rd. idea

Solo tr.

. Corsicana . Un poco grave

Solo

3. Allegrezza

4. Scherzo

5. Gigue

6. Polacca

7. Minuetto

[247]

strophe of this movement. Another pre-classical feature is the rondo-minuet finale which was favoured in J. C. Bach's concertos. Several of the Telemann movements are in strophic or rondo form, and every movement after the first sounds like the ballet in a French opera. The scoring of the first movement seems to have a parallel in certain of Rameau's 'scene setting' overtures or symphonies. Handel has a few dance movements in rondo form but very few of his overtures add more than two or three dances to the introductory movements. An exception is that to *Rodrigo* which runs to nine pieces—Ouverture, Gigue, Sarabande, Matelotte, Menuet, Bourrée, Rigaudon, Menuet, Passecaille.

Among the concertos to which we have so far referred none may have been composed as late as this one unless it be Graupner's quoted at Ex. 58—a decidedly rococo or galant piece. A great number of the Telemann manuscripts at Darmstadt as well as some at Dresden are copied in Graupner's hand, and it is interesting to note that Graupner nearly always made a full score. When Telemann was at Frankfort directing the Frauenstein players he was near to Graupner at Darmstadt, and it is plain that the two men were in close contact between 1712 and 1721. Krüger points out that certain of the Darmstadt works were certainly not for the court orchestra but for Frauenstein, for they use the chalcedon which is specified in Telemann's church works for Frankfort and was therefore played in the Frauenstein orchestra when already obsolete elsewhere. Sachs[1] records no use of the chalcedon (as well as, or instead of a bassoon) in German orchestras after 1714, but it persisted longer in France.

Telemann's autobiographical contributions do not tell us the dates of all his visits to France, but we know that there had been an earlier one than that of 1737 'which I had planned for a long time . . . and which took eight months', for he spoke of the Eisenach orchestra which he directed from 1708 as surpassing 'the famous Parisian opera orchestra which I heard fairly recently'. With our upbringing upon the classics, by which we mean largely the music of German composers—the four great 'Viennese' symphonists together with Bach and Handel—it is not easy to remember that until 1750 French domination of musical culture was challenged only by Italian. One spoke of 'the French

[1] C. Sachs, *Handbuch der Musikinstrumentenkunde*, Berlin, 1920.

style' and 'the Italian style', but rarely if at all of 'the German style'; one merely spoke of German composers and judged whether they inclined to the French or to the Italian style. Telemann seems to be the first German not merely to secure a return of admiration from the French but also to influence Leclair, Blavet and other French composers. 'If his visits to France had been longer he might have played a similar part in France to that of Handel in England,' writes Krüger. Rousseau, of course, is no reliable instrument with which to measure contemporary taste, but we may record that he and the encyclopedists thought German music too complicated and lacking in 'naturalness'. At least we know that the concerts given by Hebenstreit and Telemann in Paris were very well received, and the fact that Telemann could make French musicians admire German workmanship in absolute music should be set against what have been regarded as his major sins—responsibility 'for the shallowness of late eighteenth-century church music' and a general 'lack of earnestness' (*Grove*).

From Hamburg Burney commented upon the effect of France upon Telemann—'This author, like the painter Raphael, had a first and second manner, which were extremely different from each other. In the first, he was hard, stiff, dry and inelegant; in the second he was all that was pleasing, graceful and refined.' Reichardt in his *Intimate Letters of an Observant Traveller*[1] quoted from and commented upon Burney's opinion that Telemann's music became more ingratiating after his return from Paris: 'His first works are certainly different from his last, in which he is pleasing enough, and unfortunately pleasing (*gefällig*) to everybody.' (Reichardt may mean that Telemann would oblige anybody and would provide what he thought was wanted instead of what he himself believed best; in other words he asked if Telemann always strove towards his ideal.) '. . . If he learnt from the French how to give way to the taste of any people among whom one lives then I could say some adverse things about this visit. He sometimes pleased people of the worst taste, so that one finds among his excellent works many mediocre ones of an incredibly shallow kind.' This judgement would be unremarkable if it came from a conservative, for instance from Kirnberger or another

[1] J. F. Reichardt, *Vertraute Briefe eines aufmerksamen Reisenden*, Berlin, 1774

of Bach's pupils who loved counterpoint, or if it came from a critic
of the late nineteenth century or our own century; but Reichardt
was not born until 1752 and he later wrote with enthusiasm about
Haydn and Mozart, even Beethoven. We must consider him as
possessed of unusually shrewd and intelligent powers of discrimination, since he could be a man of his age in welcoming the
passing of the baroque solidity and the growth of mannered
sensibility and complaisance without applauding everything that
was in the latest taste.

Reichardt belonged to the Prussian court, whose musicians had
expressed the only considerable adverse criticism of Telemann;
but Reichardt succeeded the conservatives, being appointed
Kapellmeister and Hofkomponist in 1776 after Agricola's death,
and he himself had incurred much hostility from the older musicians and from his royal master, Frederick the Great. One good
effect of this was his imitation from 1783 of the Concert Spirituel
(he adopted the French name) by a series of public performances
in Berlin. These concerts included many new and unknown works
for which Reichardt supplied critical and analytical commentaries.
He was willing enough to welcome Telemann's later works when
they displayed a love of instrumental and harmonic colour yet
were not trivial in their ideas. No doubt some of the older men
thought Telemann to be merely what the French conservatives
had called Rameau—'distillateur d'accords baroques'. The Graun
who had attacked Telemann for championing the recitatives in
Rameau's *Castor et Pollux* was dead, but the two best known of
the Bendas were still active.

The last phase of the baroque concerto in Germany draws our
attention to the Hamburg of Telemann and C. P. E. Bach and
also to the very capital wherein the royal music had, according to
Burney and others, lost repute because its repertory had become
ossified and its style of playing crude. People outside Potsdam
society as well as several within it who awaited the end of the
tyranny were followers of Reichardt's public concerts of new
music. The intelligent music lovers of Berlin read Reichardt's
articles on contemporary composers and their works as avidly as
a similar section of the Hamburg public read those written by
Marpurg, and some even of the older Berlin musicians, though
restricted by their monarch's wishes when playing in the palace,

followed the changes of style between the old concertos and suites and the new symphonies. Even the Grauns, the last prominent German composers to compose without parody in solid baroque style, show in their later music the influence of younger men. Soon after the passing of the half century many Berlin, Hamburg and other German musicians were aware of C. P. E. Bach's distinction between the *empfindsamer Stil* and the *galanter Stil* but little is to be gained by asking if this composer or that work favoured the one or the other. No powerful new influence except that of the Mannheim symphonies affected German concertos after the impact of Vivaldi, just as there was no important change in *opera seria* between Scarlatti and Hasse. There was only the general trend towards lyrical mellifluousness, the replacing of solid chords by patterns of repeated notes or rests, the maintaining of a slow rate of chord change except at moments of increased tension, sometimes the provision of an agile rather than a continuo-plain bass line; in short there was a drift of the concerto towards the symphony, so that many a work composed between 1750 and 1770 could have been labelled 'symphony', 'concerto' or 'sinfonia concertante' without causing surprise. The next transfusion of blood from the opera into the concerto awaited the genius of Mozart in the late 1770s and 1780s.

CHAPTER XII

The English School

T he precursors of concerti grossi in England were advertised
by Walsh as *A Sanata Concerta Gros in 5 or 6 Parts for
Violins Compos'd by Signior Caldara* (the *Post Man*, 26–8
September 1704) and *Six Sonata's Five in Four and a Sixth in 7
Parts Compos'd in Imitation of Archangelo Corelli by Wm. Topham M.A. Opera Terza* (the *Daily Courant*, 14 November 1709)[1]
Walsh issued his edition of Corelli's concerti grossi in 1715. Thereafter the history of baroque concertos in England is distinguished
by such a veneration for Corelli that Mr. Topham's did not remain
a solitary serious parody.

Corelli was admired in France, but whereas Couperin pays
tribute with the best of his own expression in the *Apothéose de
Corelli*, Geminiani and others sought English approval by posthumous prolongation of Corelli's own expression, not merely
composing concertos in imitation of the models but arranging
Corelli's Op. 5 sonatas as concerti grossi. In 1726 Hare published
two concertos which were adaptations as 'solo concertos' of Nos.
1 and 11 of Corelli's Op. 6 by Obadiah Shuttleworth,[2] leading
violinist at the Swan Tavern concerts in Cornhill. Pepusch gave
Corelli's concertos the infrequent honour of an edition in score,

---

[1] According to W. C. Smith's Walsh bibliography this is the first reference
to a concerto in English advertisements, but Michael Tilmouth's collection of
references to music in London newspapers (RMA Research Chronicle, 1961)
gives two advertisements for Albinoni's concertos—*The Post Man*, 18 August
1702 and 18 August 1704.

[2] d. 1735. He is known to have made money by selling Corelli's works in
manuscript before and after they were printed by Walsh. Shuttleworth published nothing but the two adaptations from Corelli, but he composed twelve
original violin concertos, the MS. parts of which the present writer has not
scrutinized.

and Walsh issued *Six Concertos for 2 Flutes and Bass. . . . Neatly transposed from the Great Concertos of Corelli*. They were probably pirated from the Amsterdam publications of J. C. Schickart, a Hamburg flautist who is not known to have visited London.

It is ridiculous to regard the dominating influence of Handel as responsible for the insular love of Corelli's concerto styles and forms. To our great enrichment the number, order and structure of movements in a Handel concerto is indefinite, but Handel was indebted to almost every other significant concertist as well as to Corelli. Not Handel but the music societies or academies[1] in London, Oxford, Norwich, York, Newcastle and as far north as Aberdeen,[1] formed the taste for Corelli. Their concerts were usually led by professional musicians, 'the quality' being patrons, subscribers, officials and often performers. The German princelings sought Italian singers and players for their court orchestras and theatres; the English gentry induced Italians to return with them as private tutors and leaders in local concerts. The Earl of Essex secured the services of Geminiani, and Lord Burlington those of the Castruccis and Barsanti.

These guiding spirits and their audiences were conservative. Changes of musical fashion have always been slow to affect England. The lag persists and enables English audiences to exercise discrimination with continental novelties. It would have been smaller at the beginning of the eighteenth century if England had been an agglomerate of principalities with court orchestras whose owners travelled in Italy and imported Italian concertos as fast as they imported sonatas, but England had no established orchestra except the small royal band, and it is doubtful if London could have mustered twenty players to sound like one of the better German court orchestras until our musicians had learnt to meet Handel's demands.

Abroad or at home the English gentry and burgessy more often bought parts for their own exercise than foreign musicians to play them. Hawkins tells us of an occasion in 1724 when all twelve of Corelli's concertos were played at a sitting, the parts having

---

[1] Over fifty music societies can be counted among subscribers to parts of concertos published in London between 1725 and 1750. By 1760 there were fifty societies of from twelve to twenty players giving regular concerts by 'seasons' [not always winter because roads were bad] in the East Anglian counties alone.

arrived in a parcel containing other music from Amsterdam. This concert was as much for the pleasure of the players as of the listeners, for it was the weekly meeting of an academy founded in 1710 'for the encouragement of vocal and instrumental music', including among its members milords Essex, Egmont, Burlington and Rutland. It seems to have been a revival of 'The Gentlemen's Meeting' that had once succumbed to professionalism because its listeners had been educated by the very concerts which they could no longer accept—a process that recurs perennially in such communities as universities. Musical activities thrive by a large membership. Though their purpose is the education of participants they need both the stimulus and the financial gain of public concerts. Members hope that the vigour and spirit of enthusiastic amateurs will commend their performances more than those of *blasés* professionals; but good professionals are not *blasés*, and if they can be made to feel that a performance is worth effort they express their enthusiasm far more effectively than inexperienced performers. There must have been a great difference in quality between the professional concerts in London, perhaps Oxford or Norwich, and those in the provinces where one who brought an instrument could be excused admission payment.

In the seventeenth century, English domestic consort music had been unique; English citizens had enjoyed concerts which were private elsewhere, and England had bred one of the greatest among musical geniuses; she could hardly have been called less musical than other countries. In the eighteenth century, however, our first musical comparisons are, like Burney's, between professional performances—in theatre, concert and church; and eighteenth-century England was certainly not the leading musical country of Europe although she contained Handel.[1]

Burney's judgements upon orchestras during his European travels suggest that Londoners of his generation were quick to examine intonation, attack, expression, accuracy and rhythm— points of ensemble discipline that are noted in a modern critique; but in the first decades of the century how many Londoners knew the Italian attack and fire in fast movements or the Italian range

[1] See Stanley Sadie's *Concert Life in Eighteenth-Century England*, P(R)MA, vol. lxxxv, 1958.

of expression in slow movements? Many readers can remember the time when baroque concertos were performed by too many players in too slow and imprecise a way. Vivaldi suffered badly; Corelli less. Probably during Handel's years in London there was a change not unlike that which has affected the playing of baroque music during the past thirty years.

A few fine Italian players became available. Geminiani, Barsanti, Veracini and Pietro Castrucci arrived in 1714. Geminiani and Castrucci were Corelli's pupils and both served as leaders in Handel's orchestras. Another fine player closely associated with Handel was Matthew Dubourg, a pupil of Geminiani who was first admired while he was still a boy for his playing at Britton's concerts. Geminiani and Dubourg are known to have taken the solo parts in Vivaldi concertos. Other London players could have done so. The boy violinist John Clegg chose a Vivaldi concerto for his London debut at the Haymarket Theatre in 1753. Another pupil of Geminiani and also frequently Handel's leader was Michael Festing. Although he became a member of the king's private band he led from 1735 to 1737 the Crown and Anchor Tavern Concerts, given by an amateur orchestra like the 'Gentlemen's Meeting' which was evidently good enough for the 1732 performance of *Esther*. This was The Philharmonick Society, not to be confused with the 1813 foundation which became the Royal Philharmonic Society. None of the first-rate violinists of London was trained under Vivaldi or in Venice. Many were either pupils of Corelli or of Corelli's pupils.

Though Walsh was ready with Vivaldi's concertos almost as soon as Corelli's the London publishers issued a huge preponderance of works in the Corellian tradition for string players, flautists and oboists. (The transverse or 'German' flute was extremely popular with English amateurs.) From Walsh alone came concertos by Torelli, Geminiani, Tessarini (Corelli pupil working at St. Mark's), Gasparini[1] (Corelli pupil and Vivaldi's predecessor at the Pietà), Venturini, who became Kapellmeister at Hanover, Castrucci, Valentini, who worked first at Florence and then in Rome, and the Bolognese violinist Giuseppe Matteo Alberti.[2]

[1] Not Visconti, called 'Gasperini'. (See 'Gasparini' in *Grove*.)
[2] Not the Alberti associated with the 'Alberti bass' who was a Venetian harpsichordist with the Christian name Domenico.

None demanded a Vivaldian virtuosity even from the soloists; all would have been safe with the better music societies in London and the provinces. As for Corelli's own works, their fame may be judged from the name of the music shop in the Strand, where later the church of St. Mary-le-Strand was built—'At the Sign of The Corelli's Head'. Its proprietor was Walsh's former salesman William Smith.

Slow native advance in the technique of the violin and the limited prowess of amateur societies partly account for insular attachment to the less 'volatile'[1] type of concerto, but so surely does the equipment of most English concert rooms. One remembers no organ in the music room of a German *Schloss* or *Residenz* during the concerto grosso period, nor do organs appear in engravings or other pictures of concerts outside England. The continuo part of certain German trio sonatas of the seventeenth century is expressly marked 'Orgel' or 'organo', but these are all works in *da chiesa* style and form. Biber's sonatas are a notable instance. The few German sonatas in the fine Durham Cathedral collection of seventeenth-century consort pieces also seem to have been composed for church use. One of these, by J. M. Nicolai, a chamber and chapel musician at the Württemberg Court, specifies organ as the continuo instrument. Other church sonatas by the same composer do not mention the organ. Lacking final documentary proof we could safely assume that Biber's sonatas were played as chamber music outside consecrated walls, as were other church sonatas and concertos, and that harpsichord replaced organ. Conclusive evidence is lacking because the keyboard instrument is rarely specified in continental chamber music of the seventeenth and early eighteenth centuries. *Klavier* is ambiguous, and neither *cembalo* nor *claveçin* can be taken as precisely indicating a harpsichord.

Even if some continental music rooms contained organs they were exceptional during the concerto period.[2] Outside churches and chapels the harpsichord was the favoured continuo instrument. In England, however, an organ was usually found in a

[1] Dr. William Hayes considered Vivaldi to be 'of a volatile disposition'.

[2] The word *organo*, frequently a substitute for *basso* on continuo parts of English concertos occurs in only one German concerto known to the writer—Telemann's Concerto in G for two oboes (bassoons obbligati) and strings. Dresden, CX-180, no. 5.

7(a). Snetzler chamber
organ of a type used for
continuo in England

7(b). 'Charles
Griffiths the
Bagnigge Organist'

theatre where oratorios were given and in public and private music rooms. The favourite continuo instrument was the organ, and it is easy to understand why. We have noted that taverns acquired church organs during the Commonwealth ban on church music, and that other 'music houses' engaged organ builders. Rooms specially built or adapted for concerts followed the custom of the successful taverns. In many public rooms and in the music rooms of wealthy music lovers the chamber organ usually had no more than four stops, the foundation being a stopped eight-foot rank with a largest pipe of four feet. Surviving specimens of these instruments are no more bulky than writing cabinets and commodes. The organs installed in theatres for operas, oratorios and concerts with more than a dozen or so players were often a little larger, with eight-foot open pipes and perhaps a reed and a mutation stop. In the article which describes chamber organs in *Grove* Robert Donington quotes this extract from Mace's *Musick's Monument*:

'We had for our Grave Musick, Fancies of 3, 4, 5 and 6 Parts to the Organ; Interpos'd (now and then) with some Pavins, Allmaines, Solemn, and Sweet Delightful Ayres . . . upon so many Equal, and Truly-Sciz'd Viols. . . . The Organ Evenly, Softly, and Sweetly Acchording to All. . . . But when we would be most Ayrey, Jocond, Lively, and Spruce: Then we had Choice, and Singular Consorts, either for 2, 3, or 4 Parts, but not to the Organ (as many now a days Improperly, and Unadvisedly perform such like Consorts with) but to the Harpsicon.'

As Donington says, the little chamber organ 'lends a softness and bloom to the viols which has a peculiar charm', and to English ears it gave a fulness and bloom to the ripieno of a concerto.

Mace complains that the organ was used too often. Simpson in *The Division-Viol* (1655)[1] consistently writes in a way which assures us that the organ was the normal continuo instrument . . . 'let the Organist know your Measure before you begin', etc. Moreover the word 'organ' sometimes appears above the accompanist's staves in English fantasias. William Lawes writes 'Organ or Harp'. This English tradition no doubt helped to cover the deficiencies of amateur performance in domestic chamber music,

[1] pp. 57–9 in Curwen's facsimile of the 2nd edition, London, 1955.

R

and it survived for expert professional concerts when numbers were small, as in Britton's loft, and when the ensemble or concerto grosso was considered large by standards of the period.

While Handel was in England, concerts were still held in taverns as well as in theatres and music rooms, and concertos can rarely have been played where there was no chamber organ.[1] I do not assert that the organ was always played, for it was not always available for provincial societies, and most surviving chamber organs by Snetzler, the favourite builder, date from after 1750. Many sets of parts formerly belonging to clubs and printed in England by Walsh, Meares, Johnson, Simpson, Cooke and others include two parts with figured basses (printed from different plates), one for 'Violoncello' and one for 'Basso', 'Basso Ripieno', 'Basso del Concerto Grosso', 'Basso Continuo', or 'Basso di Rinforzo'. In several sets the two figured parts are 'Violoncello' and 'Organo', which we may interpret as one keyboard part for the ripieno and one for the concertino.[2] Many other sets have two figured parts printed from separate plates even though one of them does not specifically mention the organ. A notable example is Handel's Op. 6 wherein one of the figured parts is that of the solo cello and the other is simply called 'basso'.

Interesting information about Handel's use of organ and harpsichord during oratorios and concertos in various theatres will be found on pages 109–12 of Winton Dean's book *Handel's Dramatic Oratorios and Masques* (Oxford, 1959), including accounts of a composite instrument which enabled organ or harpsichord to be controlled by one player, and also of an organ used by Handel, perhaps the same composite instrument. At the Commemoration

---

[1] Writing about 'the Harpsichord' on p. 117 of the first edition of his *Essay on Musical Expression*, Avison gives the curious direction, 'This is only to be used in the chorus'. As he is concerned with concertos, he must be referring to the tutti sections. Was the concertino unaccompanied at Newcastle in 1752?

[2] e.g. Defesch,   'Eight Concertos in Seven Parts, op. 10' (Walsh).
Festing,   'Eight Concertos in Seven Parts, op. 5' (Wm. Smith).
Geminiani, All sets of concertos in parts.
Handel,   'Sixty Overtures' (Walsh).
    'Twelve Concerti Grossi, op. 6 (Walsh).
Hellendaal, 'Six Grand Concertos, op. 3' (Walsh, then Johnson).
Tartini,   'Six Concertos in Seven Parts, op. 2 and 3 (Le Cène).
Topham's imitations of Corelli previously mentioned (Walsh).

of 1784 Joah Bates was enabled to conduct the performers while playing both organ and harpsichord by 'keys of communication . . . which extended nineteen feet from the body of the organ, and twenty feet seven inches below the perpendicular of the set of keys by which it is usually played', and this stirred Burney's recollection of Handel's own contrivance. This evidence does not concern concertos, but it supports the growing belief that two keyboard continuo instruments, chamber organ and harpsichord, were frequently used for concertos. We know that the organ concertos played between the acts of oratorios became more of an attraction than the oratorios themselves. Handel was careful to advertise them, to promise the provision of new ones and the repetition of those which had been already notably acclaimed.

Movements in the Corellian church concerto, some of them discarded in the scheme of the Venetian solo concerto, are enriched if a chamber organ accompanies the ripieno sections and the harpsichord alone accompanies the concertino. This extra contrast must have been particularly desirable when the number of instruments was small, as they were for most fully *professional* concerts in England. Except when concertos were given in theatres during the intervals of oratorios there can rarely have been more than enough violins and 'cellos to double the concertino instruments. Adding brightness and weight to the ripieno, the little organs performed the same function as wind instruments in German court orchestras but they took less space, maintained level tone, kept in tune, and were a necessity if the strings included no violas or double bass. It will be remembered that for all his wealth the Duke of Chandos mustered neither violas nor alto singers in the 'Kapelle' at Cannons. Handel conceived both the strings and the voices of his Chandos Anthems in three parts although we normally perform his four-part versions.

Thus when the keyboard instruments were used for solo as well as continuo parts the organ concerto was peculiarly English. It was not copied on the Continent where there were fine organs and organists. It has not been consistently developed, and no subsequent generation or nation has produced a considerable repertory except primarily for the church organ. In Germany and within the Venetian style of concerto Bach's fifth Brandenburg Concerto first notably raised the harpsichord from cembalo continuo to cembalo concertato; in England Handel delighted London with extemporization and brought the organ concerto into vogue until concertos modelled upon his were superseded by harpsichord and forte-piano concertos in J. C. Bach's galant style. Astute printers published Handel's works as 'Concertos for the Harpsichord or Organ', and even the one in B flat[1] which uses the pedals (the first in the posthumous Third Set, Op. 7) can be performed with some seven strings and harpsichord. As late as 1795, four years after the death of Mozart, Smith thought it profitable to publish *San Martini's Grand Concertos now adapted for the Organ, Harpsichord, or Piano Forte.*[2]

The London composers lead us to wonder if Vivaldi was wanted in England; the London publishers show us that he was. Some of them were the agents for Roger and Le Cène. The law did not prevent a sly agent for certain publications from practising piracy with others. Walsh first advertised Vivaldi's concertos in 1715, the year in which he first advertised Corelli's. This issue was only of the first part of *L'estro armonico*, and an amusing piece of evidence suggests that he was competing very closely with Roger and was ready to pounce upon concertos 8–12. In the Strand, a few paces round the corner from Walsh's premises in Catherine Street (which led past Somerset House to Black-friars Bridge), were the French agents for the Amsterdam press. The first proprietor was Francis Vaillant. He left the business to his son, who was followed in 1711 by Henri Ribotteau. Just after Walsh had announced his intention of issuing *L'estro armonico* there appeared a counter-advertisement by Ribotteau: 'Beware of Counterfeits witness Vivaldi Concertos that are done in London and wants half, and may be had very well for a less Price being not half Compleat.' (*The Post Man*, 14th October 1714.) Walsh was ready in 1717 with the second part of *L'estro armonico* which he issued complete in 1721. He also published sonatas and 'dances' by Albinoni, and in 1720 *Two Celebrated Concertos the one Commonly call'd the Cuckow and the other Extravaganza, Compos'd by Sigr. Antonia (sic) Vivaldi.* The Cuckoo Concerto is not known to have been printed except in

---

[1] Originally a sinfonia in B♭, made into an organ concerto by one of Walsh's advisers, maybe Christopher Smith.

[2] British Museum, h.603.

England, its companion in this publication being Op. IV, No. 10.

Subsequently Walsh issued *Vivaldi's Extravaganzas in 6 parts for Violins and other Instruments Being the Choicest of that Author's work Opera 4*^{ta}.[1] This was not the complete *La Stravaganza* but five of the set (Nos. 1, 2, 4, 9, 11 in Roger's edition) together with a concerto not printed in any of the Amsterdam collections. The twelve Vivaldi concertos issued in Walsh's first *Select Harmony* are as follows:

1. Op. VIII, 7	7. Not printed elsewhere
2. Op. VIII, 8	8. Op. VII, 4
3. Op. IX, 1	9. Op. VI, 1
4. Op. IX, 2	10. Op. VII, 2
5. Op. VI, 2	11. Op. VII, 5
6. Op. VII, 3	12. Op. VII, 6

Select Harmony appeared in monthly parts and contained more works in the Corellian than the Venetian form. The third collection (1734) contained three by Geminiani and three by 'other eminent Italian authors'. 'Other' meant two, possibly one; 'eminent' was less mendacious than 'Italian', for though one of the three concertos was by a certain G. Facco and another was by a composer who remains anonymous[2] the remaining one is Handel's Op. 3, No. 5. The fourth collection (1741) was of concertos by 'Mr. Handel, Tartini, and Veracini'.

A further publication contained concertos for solo violin 'and other instruments'. Walsh was actually publishing Vivaldi as late as 1760 along with the parts of symphonies by Germans living in England—J. C. Bach, Abel and Herschel—and by Karl Stamitz and Richter, as well as 'overtures' (meaning symphonies) by Boyce, Arne, Norris and Fisher. Thus not only did the baroque concerto stay in the English repertory long after it was discarded in Germany but it also took a late turn towards the Venetian model when already affected by the galant solo concertos and symphonies which ousted it. For this phenomenon events in

---

[1] British Museum, h.43a.
[2] Identified as Handel by Hans Redlich.

Germany were partly responsible. Burney's observation concerning the musical benefit to other cities when musical mishap befell Dresden was no exaggeration. From 1756 Frederick the Great became involved in the Seven Years War and the luxury of a Kapelle was more than minor princes could afford in years which might find their States invaded or besieged, especially when they were themselves allied with an invader. Many German musicians sought a livelihood in Great Britain, even as far north as Aberdeen, which had a flourishing music society very much like Avison's at Newcastle, its performing members being largely drawn from the nobility and gentry. An inventory of its music, written in 1749, shows that it owned concertos, overtures and suites by Purcell, Rameau, Scarlatti, Corelli, Geminiani, Avison, Jommelli, Hasse and Pergolesi, but no Venetian concertos.

The amateur players were not as technically advanced as the Italian *dilettanti* yet they must sometimes have been very well drilled. Avison's Newcastle concerts included players from county families in Northumberland and Durham which to this day have continued the practical cultivation of music to professional standards.[1] Avison disliked the dispersed Germans and their music. In the preface to his Op. 8 sonatas he wrote: 'Sorry I am to instance the innumerable foreign overtures (i.e. symphonies) now pouring in upon us every Season, which are all involved in the same confusion of style.' This is vague and silly criticism, but it is quoted to show the foolishness of imputing the English fondness for Corelli entirely to a conservatism as intolerant as Avison's. If the new symphonies were 'pouring in', then plainly few Englishmen shared Avison's taste.

Until Handel dominated London's music—for at first his attention was directed towards the theatre—Geminiani seems most to have confirmed and satisfied the taste of English amateur performers and concert-goers. His concertos had a wider circulation in England than any except Corelli's and Geminiani's, which

[1] A short time before this was written, Miss Valentine Orde gave a fine performance of modern 'cello sonatas in Durham University Music School. Several Ordes from Bothal Castle were among Avison's pupils for violin, flute, etc., and played in his concerts. His op. 3 concertos, published by Johnson in 1751, were dedicated to Mrs. Orde. The present Sir Charles Orde is president of the Morpeth and District Chamber Music Society.

continued in favour after the Germans had arrived and belatedly advertised the Venetian type of concerto and the symphony. Concerti grossi appear frequently in London concert programmes between 1750 and 1780 when, as Avison has told us, a deluge of small three-movement symphonies was being produced not merely by Austrian, North German, Italian and Scandinavian composers, but by Dutch and English ones as well. It is therefore interesting to note that within this period both Geminiani and Avison collected and published in score what they regarded as the best of the concertos which they had issued in parts some thirty years previously.[1] In the process they made what they considered to be improvements. Whether we think them so or not, they show how the concerto grosso survived in England into the age of the pre-classical symphony, and also how the composers themselves were affected by the changes in style and taste.

Moreover it was not until musical style had already turned towards the pre-classical that English composers often composed concertos for solo instruments, and some of these solo concertos of the late eighteenth century are now regarded as provincial curiosities. They are certainly not the result of a belated vogue for Vivaldian concertos in the capital. In 1766 the west country organist Capel Bond published *Six Concertos in Seven Parts*, all for strings except the first which is for solo trumpet, and the last which is for solo bassoon.[2] The beginning of the first solo section in each movement of Bond's bassoon concerto is quoted at Ex. 73 to show how English concertos passed from the style of Corelli to that of the early symphonists with little intermediate influence from Vivaldi or the Germans. If there was any considerable taste for Vivaldi in England it must have continued some fifty years after those of the maximum cultivation of concerti grossi in Germany. Bond's concerto, like most others of the late eighteenth century, is cast in the three movements of a small rococo symphony, and it contains nothing to remind us of Vivaldi's bassoon concertos despite an aria-like slow movement marked 'Affettuoso'. This movement is preceded by eight bars 'Slow' in G minor for

[1] The score of Geminiani's revised op. 2 is beautifully engraved by Mlle Vandôme for John Johnson. See plate 4.

[2] Concertos by Capel Bond and Richard Mudge are available in a modern edition by Gerald Finzi, who also edited Stanley's concertos (Boosey and Hawkes).

strings alone, inserted between the first and second movement simply to give relief where all three movements are in the bassoon key of B flat.

Bond, a Gloucester man who was organist at Coventry, directed in 1768 a chorus of forty and an orchestra of twenty-five in St. Philip's Church, now the cathedral at Birmingham—the first of the Birmingham Festivals. The choral music was by Handel but Bond probably interspersed it with his own concertos, following Handel's custom when oratorios were given in London theatres. Bond could evidently employ a good trumpeter, for in the first of his concertos the violins are quite independent of the solo trumpet which soon after the fugue entry, Ex. 74A, has four bars of semi-quavers in the clarino register. The concerto is in the form of a French overture—slow introduction and fugal allegro followed by a binary minuet, Ex. 74B and C.

The conjecture concerning the venue of Bond's performances leads one to speculate further concerning a composer who seems to have engaged the same trumpeter, for one recalls no other English trumpet concertos written between 1740 and 1760, and if any were discovered it would surely reveal the decline in virtuosity between trumpet parts from the baroque to the classical period; yet the first of six concertos published by Walsh in 1749 seems to have been the very model for Bond's trumpet concerto. These six concertos are the sole surviving essays in the instrumental genera of a composer who certainly belonged to the west country. Our former loss of information concerning the years in which Richard Mudge began and ended this life has been repaired by the late Gerald Finzi, who gave them as 1718–63. Finzi also discovered his Christian name. The composer's attempt to conceal it testifies to the exquisite taste of his age, and sensitive readers must admire the reluctance of his publisher to mar on any printed page the singular cognominal distinction which fortune would have bestowed upon him even if his godparents had excelled Gibbons's in connoisseurship of euphony. Walsh treated with dignity what he had neither the authority nor the temerity to gild, issuing *Six Concertos ... to which is added Non Nobis Domine in Eight Parts by Mr. Mudge.* Did he honour talent or only cloth? For a Reverend Mr. Mudge, known to have lived in Birmingham, is the only bearer of his surname who can claim

further lyrical distinction as the author of six concertos and the strands of *Non Nobis* which Byrd left until civilization should arrive. Bach amplified Palestrina for Leipzig and Mudge amplified Byrd for Birmingham.[1]

After the trumpet concerto Mudge's set includes four concertos for two violins and a sixth for organ or harpsichord. Probably most people today who would like to hear the two concertos next to the covers, because their very conception forced the composer to invention, would be less willing to revive what are called concertos for two violins but are largely imitations of Geminiani's string concertos. Mudge was more conservative than Bond, who shows the coming of the galant style. The score-reading eye could suppose Mudge the better composer, for his study of counterpoint seems to have left him dissatisfied with second violin and viola parts that are no more than fillings; but genuine vitality of melody, rhythm or texture is hard to find. The reader can judge from the Mudge D minor concerto reprinted by Finzi, for this seems the best of the set, and look at the feeble fugue subject and still more feeble countersubjects—if they should claim that title.

Formal counterpoint does not necessarily give inner parts the quality which makes vivid to us, whether we are aware of the means or not, the sound of quite a limpid and lyrical dance or air by Purcell. Not even Vivaldi wrote fine inner parts by second nature. On the other hand, Muffat, Pisendel, Telemann, Molter and the rest of the German concertists rarely fail us in this respect when their melodic invention burns low. England was fortunate to secure from Geminiani a fine example in workmanship, though he rarely achieved the magnificent sonority of Handel's three-part writing with continuo. Apart from Geminiani and Avison the English concertists of the eighteenth century fell far behind the Germans in attention to harmony and texture.

But why first discuss these provincial composers and music of the middle of the century? Because the Bonds and Mudges are quite as representative of English taste as are the Corellians, Geminiani and Avison, or the Handelians, Stanley and St. Martini. Geminiani and Handel composed for more cultured audiences

---

[1] Finzi secured for Mudge not only a Christian name and a series of respectable curacies and incumbencies, but a home town, Bideford, which explains his appeal to a Bidefordian.

than Bond and Mudge but they were also more old fashioned. What Burney called their 'rich harmony' held in check the facile tunefulness and vapid accompaniments of the oncoming style. To be up to date in the 1750s without powers of expression and self-criticism above the ordinary—without recognizable genius or talent—was merely to have advanced towards the silliest and shallowest music composed before our modern commercial pinchbeck.

In England many of the concertos which shared programmes with Handel's, Geminiani's and Avison's tell us what sort of music charmed our cathedral, manufacturing, garrison, university and market towns before Handel's demise allowed it to charm London without challenge. Since the concertos of Geminiani, Avison and Festing were those most widely bought by the provincial music societies, their performers and listeners must have recognized a contrast between their dignified Italian style, which no doubt elicited tributes to the 'skill and science' of their composers, and a style which fell more easily upon their ears and surely drew spontaneous approval from the more naïve patrons. This second style reached great popularity in ballad operas like *Thomas and Sally* and in the programmes at Vauxhall Gardens.

Lest it be thought that only the Corellian concertos were widely purchased by provincial societies, here are a few of the subscribers to the single sets of six concertos by Bond and Mudge. (We include the names of two private purchasers merely for interest, supposing Mrs. Johnson to be the publisher's widow, who may have bought her sets of parts for retail or piracy.)

The Music Society at Cherry Orchard, Birmingham.
The Musical Subscription Concert at Birmingham.
The Cecilian Society at Lichfield.
The Lodge of Honorary Free Masons. (2 sets.)
The Philharmonick Club. (3 sets.)
The Philharmonick Club on Wednesday Nights. (2 sets.)
The Music Society at the Globe Tavern, Fleet Street. (2 sets.)
The Music Society at the King's Head in Oxford. (2 sets.)
The Ely Philharmonick Society.
The Music Society at Dedham in Essex.
The Music Society at Norwich. (2 sets.)

Mrs. Johnson. (6 sets.)

Charles Jennens, Esq. (6 sets.)

The Music Societies at Ashby de la Zouch, Banbury, Gloucester, Hereford, Leicester, Newcastle, Nottingham, Salisbury, Stourbridge, Wolverhampton and York.

The number of societies which were ready to patronize composers who were not leaders of London musical activity is as remarkable as the number which bought more than one set of parts. Players could copy single parts, and most of them knew professional copyists, for every cathedral engaged them. It was cheaper, perhaps, to order more than one set of parts when a society's meetings used two or more desks of violas and 'cellos, for the players who shared a desk did not normally share the part when they practised at home. The statement 'separate parts are also available' on advertisements and title-pages suggests that rapacious publishers were not always prepared to sell off-print extra parts of a single edition.

It has been said that an eighteenth-century publisher was very satisfied if he sold 150 copies of a work. How amply therefore must Walsh, Johnson and others have profited by the concertos of Geminiani and Avison, which ran into several editions of 500 or so, despite the circulation of manuscript copies! How mistaken would be a history of the concerto which treated the British Isles as a tract in which few ears paid attention to music more complex than ornamental variations for flute or spinet upon a favourite air!

After Purcell, England lacked native composers of outstanding genius, and in the field of chamber music she lacked even a composer of any significant originality during the early decades of the eighteenth century. Native and migrated talents could find no other expression than the one they admired in Corelli's sonatas. When his concertos reached them they had already learnt to conceive ideas that suited Corellian movements, and further imitation was not of style but of expanded designs and textures. Epigonic concertos served a laudable purpose by providing the societies with music at the technical standard they had reached in order to play Corelli. Few of them, even of Geminiani's, are worth revival.

No composer of marked originality could imitate the order and shape of Corelli's concerto movements as closely as Pisendel and

[268]

Fasch imitated those of Vivaldi's movements. Within only twelve concertos Corelli left no scheme of movements so clearly favoured as the fast-slow-fast in all but a few of Vivaldi's hundreds, nor any single movement organized on principles so established as those which govern Vivaldi's first movements or his aria-like andantes. Moreover Corelli's movements were short. The German imitator could adopt the broad Vivaldian structure described by Quantz yet remain so distinctly German in turns of phrase, harmony, counterpoint and instrumentation that one could not easily mistake his work for Vivaldi's. A Corelli concerto of five, six or seven short movements could not be imitated closely except by producing a parody, which cannot be as vital as its model unless a humorous purpose is ably fulfilled—an intention that cannot be considered.

Most of the concertos produced in England during the first half of the eighteenth century express little that was not already expressed more vitally by the models. Some of Geminiani's and Avison's were well composed only as an exercise is well composed, yet the nadir of sterility was reached by an imported set of concertos by Alberti on the Vivaldian model. Extant copies are well dispersed, and it is curious that they should have been popular with societies which apparently did not play Albinoni and Vivaldi, for Alberti used the Venetian design without making the Venetian technical challenge. Indeed his concertos sound mass-produced from a mould in Vivaldi's workshop and go almost to rule of thumb. (Ex. 75.) The opening movement is invariably *allegro e*

spiritoso with an incisive first idea ready for ritornelli, duly followed by a hey-diddle-diddle of broken chords, first *forte* then *piano*, and a stereotyped scheme of solo sections and modulations. Nearly every middle movement is *grave e spiccato* in the style of a binary aria, and nearly every finale is a Vivaldian triple-metre movement with echo effects. Particularly obsessive are the direct repetitions, with or without a change of dynamic, and the ubiquitous feminine endings to the allegro themes.

The best concertos of Francesco Geminiani (1687–1762) have a Handelian breadth of musical thought and forward thrust. Examples are given at Ex. 76 partly to show how closely Geminiani's ideas resembled Handel's, which he could not have heard at the time, and partly to show how difficult it is to pin-point the source of greater vitality in Handel; they also show Geminiani's fine command of the technique now generally called 'expanding variation'. (See Ex. 76c.) Geminiani rarely maintains for a whole movement the promise of his opening ideas, but the lines of his polyphony are usually admirable.

When Handel came to London in 1712 he was chiefly concerned with opera, not with teaching, nor concertos for music societies, nor 'lessons' (i.e. sonatas) for amateurs. Geminiani therefore had enormous prestige and influence as performer, teacher and author of various works of instruction. The phrase 'Il furibondo Geminiani' has been taken to indicate a wild nature and the dissipation of energy by a passion for painting and the writing of didactic treatises. Neither Jenkins's portrait nor what we know about Geminiani corroborates this opinion. The 'furibondo' was earned in a theatre at Naples for vagaries of tempo, to which we should be accustomed when the popularity of musicians depends upon their inability to perform consecutive passages at the same speed. The conductor who is not furibond had better pretend that he is, or his directors will find another to take the orchestra on tour and television. Presumably Geminiani kept good time when he played with Handel.

Geminiani was one of the finest violinists of his generation, and he came to England at a time when the example and teaching of a great violinist was badly needed.[1] No doubt the arrival of Veracini

[1] Mrs. Delaney wrote of his 'triumphal' public performances when he was aged 66.

76

Geminiani. Op.3, No.3.

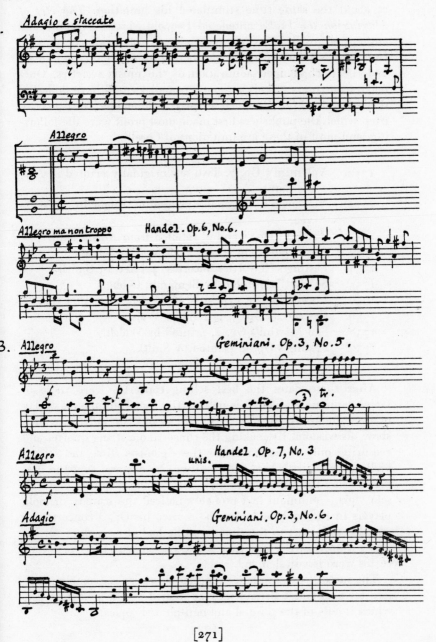

at about the same time stimulated his ambition. *The Art of Playing on the Violin* antedated Leopold Mozart's treatise and anticipated much of its commentary and instruction. It added to Geminiani's fame but could hardly add to his popularity, for he had the unchallenged admiration of the music societies. Only native composers of very strong personality could have deflected the imitation of Corelli which he made fashionable. The concertos from which the publishers first made most profit were the following, and most of these are imitations of Corelli.

1712.   Valentini's Op. 7. Two sets originally printed in Amsterdam.

1715.   Venturini's. Originally printed by Roger in the same year.

1730.   Tartini's Op. 1 and 2, retailed from Amsterdam.

1732–3. Geminiani's Op. 2 and 3, printed by Walsh.

1734.   Festing's 'Twelve Concertos' printed by Smith.

1735.   Scarlatti's, printed by Benjamin Cooke.

1736.   Locatelli's Op. 3, printed by Walsh, after Le Cène.

1736.   Castrucci's Op. 3, printed by Walsh.

1738.   San Martini's Op. 2, printed by Walsh.

1739.   Festing's Op. 5, printed by Smith.

After these dates the best selling concertos were those of Geminiani and Avison. It is noteworthy that Geminiani's outlay of instruments is not exactly Corelli's, and the difference may show his wisdom. By making the concertino a string quartet and requiring only three staves for the ripienists (first and second violins, 'cellos with bass and continuo) he ensured that the best players had the fuller harmony. This scoring required only the solo viola. Geminiani had probably noticed the scarcity of viola players in England, but when he revised his Op. 2 concertos he added a viola part to the ripieno, as he had already done for his Op. 7 concertos. Perhaps that is one reason why the Op. 7 concertos were less in demand.

The success of Geminiani's concertos in every reasonably populous town of Great Britain may be judged by the following list, which is only of the printed and non-pirated copies:

8. CHARLES AVISON

Portrait by an unidentified artist in the
vestry of St. Nicholas Cathedral, Newcastle

(Photograph by Ernest Moore.)

Op. 2 *Six Concertos in 7 Parts*
> Walsh, 1732.
> Another issue, 1732.
> Another issue, 1745.
> In score 'corrected and enlarged with some new movements', 1755.
> Revised edition, parts, Johnson, 1757.
> Another issue 'carefully correcting the errors of a former edition'. For the author, 1760.
> Another, bearing the same description, 1772.
> 'Adapted for harpsichord, or organ, or pianoforte, as performed by Mr. Cramer', Goulding, 1798.

Op. 3 *Six Concertos in 7 Parts*
> Walsh, 1733.
> Walsh, *c.* 1735.
> Cooke, *c.* 1735.
> In score, Johnson 'for the author', 1755.
> In score, a second issue, 1757.
> Revised edition, parts, Walsh, 1760.
> 'Adapted . . . as performed by Mr. Cramer', Goulding, 1788.

The six concertos which Geminiani arranged from a selection of his twelve violin sonatas, Op. 4, and the original concertos which constitute his Op. 6 and Op. 7 were successful enough to run into two or three issues, but they did not achieve the enormous popularity of Op. 2 and 3. It is strange that nowadays one frequently hears some of the Op. 3 concertos, especially a rather dull one in D minor, but none of the very good ones in Op. 7 which first appeared 'for the author' in 1746 and were then printed by Johnson.[1] The dedication of these works is worth quoting in full to enliven an uninteresting part of our story. Like Hawkins, Geminiani had to be sour towards some people when praising others.

'*To the Academy of Ancient Music*
'Gentlemen,
> 'A Dedication resulting purely from Regard and Affection, is

---

[1] Since writing, I have heard a good selection from Geminiani's op. 7 in the series of recordings by *I Musici*.

perhaps as much a Rarity in England, as in other Countries. To the Disgrace of ARTS and SCIENCE, or at least, of their Professors, almost all Dedications from such, have in all Countries alike, arisen from the same Mercenary Motives.

'From the Time of my first appearance in London, to this Hour, I have enjoy'd the Happiness of your Countenance and Favour, and such has been ever my sense of it, that I thought it highly deserving of my best Acknowledgments.

'All men are fond of Praise, and perhaps it is to this Passion, that the most excellent Compositions of every kind have been principally owing; but all Praise hath not the same Effect: That of Ignorance operates on the Understanding, like jarring Dissonance upon the Ear, it shocks the sense it was address'd to please: whereas that of Discernment, like good Malody (*sic*) and perfect Harmony, at once fills and satisfies the whole Mind.

'And here I cannot but observe, that as it hath been the peculiar Misfortune of the Science of MUSICK, that almost ev'ry Novice hath obtruded on the Publick his Crudities, which, however wretched, have nevertheless had their Advocates: So it ought to be the Consolation of every Professor who is desirous that Musick shou'd have its Standard as well as ev'ry other Science, that among You that Standard is not only held in the most religious Veneration, but is likely so to continue, as long as the Academy it Self shall last.

'To please such Judges, and such only the following Peices were design'd in the composing of which great Study and Application hath been used, to make them acceptable to the Publick, but in particular to your Academy.'

Geminiani's technical requirements were somewhat greater than Corelli's especially in 'the shift' to other positions than the third. We should note that his treatise appeared in 1751[1] just before he revised his most popular concertos, put marks of expression even on the continuo parts and altered the bow markings. He advocated continuous use of vibrato, considering that 'Even on short notes it contributes to make their sound more agreeable and for this Reason it should be made use of as much as possible.' How strongly one disagrees, as one does also with Leopold Mozart who could find no better reason for vibrato than that 'Nature

---

[1] Facsimile, edited by D. Boyden, Oxford, 1952.

herself taught it to man'! Vibrato as an effect, an interpretation used deliberately, should be a studied accomplishment; instead it is an uncontrolled disease known to singing masters as judder and produced by performers who cannot pitch notes correctly or hold them steadily. This is a very different matter from the 'tremblement qui ravissait les sens' which Mersenne enjoyed in the violin playing of Bocan.

Geminiani also published in 1755 *The Art of Accompaniament*. (His spelling.) It is difficult not to suppose that he was in some ways a queer character even if one does not believe the story that his death was accelerated by grief at the theft of a *Treatise of Music* which was to have been his most ambitious literary work. Why were other manuscripts of his stolen? The treatise on violin playing appeared as an anonymous publication twenty years before he issued it himself, and he brought an action against Walsh for illegal possession of the parts of the Op. 3 concertos, though he then agreed to let them be published with his own supervision and corrections. Had he deliberately arranged the quarrel in order to gain publicity for the concertos?

The edition in score differs from the Walsh parts, and the revisions in the edition 'for the Author' of 1757–60 are on so great a scale as to make very clear the difference in performing style (and of composition in general) between the end of Corelli's life and the middle of the eighteenth century. Robert Hernried, the editor of certain Eulenburg miniature scores, regards the revision 'in many parts to be stylistically aimless' and thinks that Burney's judgement on the Op. 3 concertos might have been less severe had he known the 'more straightforward' originals. Henried's editions are based on manuscripts which testify to German interest in English concertos. One in the hand of Bach's pupil Kirnberger is in the State Library at Berlin, and the other in the University Library at Hamburg. The latter was probably used by a member or members of Weckmann's collegium musicum, a Hamburg concert society almost as famous as Fasch's at Leipzig.

Though there is less creative vitality in Geminiani than in Bonporti, who was in some ways almost as sedulous an admirer of Corelli, Schering's harsh judgements do Geminiani less than justice. The concertos which were once admired for their unimpeachable extension of Corelli's technique, both of performance and composition, sound 'pallid' (Bukofzer's word) if they are played immediately after concertos by Geminiani's contemporaries in Italy, France and Holland respectively—Bonporti, Leclair and Locatelli. This is not because they are feeble or unduly conservative in design but because they are pedantically limited in vocabulary, and the fact is not disguised in the revised editions with their careful bowings, their coulés and other ornaments.

We should be careful not to follow the German critics by disparaging Geminiani merely because he retained early methods of concerto composition rather late in the history of the genre, for all his concertos fall within the years 1732–46. Let us hope that no modern judge can with impunity extol or disparage music for being in the van or rear of fashion, or we must let him tell us that Telemann was a greater artist than Bach. Handel and Bach lived to know that they were outmoded. Their claim to greatness is not based upon the vocabulary that occasional demand brought from them—Bach's chromatic chords at the end of 'O Mensch bewein' in the *Little Organ Book* or Handel's alternating three-eight and two-four in the *Agrippina* aria 'Bel piacere'—but upon the imagination that conceived their forms as wholes. The quoted snippets are enough to show that Geminiani had a measure of imagination—not a great measure, but remarkably well spread. His grasp of ambitious structure can be recognized by any student who attempts the mere academic exercise of adding to Geminiani's movements which combine fugue and sonata principles, relying on no ritornelli but only upon Corelli's 'expanding variation' and the *Fortspinnung* part-writing which is far harder to maintain at high quality than the crisp, sequential figuration of Vivaldi or Bach.

It seems pertinent here to comment on the tendency to hold baroque composers in greater esteem if they are proved romantic. To say that an artist has a wonderful sureness of style, commands the musical equivalent of the exactly right word, length and variety of phrase and paragraph, is to honour him as few can accurately be honoured. Corelli earns the honour. We cannot add to that honour by imagining that chromatics in a minor key betoken a more passionate creature than contemporary evidence suggests. According to Hawkins the gentle Corelli's performance was as photogenic as a crooner's, for 'it was usual for his countenance to be distorted, his eyes to become red as fire, and his eyeballs to roll as in agony'. One could mention splendid artists who are physically demonstrative and others who are externally restrained, even apparently relaxed. Corelli's and, for all we know, Geminiani's gestures were manifest in D major as in C minor; why should C minor be chosen as the clue to the composer's nature? Grateful though I am that Giegling,[1] McArtor[2] and others have undertaken careful study of Geminiani I cannot believe that his expression ought to move me more deeply than it does merely *because* he was fond of diminished sevenths, neapolitan sixths, interrupted and delayed cadences, and so on. How do we know that Ex. 76A meant any more to him than Ex. 76B?

The suggestion that if Geminiani had devoted his time exclusively to playing and composition he could have been a greater artist is surely absurd. No man by taking thought can add one cubit to his originality, and it is much to Geminiani's credit that he passed his life so fully and usefully, putting his limited talent to his own advantage and to the great advantage of hundreds of amateur and professional musicians in these islands.

Geminiani's last concertos, Op. 7, which were less popular than his earlier ones, are his finest achievements. It is curious that they embrace no new principles of construction and make no new use of dance forms, for they appeared at the same time as his ballet 'The Enchanted Forest' and seven years after Handel's Op. 6. They include compact few-movement works like No. 5 in C minor on a French overture plan, and spreading canzona-style works like No. 6 with thirteen changes of speed. Perhaps the best is No. 3, 'composti di tre stili differenti', yet one would salute the modern connoisseur of eighteenth-century connoisseurship who could allocate the movements to Geminiani's national labels. The *tempo giusto* ('Francese') is not a French overture but a fast march with two points of parody—the saccadé rhythm and the 'soli a tre'; the *andante con due flauti* (Inglese) might be Danish or Sardinian if Danes or Sardinians were as fond as British amateurs of the flutes which Geminiani here employs as a

[1] Contribution to *MGG*.
[2] M. E. McArtor, *Francesco Geminiani. Composer and Theorist.* Doctoral dissertation, University of Michigan, 1951.

77.

concertino; the *allegro assai* (Italiana) is also a fine movement, quite as Italian as a thousand others composed in England, Germany and the Low Countries. (See Ex. 77.)

The Op. 7 concertos are free from a defect specially mentioned by Schering—thickness in a texture that appeals to the eye and justifies the title-claim 'in seven parts'. If Geminiani is censured for disregarding sensuous pleasure he is in the good company of Bach, yet both men knew when they appealed to the student of part-writing rather than to the simple ear. Do their adverse critics in this matter judge by actual performance? Beethoven's quartets are proof enough that bottom-heavy spacing is less likely to offend in a string texture than in any other, provided that the effect is of 'horizontal thinking'. When played by strings the six-part ricercar from *A Musical Offering* sounds rich and impressive in places which other media make hideous. (Surely a great deal of Bach's organ music in a mere five or four parts is oppressively heavy, even if played on instruments like his own.) Geminiani, a very fine harpsichordist, shows by brilliant keyboard arrangements of his own and other composers' works that he had an enviable sense of medium and a very good ear.[1] His thickness is therefore deliberate.

[1] See examples of 'translation' by Geminiani quoted in 'Geminiani's Harpsichord Transcriptions' by Franz Giegling in *Music and Letters*, vol. xl, no. 4, October 1959.

We pass to Geminiani's pupil, obviously a charming, inspiring and altogether admirable man, yet as a composer even less imaginative than his teacher, who seems to have infected him with his pedantry. The concertos of Charles Avison[1] (1709–70) were almost as popular as Geminiani's with the music societies, even with some of those in and near London, though they were naturally most valued in the north and in Scotland. He was born in Newcastle and spent part of his youth in Italy. On his return, according to Burney, he became Geminiani's pupil in London before again settling in Newcastle as organist at St. Nicholas, now the cathedral church, and as a teacher of the flute, violin, keyboard instruments and music generally. We have only Burney's declaration that Avison was Geminiani's pupil, but Geminiani's visit to Newcastle in 1760 and the patent influence of Geminiani upon Avison's own music are sufficient corroboration of Burney. From 1739 until his death Avison conducted subscription concerts at Newcastle on a grander scale than was usual in provincial cities, and they were continued under his son until 1823. His programmes are known to have included much music by Handel, despite the common remark that he 'presumed' to criticize Handel. Great composers are not gods, and it is ignoble for a teacher to illustrate faults from the work of small men if he can find them in great artists who need not fear adverse criticism. Avison was quite sincere and he was plainly an admirer of Handel. In 1766 he directed the *Water Music* and the Coronation pieces, and in 1767 *Messiah*. He collaborated with John Garth,[2] the Durham musician, in editing an edition of Marcello's *Psalms*. The Durham choir sometimes participated in the Newcastle concerts, and Avison is known to have brought performers to Durham on more than one occasion.

Avison's respectable talent as a concertist and his authorship of the first serious undertaking of music criticism in this country deserve even more praise than they have received, but parts of

[1] Avison's name and music are strangely ignored by *MGG* and other important German books whose authors have conscientiously included all known information about quite a number of even less important English musicians.

[2] Garth was a good 'cellist and published a set of six 'cello concertos. Though a fine organist, he was not titular organist at Durham Cathedral, but was probably officially engaged to perform on the Father Smith instrument at Auckland Castle, seat of the prince bishops of Durham.

this *Essay on Musical Expression* (1752) are mere defences of his predilections. He considered Vivaldi, Alberti and Locatelli to be deficient in 'manifold harmony and true invention', and he would have withheld their music from the ears of children who were to acquire a 'correct taste'. (His admiration of Marcello was directed to that composer's *Psalms*, not his concertos.) *Remarks on Mr. Avison's Essay* by Dr. William Hayes, Heather Professor of Music at Oxford, intelligently described Vivaldi as having 'a great command of his instrument, being of a volatile disposition', and 'a certain brilliance of fancy and execution, in which he excelled all who went before him, and in which even Geminiani has not thought him unworthy to be imitated. (Footnote) *Vide* the first of his second set of concertos'. Hayes mentions the D minor concerto, No. 11 of Op. 3, as a specimen of Vivaldi's 'capacity in solid composition', and he specially commends the fugue in the first movement. Even Burney, speaking of the *Essay on Musical Expression*, considered its judgements to be 'warped'.[1] Avison seems to have been a dogged northerner, but nothing that we know about him suggests that meanness of heart assisted narrowness of taste.

Avison declined an invitation to become organist of York Minster and another, backed by Geminiani, to direct concerts and set up a teaching practice in Edinburgh. He also had similar offers from Dublin. Any of these appointments could have brought him greater fame than his work in Newcastle. Here in the north loyalty to places and people, a virtue become a fault, sometimes reaches almost to the worship of a teacher or an employer. Avison's pedantry came from his devotion to Geminiani, who could not even write a *Guida Armonica* (a set of figure-bass exercises to teach modulation) without a preface disparaging other teachers and composers; and it is surely not fanciful to see the effect of a famous and despotic teacher upon a young pupil of talent but not genius. Such a pupil succumbs without question to peremptory methods and works hard. He is never allowed to suppose for one moment that his abilities would have blossomed under any other teacher, or without a teacher. Thoroughly satisfied that the famous teacher 'made' him, he hopes that in his time he will 'make' others. The outstandingly intelligent pupil, the Handel or

[1] *A General History of Music*, p. 1013.

Mozart, can use such a teacher to his advantage; the average pupil incurs disadvantages which may do harm, especially if he sets up a local tradition and if small-minded pupils maintain his teaching tyrannously and without modification.

Avison could obviously inspire enthusiasm and hold allegiance. He lived an unusually busy life and found time to compose organ voluntaries, five sets of concertos, volumes of quartets, trios and sonatas for violin or flute with harpsichord—all for immediate use and all successful as publications. Most of his music was first published 'for the Author' in Newcastle. The following are only the editions of concertos which found a large number of buyers away from the north and Scotland:

> Two Concertos, the First for an Organ or Harpsichord in 8 Parts, the Second for violins in 7 Parts. Joseph Barber, Newcastle, 1742.
>
> Op. 2. Six Concertos in 7 Parts. Barber, also Cooke, 1740. In 1747 Walsh printed several of these 'for organ or harpsichord' (i.e. the keyboard part replacing the concertino).
>
> Op. 3. Six Concertos in 7 Parts. Johnson, 1751. This was the most popular set. It ran into many editions. Preston issued one as late as 1790.
>
> Op. 4. Eight Concertos for Organ or Harpsichord. John, then Walsh, 1755. Welcker, 1778. Preston, 1790.
>
> Op. 6. Twelve Concertos. Newcastle, 1758. Preston, 1792.
>
> Op. 9. Twelve Concertos. Johnson, Bremner, Preston—all during 1766.

To this list must be added the set of concertos 'done from Scarlatti's Lessons' (D. Scarlatti's sonatas for harpsichord) by Avison in 1744.

Avison must have shared many of our own criteria, for undoubtedly he selected what we should think the best among these works when, following Geminiani, he published 'Twenty Six Concertos . . . divided into Four Books in SCORE for the use of Performers on the Harpsichord. . . . J. Johnson for the Author, 1758.' A curious passage in *Grove* tells us that they 'compare favourably with the concertos of T. A. Arne, Boyce and Stanley'. The only known concertos by Arne are the trivial ones for harpsichord. Boyce published no concertos at all; the only one which may have been his was among manuscripts owned by his son. Stanley's concertos, which reflect Greene's teaching and Stanley's admiration of Handel, are unlike Avison's. A concert of works by Avison would reduce a modern audience to historians of music and loyal Novocastrians, but Stanley still pleases general listeners because he knew how to maintain a light touch without becoming vapid.

Avison can be heavy at times. His concertos are less Corellian and also less distinguished than Geminiani's, yet they contain a greater range of designs and styles.[1] The many music societies from Aberdeen to London had plenty of other music by which to judge them, and yet they continued in high esteem even after the new symphonies which Avison disliked had come into widespread popularity. When he is following 'the models', as in the concerto quoted at Ex. 78, we are aware that Avison is younger than Geminiani and not Italian. The adagio of Ex. 75 is no longer in the grand manner of the pompous French overture or the solemn church concerto; it has the sentiment of an English theatre song of the period and seems to demand the direction 'affettuoso'; the following fugal exposition naturally sounds more traditional, but the semiquaver retardations of the countersubject and Avison's bow marks could belong to the end of the eighteenth century. His age is naturally most observable in his less formal and freely melodic movements, and it is a pity that he did not live long enough to enjoy Haydn's orchestral music.

The British Museum copy of Avison's 1758 edition of his concertos in score was presented in 1843 by Vincent Novello, who wrote over the fourth concerto in the last set: 'This is the favourite Concerto that I have so often heard performed at the Concerts of Ancient Music. It is an excellent composition, and the last movement especially has a very tasteful and charming air. . . . The design upon which its rhythm is constructed is both ingenious and original.' The extract at Ex. 79 includes enough of the finale to justify our wonder that this music should have so greatly appealed to a man who knew much of Haydn's, Mozart's and Beethoven's.

[1] See Arthur Milner's two articles, 'Charles Avison' in *The Musical Times*, January–February 1954.

The quotation reveals one of Avison's and Geminiani's most irritating habits—the crossing of parts so beloved by pedantic contrapuntists who teach by *Papiermusik*. Bach is sometimes called in for its defence, but Bach crossed his parts chiefly in works of instruction like the *Art of Fugue* which were intended for the score-reading student, and there is much difference between Bach's crossing in order to make both parts shapely and the spoiling of one melody in order that another may be improved. The paper contrapuntist is also noticed in Avison's long notes of the fourth Fuxian species. The ties over bar lines were required for syllabification in vocal music. Their survival in orchestral music

[283]

is justified only when the composer wants a singing effect or holds a note in one part to make clear the movement in another. Handel and Mozart, despite their keen sense of instrumental idiom, did not always break or repeat the note that became a suspended discord, but the *stile osservato*, which was presumably for voices if it was for any medium at all, led minor composers and still leads apprentices into the mechanical tying of notes.

In some of Avison's concertos the teacher demonstrates. Thus in No. 6 of the last book of the 1758 edition in score there is both an alla breve movement called 'Fuga da Capella' and a lively finale in triple measure called 'Fuga del Teatro'. If no single concerto by Avison is worth regular performance, his total contains several really fine movements—not the sterile fugues and reminders of Martini's or Fux's exercises, nor the imitations of Corelli and Geminiani, but pieces with the verve of a gavotte, the lilt of a gigue, or the tenderness of a simple song to which has been added one of the composer's most commendable qualities. Novello mentioned it, in the movement which charmed him more than us. It is the avoidance of two-bar and four-bar phrasing, remarkable in an eighteenth-century minor composer who, when his concertos were written, could have heard nothing by Haydn. Irregular phrasing is easy enough to achieve; one simply prolongs the tread of harmony and postpones the cadence. Avison managed the process without labouring or faltering (as even Berlioz did sometimes) and usually in such a way that the result seems spontaneous and not deliberate. A good example is the melody quoted at Ex. 80.

At Ex. 81 there would be an equally good example of Avison's melodic rhythm if the piece were for unison violins and continuo. It is no mere assembling of Italianisms. It is distinctly national and may owe something to a Tyneside popular song. As we see it, however, it is spoilt by the crossing of the second violin part, and there seems no musical sense at all in doubling short notes by longer ones in bars 8 and 9. Did Avison want the hockets or the suspensions from the counterpoint manual? Even if the first violins had more and stronger players than the second violin part, so that the crossings did not spoil it, these doublings were a disservice.

John Stanley (1713–86) was a younger man, trained by Maurice Greene, not Geminiani. Among blind persons who have led

happy and very full lives, nobody in the history of music seems
to have been less hampered or hindered by his misfortune. As
teacher, composer, performer and family man his life was incredibly busy. Few of the items in his oratorios and theatre music have
survived in the repertory, and today he is represented chiefly by
his attractive organ pieces, some of which are not his published
'Voluntaries' but arrangements of movements from concertos.
His Op. 2, published in 1742, was a set of six concertos for strings
with the Corellian outlay. Like some of Avison's concertos, they
were also issued 'for organ or harpsichord' by retaining the
ripieno and substituting a keyboard part for the concertino.

Apart from the choice of a trio for concertino very little in
Stanley's concertos is directly modelled upon Corelli. They were
composed after Handel's Op. 6, and Stanley was obviously an

[285]

admirer and imitator of Handel. Burney called Stanley 'a neat, pleasing and accurate performer, a natural and agreeable composer, and an intelligent instructor'. Those words also suit Greene, who would be a major artist if he had left a quantity of music as fine as his one or two outstanding anthems.

There is no very moving or inspired movement in all Stanley's concertos, yet there is not a single weak one, and his workmanship is as neat as Telemann's. The first movements are either short introductions with following fugued allegros, or initial allegros like those of Italian sinfonias. The slow middle movements are usually short, and the finales are either binary and in triple measure or in the style of gavottes or bourrées. Little quotation from Stanley's concertos is necessary, for the best are available in Finzi's edition. It will suffice to show why some of them are reprinted, and why organists play voluntaries and concerto movements by Stanley while the more laboured music of Avison remains only documentary.

Certain features which Stanley observed in Handel's music and Handel's extempore playing were useful to a blind composer. Most sighted improvisers rapidly compose ideas which bear recurrence and include formulae for development; few find it easy to spread interest by maintaining it in connective portions that are not planned with main themes, and still fewer achieve long paragraphs of musical thought instead of short sequences. Unimposing movements, like that from which Ex. 82A is quoted, prove that Stanley surmounted these tasks admirably, particularly the task of spreading the interest. A simple dance-form, such as that begun at Ex. 82B, better enables him to display his attractive melodic invention by removing the other difficulties.

Stanley has been praised for his fugal movements, and it must be admitted that they are enjoyable at a first hearing. They are not stiff, because they do not follow taut and continuously cumulative designs. Their recurrent episodes for concertino or light texture give them the symmetry of non-fugal allegros. Experience in extemporizing such movements proves them to be superficially effective with less genuine invention than must be expended on a really attractive air or dance, and that is probably why the listener finds Stanley's fugues less impressive at a second or third hearing than at a first. Conventional fugues have been likened to Japanese paper flowers which expand in water, for they leave nothing to discover when we have once seen the process. Stanley's expand from their proposed materials more elegantly than do fugues by most English concertists, but they provide us with no fascinated uncertainty at any point in their course. Indeed Stanley left no deeply felt or powerful movement, for even in minor keys he avoided ideas that incurred risk of anticlimax; but his professional competence and consistent invention make him the only native English concertist of Handel's time whom we can rank with Fasch, Graupner, Telemann and the other German court composers.

Discussion of most later concertos published in England is withheld for the final chapter. More space has been given to Geminiani and Avison than their music warrants (by comparison with that of German concertists) because they represent the state of music in England and the enormous dissemination of epigonic Corellian concertos during the most vital period of concerto composition in Germany. It is not proposed, however, to examine in detail the many minor talents among concertists who lived in England. The closest rival of Geminiani and Avison with the music societies was Michael Festing (c. 1680–1752), a pupil of Geminiani and a member of the royal band. He has already been mentioned as leading The Philharmonick Society at the Crown and Anchor Tavern in the Strand. To this 'Gentlemen's Meeting' he dedicated his *Twelve Concertos* which were published by Smith in 1734 without opus number. They cannot be distinguished from Geminiani's except by their ponderous dullness. His other concertos are *Eight Concertos in 7 parts*, Op. 5 (Smith, 1739) and *Six concertos in seven parts . . .*, Op. 9 (Johnson, 1756). In 1737 he became a director of the Italian Opera, and he was put in charge of the music when Ranelagh Gardens was opened in 1742.

Castrucci's *Concerti Grossi Op. 3*, issued by Walsh in 1736, have the same full Italian title as Corelli's, which they closely imitate. So do the *Six Concerto's in seven parts, for four violins, a tenor, a violoncello etc.* by Dr. John Alcock, 'printed for the Author' in 1750. Only slightly less Corellian, because they do not use the string concertino, are *Six Concertos in Six Parts, for a German flute, two violins, a tenor, with a bass for the harpsichord and violoncello, Opera Terza* by Filippo Ruge, printed by Walsh in 1753. 'Ruge's Concertos' appears on several publishers' advertisements, and works for the flute, being in considerable demand, were much favoured by piracy.

We should expect the concertos of a Dutchman to be influenced by Vivaldi, Locatelli, or German composers, but the concertos of Willem de Fesch are unadventurous. He was baptized at Alkmaar in 1687 and became organist of Antwerp Cathedral. After his dismissal in 1731 he lived in London and died there in 1761. He composed for Marylebone Gardens, where he probably directed the music, and Walsh published a whole volume of his songs which had been used there. He was also on more than one occasion first violin for Handel. His Op. 10 was entitled *8 Concerto's in seven parts. Six for two violins, a tenor violin, and a violoncello, with two other violins and thorough bass. . . . One for a German flute, with all the other instruments, and one with two German flutes. . . .* It first appeared in London in 1741 but the publisher has not been identified. There is a Walsh edition of 1745. Not even the flute concertos show any advance. Although some of Defesch's music was given by Vivaldi during his visit to Amsterdam, many would agree with Burney that he was 'a good contrapuntist' but that his concertos are 'dry and uninteresting'.

Altogether more admirable is another Dutchman's work, recently edited by Hans Brandts Buys as Vol. 1 of *Monumenta*

9. Norwich Music Rooms

Musica Neerlandica. This is the Op. 3 of Pieter Hellendaal (1721–1799), *Six Grand Concerto's,* printed 'for the Author' and sold by Walsh, then reprinted by Johnson. As well as the British Museum copy (g. 960) there are copies in Cambridge libraries, for Hellendaal became organist at Pembroke College and succeeded Randall at Peterhouse. Son of a Rotterdam candle-maker, he went at sixteen to study under Tartini at Padua. Evidently the patron who financed him could not show him adequate prospects in his native country and he gravitated to 'Little Holland' across the sea. There were more flourishing music clubs in East Anglia than anywhere else, and our collegiate universities required many organists and leaders of musical activities. Hellendaal came to London in 1752, settled in Cambridge ten years later, after a short time as organist at St. Margaret's, King's Lynn, and played the violin at concerts in Norwich, Bury St. Edmunds, and as far afield as Oxford.

His concertos are notably distinct from the average purveyed to clubs and called by Burney 'servile imitations of Corelli'. His wit betokens a past-mastery of musical phraseology, and the second violin and viola parts are of a rare quality. His fugal movements, for all their brilliant facility, hold attention as do the best of Handel's. These magnificent string concertos follow designs like those in Handel's Op. 6 which resemble concertized French suites, for they are not at all Corellian in form or style. The broad and splendid movements are basically ripieno but contain solo passages.

Apart from these works by Hellendaal few concertos of the English School reveal the experience and craftsmanship of the pedestrian kapellmeister concertos of German courts, or show a degree of invention that makes them more than very small foothills to Handel's eminence. It is hard to understand how any connoisseur believes that Handel 'stifled native genius', which is usually stimulated rather than stifled by what it admires. England lacked any great genius to stimulate or stifle, but she did not lack valuable minor composers who, to a man, knew their debt to the Italians and Germans, above all to Handel.

The number of works which have not been discussed in this chapter, lest it swell inordinately, is evident from a glance at the advertisements on Walsh's and other publishers' covers, or at the

T [289]

manuscript catalogues often prepared by club secretaries. For instance among the works owned by the Oxford Music Club were:

> Hebden's Concertos in 7 Parts.
> Mudge's Medley Concerto, with Horns, etc.
> Humphries's 12 Concertos, with German Flutes, Hautboys, Trumpets, and Kettle Drums.
> Bates's 6 Concertos in 10 Parts, with Hautboys, French Horns, and Trumpets.
> Ricciotti's 6 Concertos.

Richard Gorer's remarks in *Grove* upon the Op. 2 and Op. 3 of John Humphries (d. 1730), suggests that they are better works than many upon which I have commented. At the comparatively early date their full instrumentation is remarkable for English concertos. The Op. 2 set was for strings, but the composer 'suggests alternative instrumentation for some of the concertos'. Bates's concertos cannot be remarkable for the same reason, being much later; the composer's dates are not known but he was popular chiefly as a theatre and Vauxhall Gardens musician between 1760 and 1780. Ricciotti, migrant to The Hague, is suspected as a plagiarist, but the authorship neither of the 'Concerti armonici' (issued by him in Holland and reprinted here by Walsh) nor of their part-source, the 'Concertini' listed among the works of Pergolesi, has been conclusively established.[1]

Concertos of English provenance have already been discussed at greater length than better ones, not merely because an English writer is expected to do so but because writers of any country could compile an interesting commentary upon the status and fortunes of eighteenth-century musicians merely by considering migrants to these islands. Only a few Italians and Dutchmen have been mentioned in the foregoing pages, and it is a pity that J. B. Loeillet could not also have been considered.[2] Will no concertos by him be discovered? If not, why was so notable a player

[1] See C. L. Cudworth's 'Notes on the Instrumental Worke Attributed to Pergolesi' in M and L. Vol. XXX, 1949.

[2] Loeillet, 1680–1730, came from a Ghent musical family. Although some of his works are dedicated to French patrons he cannot have stayed long in France before settling in London and doing well, not only as harpsichordist, flautist and oboist in theatre and concert room, but with his lucrative teaching practice. If he did not introduce the transverse flute into England, he did much to make it popular by his brilliant playing and many fine sonatas.

and composer not urged to play and compose flute concertos? The envied peculiarity of English social and political conditions had an effect upon musical activities, and composers as well as performers catered for a wider diversity of tastes than was found in other lands. England is the country which historians of the baroque concerto leave last and historians of the galant concerto visit almost first. For these facts the migrants were largely responsible. If Mozart had become one of them—if he had lived another year and carried out his resolve to follow Haydn's advice—England might also have provided some fine pages for historians of the classical concerto.

CHAPTER XIII

Handel's Concertos

Handel has been too summarily called a Corellian concertist, classified with Geminiani except in genius; but Geminiani was Corelli's pupil who left Italy before he was affected by the Venetians, whereas Handel was a migrant Saxon influenced by north German concertists and by French suites. Geminiani may have been influenced by Kusser during his years in Dublin but the effect could not have been shown in his works, for they were already published. If our survey had been arranged by stylistic instead of regional schools Handel would have been considered along with Muffat and Telemann who 'concertized' suites. We do not readily think thus of Handel for he was never drawn like Telemann to comment upon the music which he admired. His university was not Leipzig but the small one at Halle, yet Telemann's friend must have been familiar with the francophile aesthetic of Leipzig and with the French elements in Telemann's music, which he so often purloined.

Living in the same century as Handel, Mozart was in some ways more able than we are to recognize certain characteristics of Handel's music. When we first play Mozart's *Overture in the Style of Handel* we wonder how so shrewd a parodist fell short of the Italianate high baroque mannerisms that are elsewhere served in supposed imitations of Handel. There is, of course, far too much of Mozart in this work for any item in it to be passed off as Handel's, but the average student could not be reproached for asking if

[292]

Mozart, like Beethoven, planned two overtures in honour of Bach and Handel, finished only one of them, and copied it under the wrong title; for the *Overture in the Style of Handel* is more like a French suite by Bach than like anything by Handel. Certainly what Mozart parodied was a German-French overture, and certainly he recognized the French elements in Handel's music.

Most of Handel's overtures are versions of the French design, and though no pieces in his operas and oratorios are exactly like Rameau's storms, shipwrecks and scene transformations, the great orchestral genius of France would have admired many a piece of scoring by Handel—the dances in *Alcina*, the sleep-enchantment and awakening in *Orlando*, the scene complexes (mixtures of orchestrally accompanied recitative and arioso) in several operas, the nightingale chorus and other love scenes in *Solomon*, the harps and muted strings for Cleopatra's languishings in *Giulio Cesare*. These observations are pertinent while Handel's concertos are considered chiefly as part of the apotheosis of Corelli which constituted the main British contribution to the history of the concerto grosso. The *Music for the Royal Fireworks* not only provides a suite that is as French as any by Telemann but also four final movements—*La paix*, *La réjouissance* and the two minuets—which are more like items in Rameau's ballets than any other music composed outside France itself.

The title *The Oboe Concertos*, by which Handel's six Op. 3 concertos are still commonly known,[1] seems to have been given to them by English audiences as soon as they heard them. This may indicate that neither the privileged auditors at Cannons nor those in London had formerly heard concerti grossi with essential wind instruments. Chrysander dates some of them as early as 1711–12 and may have been correct in his opinion that they are taken from Handel's compositions as Kapellmeister at Hanover. They could well represent the most advanced concertos of a German court before the full spate of Venetian concertos. Several of them begin like a French overture and include one or two dance movements. Some which have no initial slow introduction and allegro fugato can still be regarded as Italianized French suites. The opening

[1] Although the autograph of Op. 6 also provides oboe parts for four of the concertos.

movement of No. 4 in F was used as the overture to *Amadigi* at
its 1716 revival; the fugue of No. 2 in B flat was used in the setting of Brockes's *Passion* and also appears among Handel's
harpsichord works; the second and the last movement of No.
6 in D minor also occur in the third harpsichord suite and the
tenth organ concerto. Hawkins says that the Op. 3 concertos
were performed in March, 1734, to celebrate the wedding of the
Princess Royal.

By comparison with concertos composed in Germany after
about 1716 Handel's Op. 3 hardly seems like a set of concertos,
for the concertino is not a distinguishing mark. In *The Water
Music*, the overture has a concertino for two violins, and Nos. 3
and 6 a concertino for two oboes and bassoon; No. 2 is exactly like
the slow movement of a concerto for solo oboe, and in some movements the oboes, bassoons and horns concertize as in Bach's first
Brandenburg Concerto. In Op. 3, as in *The Water Music* and in
Scarlatti's sinfonias, most of the concertino sections are simply
episodes which relieve the tutti, forming a persistent rather than
a contrasting part of the structure, for the music could be
arranged for strings.

Handel's Op. 3 differs from his Op. 6 not only in quality but in
purpose. He need not have composed Op. 6 for any other reason
than delight in showing his powers, for he had at hand plenty of
concertos to use during oratorios, and most concert-goers would
rather hear a favourite work than a new one. (Burney's choice of
concertos for the Commemoration shows that his favourites were
not ours.) Handel composed Op. 3 as *Gebrauchsmusik*, and it suggests the average complement of a ducal band when trumpets and
drums were not requisitioned. Whether these concertos were used
by Handel in Hanover or not, Arnold believed that they were part
of the fulfilment of a Kapellmeister's contract. Arnold also gave
permanence to the popular description 'Oboe Concertos' for the
title-page of his edition runs: 'Concertos (commonly called the
Hautboy Concertos) for two Violins, two Hautboys, two German
Flutes, two Tenors, two Bassoons, two Violoncellos and a Basso
Continuo, chiefly composed at Cannons in the year 1730.' (His
date has been proved to be a year too late.)

Only an idolater would claim that Op. 3 is a fine sample of
sustained musical invention and thought comparable with Op. 6,

and one sometimes wonders how often its concertos would be performed, reprinted or recorded if they were attributed to Telemann. They are not disparaged because little is unusual in their harmony or design, for Handel's best work is fully evident when the general style of a movement looks conventional to the score-reading eye. The few movements in Op. 3 which strike us as uniquely Handelian are not those in the grand manner but the best dances. We are glad to have Op. 3 for the charming movements rather than those which the first audiences probably found impressive. Particularly attractive are the sarabande which forms the middle movement of No. 1 (the only movement with flute), the gavotte and variations (not so labelled) at the end of No. 2, and the minuets of No. 4.

The manuscripts of these works are lost, but not that of a fine C major concerto called by Arnold 'Concertante'. It bears the date 25th January 1736 and was known as 'The Concerto in *Alexander's Feast*' after the first occasion when London heard it. It was the first item in Walsh's fourth collection of *Select Harmony*, which is thought to have been issued in 1741. The ripieno includes two oboes but the concertino is the Corellian string trio. Walsh also published two other Handel concertos which need not detain us here. The student can find them all, as well as those of Op. 3, in a handy volume of Lea Pocket Scores (New York).

Before doing homage to the most wonderful of all concerti grossi we may take as a point of departure Chrysander's remark that the Op. 3 concertos show 'a bewildering variety of form'. If 'design' and 'form' are regarded as synonymous, then any work that is not epigonic should bewilder us, and Handel's Op. 6 should serve a feast of bewilderment. Because words will no more describe the form than the expression of music, for the form *is* the music, we measure the parts of a musical design instead of learning a piece by heart in order to judge its form. One artist does not excel another because he has used a more complex design, but because his form is more organic, which means that the ideas and their growth are of the right quality and quantity for the expression. When equally sensitive and intelligent judges of music have different opinions concerning the quality of ideas and the forms into which they grow, their argument often settles upon design—how many themes are used, how many are germs for motivic growth, where and how contrast is made, where and how it is avoided, whether the themes are curved or angular, rightly or wrongly lacking in colour—and behind the description is the implication that one design is superior to another, a fugue with stretto superior or inferior to one that is as effective through well-timed entries between non-derived episodes. Thus too often we think of form as a relation of A to B, of a movement as being fine if C, instead of D, follows B at a certain point; sometimes this pseudo-explanation may in fact support truth, but we grasp the symbols of the truth instead of the truth itself.

Beethoven had neither the education nor the natural ability to use words explicitly. On his deathbed, having no further need to regret his limitation or to cure it, he pointed to the Arnold volumes of Handel which had just arrived and said 'There is the truth'. On a previous occasion Beethoven had said of Handel: 'He was the greatest composer who ever lived. I would uncover my head, and kneel before his tomb.' Among Beethoven's eccentricities we cannot number that of seeking to impress company by aesthetic and musical judgements. Men with the greatest insight into music use one life in its pursuit and lack another in which to command words in a way that effectively communicates their musical judgement. Beethoven's words are often incoherent, but when we grasp their purport we find them true. 'Ah, my dear Ries, he was the master of us all in this art'—Beethoven was speaking of Mozart and the art of the piano concerto. He did not flatter. Mozart was and still is the master in that particular art. Beethoven did not say that Handel was the greatest *Künstler* but the greatest *Komponist* that had lived, and he would have been right if the only existing proofs of the fact were the Op. 6 concertos.

In each of these superb works the four, five or six movements seem like facets of one personality; so we have twelve essays of an integrity comparable with that of the best classical symphonies. These concertos embrace most of the musical expression that belonged to the concert room of their time and much that belonged to the theatre, and they exclude only the morbid, bizarre, extremely tragic, directly programmatic and religious—in short what was then reserved to illustrate words or drama and to dignify worship. This marvellously comprehensive expression

[296]

would not make us willing to doff and kneel with Beethoven unless it were conveyed in sublime examples of almost perfect form, none bewildering unless we try to explain it by the vocabulary of what should be called design. 'The opening movement is a French overture fertilized in its slow introduction by the Handelian sarabande-like sacred aria, and in its fugato movement by the Italian sonata-allegro.' This tells no intelligent musician anything about Handel's success or failure to achieve form, yet a sympathetic listener who does not know the design of a French overture may perceive Handel's achievement. The empty grandiosity of certain items in *Joshua* or *Judas Maccabeus* fulfils designs which, according to text books called 'Applied Forms' and 'Applied Strict Counterpoint', ensure safety for any composer who can invent or borrow ideas to suit the designs. The opposite of 'applied' is 'organic', and because they are all organic the Twelve Concerti Grossi are one of the greatest feats of musical composition.

It has been well said that some of Handel's best movements defy analysis because they are improvisatory—a word which can be pejorative. We are not intended to listen more than once to an improvisation. It satisfies us if we are pleased with the music as it passes, and if it is congruous. Improvisation, however, is the first stage in written composition, and if mechanical reproduction of an improvisation forces us to listen a second and a third time we are like the composer who scrutinizes his first draft and decides what should be pruned and what extended. Sometimes we are dissatisfied not with the unchecked fancy of the improviser but with our recognition of pre-fabrications, 'applied forms', modulations and developments introduced exactly as in other extemporizations. To extemporize from a preconceived design or upon ideas given by an auditor is splendid exercise, but at best only portions of the exercise can be significant artistic expression—in short, form. When, however, a whole written piece seems to have grown by impulse, and when both the ideas and their growth are of superb quality, we can hardly praise it more highly than to say that it sounds spontaneous throughout, and still sounds so when we hear it for the hundredth time.

Comparatively late in his career Handel impressed shrewd judges by his organ extemporizations, and though it is unthinkable that the ideas and developments had the breadth of those in his published work, Handel had more ability then most musicians to extemporize whole sections within a well-proportioned whole. How often in composing the Twelve Concerti Grossi he proceeded by deliberation and how often the music welled forth without his conscious control we shall never know, and that is one tribute to their greatness.[1] They are said to have been written in a few weeks of 1739, yet they contain no sign of careless or hasty work. The borrowing of one opening from Cleopatra's *Piangerò la sorte mia* and another from Semele's *Myself I shall adore* does not negate the last assertion. Most of the movements are an exception to the general criticism that few of the greatest works of music are well composed throughout. Conscientiousness cannot make them so; otherwise the forms of Brahm's long movements would be as wonderful as Handel's or Beethoven's. Fortunately we rank the imperfect fulfilment of a noble ambition above the perfect management of trivialities and musical platitudes. Not a single movement in Handel's Op. 6 is pedestrian; no concerto fails to suggest verve and joy in the process of composition.

Even if the Op. 6 concertos lacked their distinguishing breadth of conception and their splendid musical ideas they would still differ from Corelli's for two main reasons: (a) some of them are dramatic in the strict sense of the term—they are the work of a theatre composer; (b) a great number of them come from the German-French suite. It has been admitted that Geminiani, who was almost entirely Corellian, occasionally achieved Handel's breadth of musical thought; but he did this only when composing contrapuntally or by the Corellian continuation technique without motive development. Handel achieves a huge breadth of musical thought when composing almost mechanistically in the least weighty of styles. (Ex. 83.)

This quotation illustrates a second point, Into the light figuration of the violins erupts a contrasting idea by the bass instruments. It may have been introduced to give a touch of humour or to prevent the developmentfrom being too simple and mechanical; yet it is surely not accidental that, when the whole flight reaches its conclusion in four

[1] The dates and circumstances of their composition are fully discussed in Deutsch's *Handel: A Documentary Biography*, London 1955.

bars of plain ripieno harmony, the paragraph is clinched by the solid rhythm of this interruption. Whether Handel planned it as he began the movement or whether it occurred to him as when improvising, this way of integrating the movement was exactly right in this place, and sensible people may call it a symphonic way.

The last phrase seems discourteous, but it seems justified while critics spoil enthusiasm by asking us to value old music if its methods anticipate later ones. Thus we are told that some passages by Bach are almost atonal, and that they prefigure Schönberg. Nothing by Bach is like anything significant by Schönberg. Misinterpreted by ears and minds which inherit the work of both composers, passages by Bach wherein 'horizontal' thinking temporarily dominates the 'vertical' thinking of continuo harmony remind us of atonal polyphony. We are delighted by the unusual ascendance and stimulus of discord, the pleasure of which would have been lost to Bach (and would seem incongruous to us) unless it brought with it the pleasure of restored tonal bearings and ultimate concord. The mere fact that we call it discord shows that there is little in common between Bach and Schönberg except recourse to the devices of counterpoint. Similarly we should be careful not to pretend that Handel's movements are Beethovenian because they are often dramatic, often include passages of motivic development and often show energy and urgency that is rarely found before Beethoven.

'Handel points to Beethoven' is a meaningless comment. Tubal Cain points to Sibelius. It is also accidental that Beethoven the man, beneath the eccentricities which may have been caused by misfortune, had some of the known characteristics of Handel, and that like Handel he was in no way a wild or revolutionary artist. His music and Handel's changed gradually from early acceptance of inherited designs and styles. Without alteration they could not serve their expanding ideas, and when we set their first forms beside their last we observe a much larger change than between the first and last work of most revolutionary composers. The important parallel between Handel and Beethoven lies in their recognition of *comparable*, not similar means of maintaining movements on a large scale, especially when their materials suggested energy and urgency. These qualities in Beethoven would

not have their peculiar effect if Beethoven had not been primarily
a musical architect with an innate sense of symmetry and poise.
Like Beethoven, Handel sometimes delights us by seeming to
release uncontrollable energy and then to remember symmetry
and poise reluctantly, staying the heat of speed just in time to
prevent it from becoming monstrous. The process is as intention-
ally playful as the unexpected turns of effervescence in Beethoven's
scherzos.

A wonderful example of this is the finale of Op. 6, No. 4, which
one is tempted to quote in full. The forward thrust of what
promises to be a monothematic improvisation is held in check
(a) by breaking the rate of chord change and holding several bars
to the same bass, (b) by inserting echoes between concertino and
tutti, (c) by cunningly shifting to episodes which maintain the
metrical pulse but change the rhythm, (d) by counter-melody in
longer notes. (Ex. 84.) This superficially unimposing movement
marks the past master of composition who, having at his finger-
tips most of the musical craft of his time, could lightly achieve
spontaneous form without relying upon formal design. This, and
not only the pathetic, luxurious and grandiose expression for
which Handel is justly admired, should convince us that at his
best his skill was not inferior to Bach's.

85.   'Fireworks Music', No. 1.

Allegro

A.

B.

What seems marvellously and instinctively right in Handel's
forms is paralleled in his formulae. Let the point be illustrated
from the tiniest detail one can find—a mere semiquaver in a
movement marked *Allegro*. Towards the end of the overture to
the *Fireworks Music* there occurs the little sequence seen in Ex.
85A. Suppose the figure to be altered by one semiquaver as at
Ex. 85B. We still have nothing that does not belong to the style
and might not have been written by Handel himself. Moreover

[301]

the alteration would be perfectly suited to the trumpets. Why is it so much an alteration for the worse? Because it is less peremptory and, as we imagine, less characteristic of the man? Perhaps, but the most probable reason is that it anticipates instead of withholding the upward destination of the whole passage. The graded terraces are spoilt. The point is extremely subtle, but of subtle points the supremely great composer of Op. 6 was as much the master as he was of the broad paragraph.

The range of Handel's forms prevents our calling him simply a Corellian or simply a Vivaldian. The most frequent features of his musical vocabulary link him with Corelli and Scarlatti, but initial and final movements of Venetian concertos are sometimes almost Handelian—an example is the first movement of Albinoni's ripieno concerto in B flat, the first of his Op. 5 set. Handel's larger movements begin either with a grandiose or otherwise memorable main idea or with a large paragraph derived from a memorable motive; he then often passes to a contrasting idea which is lighter than his first in rhythm, harmony or texture, and may be presented like most of the Venetian ancillary ideas in a pattern of sequences; but Handel could achieve a broad symphonic play of tensions and climaxes when he continued in the asymmetrical way which we associate with Corelli and Bonporti rather than the Venetians. The slow descent of the first violins and the gradual release of tension in Ex. 87 will serve as well as more famous movements to illustrate the breadth of Handel's melodic and harmonic thought.

Sometimes, as in the first movement of Op. 6, No. 11, Handel kept his main idea to strong, simple harmony and primary diatonic intervals in the melody but introduced chromatics in the ancillary materials. The recurrence of a grand first idea is well illustrated in the first movement of Op. 6, No. 2, although its

[302]

7. *Largo, e piano*

Handel. Op. 6, No. 7.

finish shows it to be an introductory movement. How well these recurrences are timed! The majestic tread of chords is offset by the more static and repetitive harmony of the concertino episodes. If Geminiani, ambitious enough in his requirements from the players, had thus advanced from Corelli's methods of structure, his movements would have been more imposing. Had he been less than a very inventive musician his concertos would not have survived.

Handel employs a symphonic contrast of materials even in fugues, for when short sequential episodes and non-derived concertino passages come between entries of a memorable subject, and when that subject has verve but is unfit for ricercar devices,

[303]

the broad plan of the fugue is similar to that of a Handelian sonata-allegro. This is true of the fugues in Op. 6, Nos. 1, 2, 4, 7, 10, 11 and 12, but not of the fugues in Nos. 3 and 6. These two are not symmetrical, and though they make little use of the traditional devices their effect is of unbroken cumulation, even during the derived episodes. Both of these are short, concentrated fugues which call for no marked halt of their intensity and are not on a symphonic scale.

The fugues thus illustrate our main point, that length demands either wealth of materials or much contrast in their treatment. It does not demand that materials be grand or imposing. Could they be lighter than the two ideas quoted at Ex. 86? One is a mere dip and shake, the other the upper tetrachord of a major scale. But could two ideas of their time make a more brilliant contrast? And how perfectly both belong to the string medium! Neither is effective in translation, and only one medium can produce the thrilling effect of a unison of tremolo bowing.

Bülow spoke of Bach's Forty-Eight and Beethoven's sonatas as the pianist's Old and New Testament. Despite one or two fine pieces like the fugue in E minor Handel left nothing for the keyboard that is comparable with Bach's rich legacy; but musicians whose interests range beyond what their two hands can encompass need no more wonderful Old Testament than Handel's Op. 6. Those who know it by heart carry with them a perennial source of joy and wonder—joy because no scores of the period, not even Rameau's, are so exquisitely sensuous within the bounds of strength and sanity, and wonder because organic form, the fulfilment of great ideas in great style, is the most wonderful phenomenon both of the natural order and also of that order in which a divine hand is withdrawn so that the creature may share the experience of creation. How lavish a bounty is showered on the few from whom not even the perfection of form is withheld! How much is denied to an artist who receives a second share of endowments! A hundred years of orchestras, fifty years of concertos, the pains of living and working to perform and compose them well—all would have been justified if every one were lost, provided that we still had the Great Twelve. 'There is the truth.'

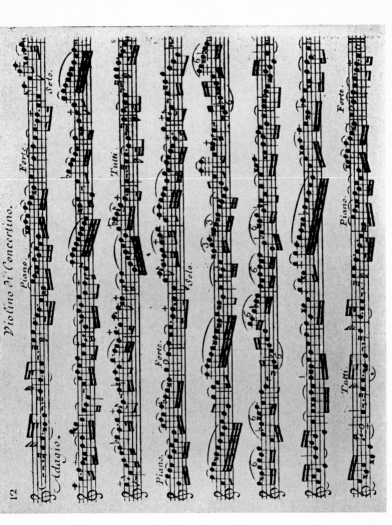

10. Middle movement of a concerto by Leclair, showing the composer's attention to bowing. Printed by Leclerc of Paris c. 1757

CHAPTER XIV

Bonporti and Leclair

Why allot a separate chapter to composers for whom we
cannot claim Corelli's and Vivaldi's historical importance nor Handel's and Bach's musical importance?
Bonporti and Leclair are linked in no other way but the fact that
they composed very fine concertos. Leclair was by twenty years
the younger; his concertos followed Bonporti's by an even longer
interval, and his designs and styles differed from Bonporti's as
greatly as Vivaldi's from Corelli's. My first defence is simple
enough. I could not class Bonporti with Corelli's contemporaries
nor with the Venetians, and the cult of concertos by native French
composers did not justify a separate chapter. My second defence
explains my happiness at finding Bonporti and Leclair 'left over'.
Their musical styles are almost disparate, but they have in common certain qualities which I value more than others, and could
not have found in any other concertists but the supremely great
ones. Defective planning thus gives me opportunity, before finishing the book, of speaking about the standards by which we judge
or misjudge music of the past.

Francesco Antonio Bonporti (1672–1749) described himself as
a dilettante, more precisely as 'Gentilhuomo di Trento' on his
first book of sonatas (1696) and 'Dilettante di musica' on later
works. Though a contemporary of the great Venetian dilettanti,
Albinoni and the Marcellos, and though a priest like Vivaldi,
either his isolation in the north prevented his direct acquaintance

with the Venetians or he wilfully sought his own way of advancing sonatas and concertos from Corelli. The second seems the more acceptable explanation, for it is hard to believe him so chained by duty in his cathedral at the alpine frontier that he could not hear the concertos which had spread beyond Venice by 1720, and still harder to believe that such a wonderful violinist failed to study the printed parts of works by Albinoni, Vivaldi and Benedetto Marcello. If, however, Bonporti's concertos were published before he knew Vivaldi's Op. 3 then let us be thankful, as we are that Bach became a cantor and student of keyboard playing and not another adept composer of 'neapolitan' operas. At his level Bonporti is as distinct, idiomatic and unclassifiable as Bach, and that is one reason why he can be ranked with Leclair.

Bonporti was an aristocrat and an intellectual, and though his music is sometimes as romantic and passionate as Vivaldi's, much of its vocabulary and syntax is conservative. Its proud baroque harmony and melody, without displaying fugal devices, comes from an expert contrapuntist's part-writing. Thus Bonporti reminds us of Handel, who is more consistently grand because he is superficially more simple, and he strongly differentiates a theme from the episodic matter between thematic recurrence. Bonporti binds his allegros with memorable main themes but is more prolix and diffuse than Handel, and he puts chromatic notes where Handel did not. Handel's concertos are not chiefly a development of Corelli's, and their tribute to Corelli lies in the adoption of a trio-concertino and in turns of style in *some* types of movement. These turns of style are not peculiar to Handel and Corelli, and not a single movement in one of Handel's concertos could be taken for any by Corelli, who was not among the composers from whom Handel borrowed. Bonporti, not Handel, is Corelli's most handsome musical child. Like Geminiani, he was Corelli's pupil, but he has much more character of his own, much more originality than Geminiani.

After a good general education in Trent, Bonporti studied at the Jesuit College at Innsbruck and left it with a doctorate in philosophy. He then went to the German College in Rome and was enabled to study counterpoint and music generally with Pitoni and the violin with Corelli. He had already been ordained to full priesthood, and he returned to the cathedral at Trent to occupy a minor canonry with status and duties like those of pre-centor in English cathedrals of the 'old foundation'. From 1695 until 1740, nearly half a century, he served the cathedral as director of music. He is known to have published eleven sets of instrumental works. He probably composed many more. The original place of publication was usually Venice, but at least once it was Bologna. The original editions may have been at his own expense, for he sent copies to various ecclesiastical and secular grandees with flattering dedications and, after 1717, letters begging for appointments or for the influence that might secure for him a canonry at Trent. Apparently the sole mundane advantage they brought was from the Emperor Charles VI, who made Bonporti an aulic familiar in 1727, after which he styled himself 'Maestro dei Concerti' to his imperial and catholic majesty.[1] For this reason historians mistakenly thought him to have been employed in Vienna.

One can understand the vulgar man's desire for rank in society or a profession, especially in days when we are taught to admire rather than pity it, and when many second-raters holding positions formerly reserved for few behave as if those who have not clambered and smirked to their eminence must be dullards. One cannot easily understand the pathetic yearning for promotion in a man of Bonporti's intellect, education and breeding, any one of which should have taught him the vanity of popular esteem or social rank and the truth that one can enter heaven or hell as easily from a parlour in Trent as from the grandest saloon in Rome, Vienna or Paris.

Unless we are to think poorly of a man who seems to have followed his clerical vocation sincerely we must consider the time in which he lived. His emoluments in a minor office at Trent Cathedral were poor for a man of his culture, and the little city offered him little congenial society and no powerful patrons. Trent was well off the map of princely patronage. Its setting is lovely and wild, at the foot of mountains and near the Italian lakeland; but the eighteenth century thought wild nature horrid and saw beauty in fine cities, mansions and parks. Bonporti may have felt as stifled in Trent as Mozart in Salzburg. He may also

[1] All facts about Bonporti's life are taken from G. Barblan's *Un musicista trentino. Francesco A. Bonporti: la vita e le opere*, Florence, 1940.

have endured the disdain of unimaginative superiors. Had he the company of any other musicians of his own calibre? With a canonry he might have been able to appoint talented players, and we may note that when he retired from Trent he went to live in Padua where there was plenty of cultivated and musical society, including Tartini and his circle.

There are several assurances that Bonporti's work became well known, especially in German-speaking countries, while the man remained an obscure priest over whom a succession of far less worthy candidates secured the Trent canonries. Editions of his sonatas were issued in Amsterdam, Paris and London, either by private arrangement between publishers or just by piracy. Evidence of his fame illustrates a phenomenon that could recur only exceptionally after the enactment of international laws concerning the copyright and performance of music. When Veracini travelled in northern countries between 1713 and 1735 his playing of works by Bonporti enormously enhanced the composer's reputation. Veracini was most anxious to shine in Dredsen where, under Pisendel's direction, could be heard the finest orchestra of the concerto grosso period, and the State Library at Dresden is one of the present locales of complete parts of Bonporti's concertos (which require brilliant solo performance in the sixth position on the E string) and of several of his sonatas. Yet there is a considerable list of '*Bom*porti's solos' and '*Bom*porti's sonatas' in English archives.

The gibe, 'X composed not N concertos (or sonatas) but the same concerto N times' could not be more badly misapplied to any baroque composer than to Bonporti. Wrongly taught, as most of us were, to think highly of baroque music when it supposedly anticipates later music, we might support a high estimate of Bonporti by quoting a list of unconventional details, including difficult passages for the solo violin. Let us do so and be done with what I regard as quite a secondary ground for admiration. At Ex. 88 is the sort of detail which we may soon be told 'might have come from Mozart', to which I hope we shall answer: 'Obviously it did not.' At Ex. 89 is part of the long, impassioned middle movement, called 'recitativo', which 'anticipates' Bach, Beethoven, Franck, Krank or Flügelstosser. These examples happen to occur in exceedingly fine movements; but *most* of Bonporti's movements are

90.

exceedingly fine, and no less fine than the 'recitativo' is the movement that precedes and acts as a foil to it—in all concertos the unique first movement that begins and ends in the unemphatic way shown in Ex. 90.

Perhaps a different kind of idiosyncrasy points to Bonporti's intention to avoid epigonic mass production and prefabrication. His Op. 1, 2, 3 and 4 trio-sonatas and his Op. 7 'solo' sonatas are sets of ten, not twelve, and all his publications are separated by intervals of from two to five years. They are crowned by the *Concerti a quattro con violino di rinforzo*, Op. 11 which are thought by Barblan to have been composed between 1715 and 1720, the first edition being undated and less easy to assign to an approximate date than the numbered productions of the Amsterdam press.

Readers may well ask: 'If Bonporti is so splendid a composer, why have we not heard these concertos before, and why do we not frequently play the sonatas?' A plain answer is: 'I am old enough to remember the time when not more than two or three concertos by Vivaldi were well known by most professional musicians, and these few were regarded as works for amateur string orchestras.' Bonporti suddenly came into public notice when Alfred Dörffel was found to have attributed to Bach Nos. 2, 5, 6 and 7 of Bonporti's *Invenzioni a violino solo*, Op. 10, and to have included them in No. 45 of the Bachgesellschaft volumes. The error was a measure of esteem. The *Invenzioni* are the sixth set of sonatas known to have been published by Bonporti. (Despite their full title, the violin is accompanied.) They were deliberately intended to represent the composer's most extreme flights of fancy, for he used such titles as 'Capricio', 'Bizaria', 'Ecco Adagio' and 'Scherzo'. The specimens of these pieces which have been recently issued in *Hortus Musicus* show a grip of form that inclines one to quibble with the excellent contributor to *Grove* who thinks that they show a 'freakish mind'.

I need not know the point from the nut of a fiddlestick to put on paper a transcendental arabesque in the twenty-fourth position. I need only the eye to draw leger lines. Any fool can be idiotically novel. The attitude of professional musicians to baroque music that is merely unconventional should be Dr. Johnson's: 'Sir, a woman who composes verse is like a cow who walks on her hind

legs; it is nothing in the performance that you admire but that
she does it at all.' What man who has tried to compose 'admires'
some of Vivaldi's novelties more than the fact that so fine an
artist sometimes failed to give them a worthy context? Few of
Vivaldi's contemporaries had the imagination to secure the evoca-
tive and onomatopoeic sounds in the 'Four Seasons' but many
could have produced concertos as novel, and without regarding
Vivaldi as less than one of the finest artists outside the very first
class, do we not recognize that the 'Four Seasons' contain very
few movements that are more than superficial, and that these four
concertos are much inferior to the dozen or so best of Vivaldi's?

Comparison of Vivaldi with a composer who published only ten
concertos would be stupid, and in any case I am not setting up
Bonporti as greater than Vivaldi. All I want to emphasize is that
the very concertos and movements in which we see Bonporti's
most brilliantly original strokes are those in which we also recognize his broad command of form and feel the inexorable purpose
of his harmony and texture. Where he is most original he is no
less the nearest predecessor of Bach except Albinoni, and no less
the nearest predecessor of Handel except Pez; the flush of passion
or quirk of humour is the more appealing for its transitory relief
of the grand manner and the *da chiesa* polyphony.

The point may be illustrated from the concerto which, among
the ten, maintains the most conservative features of the grand
manner. The quotations at Ex. 91 do *not* 'anticipate' nineteenth-
century ways of relating movements thematically, nor does such
a work necessarily cohere better than one in which themes and
movements are superficially heterogeneous; but the conservative
and radical are wonderfully unified in the creator of such a concerto as this. We are not surprised to find in the same composer
other forms of apparent 'anticipation'—for instance the finale
with brilliant solo and tutti variations (Concerto No. 6 in F major)
which the ear imagines to be a minuet-finale, or the opening
allegro of No. 8 in D major, with its clearly defined and developed
'second subject'. A sonata hunter's early catch? So might be an
entirely puerile experiment, and the very rarity which makes the
early capture exhilarating gives it almost no significance in the
history of music. If an Austrian composer of 1790 had used Bonporti's two main themes in a classical sonata it would have been a

poor piece; and if Bonporti had 'anticipated' a classical sonata in this concerto he would have done nothing to extol but something to condemn, for he would have published as music, as expression in form that is part of oneself, a mere experiment in design.

Just as Bonporti's sonatas were entitled 'da camera', so his concertos are all cast in three long movements, none reminiscent of the church concerto in *shape*, but many recalling the dignity and magnificence of a cathedral festival. The technical points of procedure which make Bonporti's movements so impressive are the prolonged or delayed cadence, the polyphony-producing bass, and the interruption less often of a close than of the tread of harmony in the bar before most composers of his period would have made a close. Of course this way of forming huge and noble paragraphs is also a limitation. Handel used it, but far less extensively than Bonporti, making splendid variety between the long paragraph and the episodes which, even if joined into an urgent stream of melody, were often the recurrence or assembling of units based on a short chord-formula.

Though Bonporti often opens his allegros with a long initial tutti which closes in the tonic, the effect of later references to it is rarely that of the clearly distinguished ritornelli of Albinoni and Vivaldi, but more like Handel's symphonic returns to a grandiose rhythm and theme. Frequently the solo and tutti parts are not strongly opposed, for the solo may have an independent and brilliant part even during the initial tutti. Bonporti's conception of the concerto is implicit in the last phrase of the title—'con violino di rinforzo', not 'violino principale con due violini . . . di concerto grosso'. Yet our quotations are enough to show that his solo violin parts are no less virtuosic than Vivaldi's; indeed in some concertos they are as exacting as the most difficult of Vivaldi's, and they have been compared even with Locatelli's, though with little point.

The chief point to emphasize is the contrast between Bonporti and his Venetian contemporaries. Many of the new features of Venetian concertos became traditional; Bonporti's originality is a connoisseur's luxury, for it was unnecessary to the development of the concerto.[1] Exactly the same remarks could be made about

---

[1] Four concertos from Bonporti's op. 11 are excellently played by 'I Musici' on Philips' A.00449, which was issued just after these remarks went to press. They convince me that my claims for this composer are not exaggerated.

Leclair, though he brought an original mind to bear upon an eclectic and international style. Leclair's concertos are not obviously French as Bonporti's are obviously by a north Italian who admired Corelli and Scarlatti.

The only great French baroque concertos are those in two volumes, each of six violin concertos, published *c.* 1737 and 1744 by Jean Marie Leclair, who was born in 1697 and murdered in 1764.[1] Though his father was a master lace-maker in Lyons, five of Leclair's brothers also became professional musicians and most of them were violinists. Two published admirable violin sonatas and also composed symphonies, divertissements and ballet music. The concertist is called Jean Marie Leclair *l'aîné* because his most distinguished younger brother, *le cadet*, bears the same Christian names as he. Unlike his brothers, Leclair did not originally make violin playing his chief musical pursuit, but during his visit to Turin in 1722 the dances he composed for inclusion in operas by Italians greatly impressed Somis, who induced him to begin an intense study of violin playing. Leclair returned to France. He soon made a second and longer visit to Italy and presumably continued his study of the violin, for between 1728 and 1736 he was regularly acclaimed at the Concert Spirituel and he was the most admired performer in the royal band. A period following this, during which we do not hear of him as a public performer, covers the publication of his finest compositions, including the sets of concertos. It is noteworthy that a Frenchman should compose little else than sonatas and concertos, use no 'literary' titles and write tempo indications in Italian.

For the lack of any other considerable French concertos we have ample compensation in the superb quality of every single one of Leclair's, and it is much to our shame that they are not issued in a modern edition and often played. The composition of their movements is more highly organized than that of most German

[1] A set of ten concertos, wrongly called the first examples of the genre composed by a Frenchman, was issued in 1735 and 1739 by Jacques Aubert (1689–1753). After serving the Duc de Bourbon, Aubert became a member of the royal *vingt-quatre violons* and was also first violin at the Opèra. The concertos are for 'Four violins and a bass', and of no great musical interest except as showing the influence of Venice even in France. Boismortier's Op. 15 dates from 1727.

concertos, except Bach's, and their solo parts are more exacting
than those of such famous post-Vivaldians as Tartini. In his solo
requirements Leclair was matched only by Locatelli, who had
taken up residence at Amsterdam and had published *L'arte del
violino* and his notorious Op. 9 Caprices. Leclair was determined
to hear him, and he had opportunity to do so in 1743 when he
was invited to Holland by the Princess of Orange. He employed
all the Vivaldian brisures and bariolage and wrote whole movements without relaxing the demand for double and triple stop-
ping, but—a far more creditable achievement—he maintained
the high musical quality of his thematic development during the
virtuosic solo display.

He cast his concertos in Vivaldi's three-movement form, adding
an introductory slow movement to two of them. His allegros are
further advanced towards the classical, post-symphony concerto
than any in Vivaldi's printed sets. A certain degree of this advance
would not have been remarkable, for the last set of concertos
printed by Vivaldi, his Op. 11, must have been composed before
1730; by the time Leclair's first set appeared Sammartini's G
major symphony had been enthusiastically acclaimed in Milan,
and by the time Leclair's second set appeared not only Sammartini
but also the elder Stamitz, Monn, and other composers were producing concert symphonies on a scale comparable with that of
Haydn's symphonies up to Op. 30 or Mozart's to K.200. Yet the
advances shown in Leclair's movements and the secure vision and
workmanship with which he made them should be acknowledged
as quite personal.

Within his smaller field, Leclair reveals a trait which is rarely
observed outside the music of much greater artists, for instance
Beethoven or Bartok. I refer to the constant extension and variation of his ideas. He does not often repeat them exactly (when he
needs them in a new key), nor present them in a former context
except where the repetition serves a better purpose than development. Hence the otherwise far-fetched mention of Beethoven and
Bartok, to which one might add Wagner—composers with whom
most parts of a movement are 'developments', so that even while
announcing a musical idea they seem to be dealing with living
spores and can scarcely restrain their activity. One does not wish
to suggest that Leclair is less than thoroughly baroque, or that

[315]

his sense of rhythm and form anticipates that of Beethoven, but that no other baroque concertist is more prone to use ornaments and variations that are urgent and not merely decorative.

If we play only the principal violin part in the first movement of his first published concerto (Ex. 92) we recognize a vitality that avoids rest however much, as the man of his age, Leclair seeks clarity and balance. The opening tutti is as strong and clear as one of Albinoni's or Vivaldi's but it does not halt before the solo entry. The solo quits the main theme after the first phrase and becomes more and more impulsive until the second tutti interrupts it; but this is not strictly a ritornello, for Leclair did not restrict the advance of new ideas to the solo. This second tutti begins with sequences upon an entirely fresh idea, proceeds to a ritornello in the relative major which comes from the opening of the initial tutti, abandons it for free development, and then returns to the sequences. So great a freedom and fertility in tutti sections is unique before the second half of the century, and it is also Leclair's regular practice. We see it even more clearly in Ex. 93 and some of the other movements quoted here.

When Leclair composes in a major key and an extravert mood, he is the most Italianate of French composers (see Ex. 94) until he chooses a type of melody or rhythm that is derived from the French divertissement. When, however, he composes in the minor key, he is impetuous and chromatic in a way that is far from common in Vivaldi, Tartini or any Italian composers before 1740, except in their dramatic slow movements, for Leclair infuses vigorous allegro movements with the impassioned lyricism and solo virtuosity of Italian adagios. One could as well point to fast movements such as Ex. 93A as to a richly emotional adagio like that seen on Plate 9 in order to refute writers who, surely upon inadequate acquaintance, tell us that Leclair commanded exquisite grace and finesse but little pathos or deeply-felt expression.

Leclair marks the bowing on his parts more fully than other composers of his day and leaves very little ornamentation to the performer's whim. Like Bach he writes out the embellishments and he seems to use very few abbreviations, the only common one being the small 'plus' above or below a note. This cross can normally be taken to indicate a mordent, but in some contexts it

[316]

92.

Leclair. Concerto 1 of Set 1.

93.

(a) Vivace

(b.) Largo *

* Printed '6/4'

(c) Allegro assai

Leclair. 1st. movt. of Concerto VI, set 1.

could be congruously interpreted as a shake or an inverted mordent. Leclair's instrumental parts, from the agile basses to the wide compass and nimble rhythms of upper strings, need alert players, and his parts for the solo violin are still regarded as exacting enough to prevent a mediocre performer from sounding like a very good one after strenuous practice of a single work. Yet these are not the points upon which to champion Leclair. Any zealous musician can decide to work with the *avant garde* of his time though he lacks originality apart from modish novelty. Our quotations are enough to show that Leclair's melody and harmony are of the age of J. S. Bach, not of Bach's sons; but the fact should not prevent our acknowledging him as one of the six best concertists mentioned in this book—surely a high distinction when we know what claims have been made for Geminiani, Tartini and others who are very much Leclair's inferiors. We cannot allow Leclair the same importance as Albinoni and Vivaldi because he was so much their beneficiary and because he did not publish as wide a range of forms as theirs; but he was undoubtedly both a genius of great imagination and also a magnificent craftsman.

No French School can be justly grouped around Leclair's concertos yet the fine works by Boismortier and Blavet now issued by Ricordi not only provide for cellists, bassoonists, flautists and oboists who are less richly served with concertos than are violinists and pianists, but prove that we have yet to explore a field of French concertos in which there are works as attractive as Telemann's, which they notably influenced, and sometimes quite as distinguished by technical skill. Concertos did not appeal to French ears until they framed notable solo parts.[1] A fine soloist might persuade an employer or patron to hear more concertos in a season than could have been heard at Versailles or at Philidor's concerts. Thus Blavet's excellent flute concerto in A minor was almost certainly played at Berny, where the composer directed music for the Count of Clermont who had a theatre, and we note fully Vivaldian proportions along with parts only for the solo, two violins and continuo. For still fewer instruments are the two little concertos by Boismortier subtitled 'Zampogna' (bagpipe) in which the two solo instruments supply their own tutti sections. (The first work is for flute and oboe with continuo, the second for two oboes, though violins may replace the wind instruments.) Indeed these works were included within the composer's Op. 23 sonatas, just as the splendid Boismortier cello or bassoon concerto in D

---

[1] French musicians and publishers were well enough informed about Italian concertos, but France lacked the many court orchestras of Germany or music clubs of England. A lengthy royal privilege of 1739 was granted to the piper Nicolas Chédeville enabling him to copy concertos by Corelli, Vivaldi, Albinoni, Veracini, Tartini and many others.

among his Op. 26 sonatas for those instruments; yet the Venetian structures, the closed initial tuttis and ritornelli, at once distinguishes them as concertos. Moreover the first movements and finales might be mistaken for Vivaldi's, but the middle movements are too plainly French to be mistaken for Telemann's. Blavet has a delicious pair of minor-major gavottes, worthy of Rameau at his best, and although Boismortier usually writes *Largo* or *Adagio*, what follows is a slow air in Lullian tradition, not an impassioned Venetian aria or chaconne.

Most French concertos are cast in the Vivaldian three movements, beginning with Boismortier's Op. 15 *Six Concerts pour 5 flûtes trav. sans basse*, 1727, and his further six for flute or oboe issued a year later. (I have not seen Carlsruhe MS. 49—Boismortier's four-movement work, *Concerto a quatre parties pour flûte, 2 violons, basse non chiffrée*.) Noticing the diversity and technical efficiency of these French concertos for small groups, and imagining Telemann's debt to them in his concerto-like suites for various combinations of players, we may wonder how rich a French School of concertos we should inherit if other composers of fine sonatas, such as Mondonville, Francoeur and Senaillé, had been urged to compose them.[1] Meanwhile we have compensation from Leclair, whose sonatas alone tell us that even in a galaxy of French concertists he would still have been the brightest star.

---

[1] A set of six by Gaviniès is less worth revival than any of the three concertos by his pupil, Leduc, happily reprinted in the *Collection Fernand Oubradous*, or of the six notably Vivaldian concertos for strings and flute by Michele Corrette.

CHAPTER XV

The Last Phase

After hearing the Mannheim orchestra Burney wrote:
'It has long seemed to me as if the variety, taste, spirit, and new effects produced by contrast, and the use of *crescendo* and *diminuendo* in these symphonies, had been of more service to instrumental music in a few years than all the dull and servile imitations of Corelli, Geminiani, and Handel had been in half a century.' (*History*, vol. ii.)

A genre is decadent when even great artists seek no important change in its growth, when their expression shapes itself within the inherited forms and their imagination is bent only to make the leaves more graceful, the blooms more colourful, the detail more neat or more elaborate. No years in the history of European music as a whole can be called the decadent period of the concerto grosso; we can only say that early forms passed through a decadent period in England long after they had been forgotten in Italy and that some of the late blooms were beautiful. In 1760 Walsh newly issued the instrumental parts of Vivaldi's concertos in volumes which contained those of symphonies (called overtures) by Stamitz, Abel, J. C. Bach, Richter, Norris, Herschel, Fischer and Gossec.[1] This longevity of early models, the welcome of Handel's concertos in Germany and the growth of academies of ancient music are all signs of a decadence, yet we prefer to speak of a last phase. If the concerto grosso had entered a period of general and

[1] There is a copy in the R.C.M. Library, London.

[322]

not just local decadence, it would have been noticeable in the work of Italian composers who did not migrate; yet in Italy, and at the hands of composers who were themselves symphonists, the concerto grosso grew into the symphony when Vivaldi's flesh was scarcely cold. Our ears alone cannot tell from symphonies some of the ripieno concertos composed between 1735 and 1755. Nor was there any general decadence of the solo concerto. It is true that the harpsichord concertos of C. P. E. Bach, J. C. Bach, Vanhall, Wagenseil and others seemed to be novelties in Vienna, Paris and cities which, unlike London, had not heard Handel's and Stanley's organ concertos and arrangements of string concertos 'for organ or harpsichord'; but the solo violin and flute concerto passed from the baroque to the classical period by stages as imperceptible as those by which the ripieno concerto passed to the symphony.

The symphonist composers of the last concerti grossi show both baroque and classical features within the same pieces. The quotations at Ex. 95 are from the *Concerti Grossi* of Francesco Barsanti 1690–c.1775) who was only five years younger than Bach and Handel. They were published at Edinburgh during 1743 in two sets; in the first set only horns and drums are added to the strings, and in the second set only two oboes and a trumpet. The wind instruments and the two timpani form a concertino, and because of this feature and others Barsanti can have been in no uncertainty as to whether he would call them concertos or symphonies; he did not score them for oboes *and* bassoons, or for trumpets *and* horns. In a work for the delectation of a North British music society before 1750 we expect to find a style such as Burney, a few decades later, would have thought proper for an academy of ancient music. The specified instrumentation is also baroque; but the scoring, the texture as distinct from the initial choice of instruments, is often that of early symphonies, for remote Scotland had early knowledge of Mannheim symphonies.

Barsanti came to England with Geminiani and was first engaged at London concerts and operas as a flautist and oboist. Soon after 1740 he settled in Edinburgh, for his 'Collection of Old Scots Tunes' is dedicated to Lady Erskine whereas his pieces for flute had been dedicated to the Earl of Burlington. The concerti grossi were his Op. 3, but within two years his Op. 4 appeared—nine overtures or symphonies. The Erskines were

95. A.

apostles of advanced musical fashion. According to Burney, Thomas Erskine, Earl of Kelly,[1] 'shut himself up at Mannheim with the elder Stamitz, and studied composition and practised the violin with such serious application, that, at his return to England, there was no part of theoretical or practical Music, in which he

[1] Not the husband of Lady Erskine, Barsanti's patroness. The Earl of Kelly was a bachelor.

was not equally versed with the greatest professors of his time'. Erskine's own Op. 1 is a set of symphonies published by Bremner, but they were offered as 'by J. Stamitz his pupil the Earl of Kelly and others' and share so many points of style that assignment is impossible by internal evidence.

Barsanti was not the only musician in these islands who composed both concerti grossi and symphonies. Probably the most popular one was the 'London Sammartini' to whom we shall refer as St. Martini. His name appears in at least five forms, and we choose the most English one because his brother in Milan is usually called Sammartini. Giuseppe St. Martini (c. 1693–1750) was admired by Quantz for his oboe playing in Milan where he composed at least one opera. He came to London in 1727 and stayed there for the rest of his life as a composer (chiefly of sonatas), teacher, performer, and eventually as director of the Prince of Wales's chamber music. Burney said that 'As a performer on the hautboy, Martini was undoubtedly the greatest that the world has ever known . . . by great study and application, and by some peculiar management of the reed, he contrived to produce such a tone as approached the nearest to the human voice of any we know.'[1] Yet Giuseppe was famous as a composer, so much so that 'Mr. St. Martino' and 'G. St. Martini' were taken to refer to him in publications which were really of works by his younger brother, Giovanni Battista (1698–1775) who stayed in his native Milan as organist and composer.

The common first initial, in Giuseppe and Giovanni, issues of the same works by different opus numbers, and the lack of dates on most publications by the brothers have made an unusual bibliographical confusion in which one has no desire to paddle, for it has baffled the clear heads of Saint-Foix and La Laurencie. The reader who seeks to know which opus numbers and dates should be assigned to one or other of the brothers may try to continue where Henry Mishkin leaves the problem in 'The Published

---

[1] We hear about 'management of the reed' in modern critiques but anybody who has tried to play an oboe knows that management of the breath as the servant of musical intelligence is what chiefly tells a good player. Critics sometimes imagine that double reeds must have been harsh and oppressive in works like Boyce's symphonies where oboes double violins; but until the end of the eighteenth century oboes were less penetrating than ours, having reeds shaped like those of a bassoon which are easy to control.

Instrumental Works of Giovanni Battista Sammartini' (*The Musical Quarterly*, vol. xlv, no. 3, July 1959). We shall speak here only of concertos which we know to have been by the London oboist, St. Martini. He was an artist of more limited scope than his brother. He 'composed to live', or at least to please amateur flautists, violinists and harpsichordists; but he had a high standard of workmanship and invention. The concertos which were published in England as St. Martini's are given here with the opus numbers originally attached to them, even where they are known to be incorrect.

Op. 2. 'VI Concerti Grossi con due Violini, Alto-Viola e Violoncello obligati e due Violini e Basso di Rinforzo. . . .'
(N.B. the Geminianian form of concertino. The set sold very well. First issue by Simpson 1736. An edition of 1738 is marked 'Scolp. da B. Fortier, Londra'. Two Simpson editions appeared in 1745 and Johnson printed a new one as late as 1760.)

Op. 5. 'Concerti Grossi a due Violini, Viole, e Violoncello obligati con due altri Violini e Basso di Ripieno. Composti da Giuseppe San Martini Opera Quinta. Questi Concerti sono composti dalle Sonate a due Violini e Basso dell Opera iii.' Walsh, 1760, printed along with the Op. 8 concertos.

(Not the original Walsh publication of the Op. 3 sonatas arranged as Geminianian concertos, but we have chosen the issue with this late date because the previous volume, advertised by Walsh as 'St. Martini's Concertos', bore on the title page 'Concerti Grossi. . . . Opera Sesta di Gio Batta St. Martini.' Mishkin shows that it contained work by both brothers.

Op. 8. 'Eight overtures Op. 7 and Six Grand Concertos for Violins, etc., in eight parts, Op. 8.' Walsh, 1752, 1754 and 1760. In 1790 Wright printed '8 Overtures Op. 7 and 6 Grand Concertos now first adapted for the organ, harpsichord, or piano forte by the Composer of "Young's Night Thoughts".' In 1795 appeared 'Martini's Grand Concertos Op. VIII and IX (?) now adapted for the Organ, etc.'

Op. 11. 'Six Grand Concertos', Johnson, *c.* 1756.

96.

A. *Allegro* [2nd. movt. after *Adagio e staccato* of 16 bars] St. Martini. Op. 7, No. 3.

Soli.

for 130 bars ending :—

Adagio

Segue finale

B. Finale. *Allegro*

In St. Martini we see the obverse of Barsanti. Whereas in Barsanti's concerti grossi the general style was 'ancient' and the scoring 'modern', St. Martini's outlay of instruments is 'ancient' yet the general style so advanced as to remind us of Haydn or Mozart. For instance Ex. 96A is very like the main allegro of Mozart's two-piano Adagio and Allegro in F minor-major, K.594, originally for a mechanical organ, and like some of the contrapuntal movements in Haydn's quartets and symphonies. (The Mozart piece was plainly an essay in the 'ancient' manner.) In no movement by St. Martini does the harmony suggest that the work was composed before Boyce's symphonies or Stanley's concertos, or by a musician who was Handel's junior by a mere eight

[327]

years. Yet the order and design of movements as well as Geminiani's quartet-concertino are conservative. The composer wanted
the favour of English music societies. He certainly sought popularity, for he destroyed both the plates and unsold copies of the
1738 edition of his Op. 3 sonatas and 'the gossip thus occasioned'
did much to boost a new issue by Johnson.

Hawkins says that the Op. 11 concertos were originally published in 1738 'for the author', but that 'in an evil hour'
Martini destroyed the plates. He died during the preparation of
Johnson's edition, which was in such demand that a new issue
was made in 1760. In this set the concertino is for two violins and
'cello, the viola being restored to the ripieno. Apart from the
grace notes and other features, which resemble the additions and
alterations made by Geminiani when he revised his concertos,
there are several indications of the effect of the imported symphonies. The bass of the concertino is not figured, and the texture
of the ripieno hardly needs the keyboard continuo although the
figures are supplied. Most of the concertos begin with a slow
introduction and a fugue, but the following middle movements
are mere gestures of a few bars, separating what is traditional
from what is more in favour with a wide audience—a really
long and attractive gigue and, as in several Handel overtures, a
final minuet.

The persistence of concerti grossi leads us to suppose that the
new symphonies took as long to arrive in this country as the
concerto grosso itself. On the contrary, the Mannheim symphonies were in London almost as soon as in Vienna, Paris and
Amsterdam. Corelli's concertos had come as a new genre; the
symphonies were only a transfer of Italian overtures from theatre
music to chamber music. Three-movement overtures had been
composed for the English theatre within a few years of Purcell's
death. Some eighteenth-century English composers, including
Maurice Greene, took care to distinguish between 'Overture' and
'Sinfonia', using the first title only when the opening movement
was of the slow-fast French kind, but on London programmes and
title-pages both types were called overtures. Did Haydn see his
London Symphonies advertised as 'Grand Overtures', and did he
comment?

German symphonies entered London programmes late in the

1750s and flooded them during the 1760s; then Bach and Abel were adding to their number and a whole school of minor native composers—Rush, Bates, Collett, Norris, etc.—were composing overtures and songs for ballad operas, plays and entertainments at Vauxhall or Marylebone. Assisted by the publishers, they put to concert use as symphonies what had been originally composed as overtures for these entertainments. We should not judge them merely from the specimens which we value most, such as the Eight Symphonies of Boyce which date from the mid-1750s. The first movements of these are either in binary design with a double bar, or are 'overtures' in the stricter sense. We most easily trace the effect of the symphony upon the concerto in English composers; but we also notice as in no continental music except Sammartini's the effect of the concerto grosso upon the symphony. Arne's overture to *Alfred*, which may have been composed before 1740 but cannot have been composed later, is enough to verify this point, for it contains frequent passages for solo violin and for a concertino of oboes and bassoons.

The passing of the older kind of concerto grosso in London, while it still formed the staple repertory of 'Country Concerts', was expedited by the favour which Handel brought to its progeny, the organ concerto. From about 1740 to 1750 organ concertos reached their maximum popularity, though only Handel's and Stanley's are worth hearing today. As we have seen in St. Martini's case, publishers continued until the end of the century to issue concerti grossi arranged 'for organ or harpsichord', that is to say with a two-stave keyboard part instead of the concertino. Johnson published the organ-harpsichord concertos of the Rev. William Felton, said by Burney to have been a fine keyboard player. His Op. 1, 2, 4, 5 and 6 are all sets of 'Six concerto's for the organ or harpsichord with instrumental parts', and his Op. 7 bears the same title but contains eight concertos. Felton's Op. 1 was issued in 1744 and his Op. 7 in 1762, and the sets between them share their pretty complacence. We should note the effect of using the organ or the harpsichord as a solo instrument. The organ was formerly the continuo for the ripieno. Was the solo organ also the only keyboard continuo instrument, did it change places with the harpsichord and let that instrument accompany the ripieno, or did the ripieno dispense with all keyboard continuo

[329]

except an organ bass maintained *tasto solo*? This is an important matter in the change of style from baroque concerto to classical symphony.

Soon after 1760 the keyboard continuo may often have been omitted, or used only for certain sections of works when the conductor, directing from the keyboard, felt a desire to play. The conservative Avison gives us an interesting piece of evidence to support this belief. In the section of his *Essay* which deals with the harpsichord (p. 117 of the first edition), he says: 'This is only to be used in the chorus.' As he is concerned with concertos he must be referring to the ripieno, and we may therefore assume that the concertino was unaccompanied at Newcastle in 1752. Otherwise one would suppose that it became casual in symphonies but persisted in concertos *because* the solo instrument or concertino needed harmonic and rhythmic support whereas the 'chorus' did not.

Concertos for non-keyboard solo instruments, especially the favourite flute, also speeded the passing of the older designs, for nearly all the concertos for solo instruments favoured the Vivaldian three-movement scheme and, in England, very short slow movements. The best seem to have been those by Pepusch's pupil William Babell (*c.* 1690–1723) whose earliest reputation in London was as a harpsichordist.[1] It has been claimed that Babell led the fashion of arranging airs from operas as harpsichord lessons. He was also an organist and a violinist in the royal band. His works were in favour on the Continent and are found in libraries as far apart as Paris, Amsterdam and Hamburg. Unfortunately neither York Minster Library nor the Henry Watson Library at Manchester possesses the essential solo parts of his 'Concertos in 7 parts. The first was for violins and small flute and the two last for violins and two flutes, Op. 3', published by Walsh and Hare *c.* 1730, but the string parts quoted at Ex. 97 and 98 show the Vivaldian three-movement and ritornello style of the German solo concertos with which he may have become acquainted through Pepusch.

It is not true that where symphonies were played the older concertos disappeared. It would be more nearly true if applied

[1] The Swedish concertist and symphonist, Johan Helmich Roman, was also a pupil of Pepusch in London for at least a year.

only to Italy and France, but in France the concerto grosso never took a firm hold, and elsewhere 'ancient' and 'modern' were both enjoyed. In England and Germany the growth of a historical culture of music would have been evident without the testimony of writers. When the Academy of Ancient Music in London, which met at the Crown and Anchor, was instituted in 1710, it naturally performed nothing by Handel the modern. Within a few years of his death, however, Handel could 'assume the dignity of an Ancient' (as Johnson said of Shakespeare), although he was honoured chiefly by an entirely different series of meetings which were begun in 1776 and called the 'King's Concerts' or 'Concerts of Ancient Music', being regularly attended by George III. There were similar societies in Germany. Through Mozart we know much about the one organized in Vienna by Baron van Swieten, who founded it in 1778 immediately he arrived back from the Prussian court where he had been ambassador. At Potsdam there had been too much ancient music and too little modern—a condition that was probably to Van Swieten's taste, for he heard and requisitioned plenty of music by Handel and plenty of old-fashioned concertos.

The least conservative centres of music—those in which one hears of no cult of ancient music but of continued acclaim for the new—were Venice, Milan and the Italian cities which had enjoyed the new concertos of a series of violin virtuosi, each more astonishing than the last. When histories of music reach the middle of the eighteenth century they draw our attention to Mannheim and Vienna, and we tend to forget Italy except as the home of opera. Vivaldi is the last considerable Italian instrumental composer we have in mind unless we are fortunate enough to have heard and valued sonatas, concertos and symphonies by Locatelli, Sammartini, Rinaldo di Capua, Galuppi and Pergolesi.

'There are few phases in the history of art so little explored yet so categorically settled in manuals and even in learned dissertations as the preclassical symphony and sonata. Our knowledge of this field was until recently restricted to Riemann's discovery of the so-called Mannheim school; but even this school has not been properly investigated and so is popularly supposed to be an autonomous German school in the Palatinate, whereas actually its members formed a colony of Austrian, Sudeten-Bohemian, and Italian musicians whose activity was a logical chapter in the movement which started in Italy and received encouragement from northern Germany.'[1]

Since Riemann, other writers have put forward Mysliweczek, Rinaldo di Capua, Sammartini or Galuppi as 'the father of the symphony', and Pincherle asks what changes in their forms, as distinct from their style, gives them more right than Vivaldi to the title. The best supplement to Riemann's work is still Torrefranca's article of 1913 'Le Origini della Sinfonia',[2] which was continued two years later and dramatically vindicated by Saint-Foix's commentary[3] on the newly discovered Blancheton Collection of Italian symphonies and concertos in the library of the Paris Conservatoire.[4] Torrefranca recognizes that nothing is gained by seeking the first 'real', 'true' or 'genuine' symphony.

One can hardly describe the last phase of the concerto grosso without touching upon the early history of the symphony, but a first point to be made clear is the uselessness of saying that the general style of a work is concerto-like or symphonic. Concertos during the phase of transition often proceeded by *Fortspinnung*, but sometimes they were largely motivic, and sometimes had long movements built from only a few clearly defined themes. Haydn, Mozart and Beethoven can supply us with each of these three types of movement, and it is fallacious to put forward, say, the highly motivic type or the type with few themes as belonging to *the* symphony while relegating the more spreading type with a plethora of musical ideas to *the* concerto. Still more should we guard against regarding one type as superior to or more advanced than another. With minor talents the motivic integration of a piece may constitute an attempt to cover poverty of invention; with Beethoven it may accompany great fecundity of invention, as we can see in the first movement of the D major sonata, Op. 10, No. 3, and in others of that period, or in the first movement of the *Eroica* symphony.

[1] P. H. Lang, *Music in Western Civilization*, New York, 1941.
[2] *RMI*, vol. xx, 1913 and vol. xxii, 1915.
[3] G. de Saint-Foix, 'La chronologie de l'œuvre instrumentale de Jean-Baptiste Sammartini', *SMIG*, vol. xv, January 1914, p. 309.
[4] See Lionel de la Laurencie, *Inventaire critique du Fonds Blancheton*, two vols., Paris, 1930. (Vol. ii, pp. 29–47 deals with Sammartini.)

We are thus forced to recall a point that we made early in this book. It is as profitless to seize upon one composer as the father of the symphony as of the concerto, or upon a specific work as the first 'true' concerto or symphony. An initial tutti closing in the tonic and followed by concertino or solo passages was one defining but not obligatory feature of the concerto; is there a defining feature of the symphony? Vivaldi composed works which are called sinfonias on some manuscripts and concertos on others; at least one title-page shows his crossing out of 'sinfonia', and another some corrections which turned solo parts into tutti.[1] What made Vivaldi and others choose between the two titles? No good answer has yet been made to that question. Nineteenth-century editions of reference books regarded a clear theme (as distinct from *Fortspinnung* and added figurations), introduced after the exposition had established the dominant key, as a defining point of 'sonata form'; but when the writers looked for this new theme they had to admit that Haydn did not always set it in clear contrast with previous materials. In Parry's words, it sometimes occurred 'almost like an afterthought' at the very end of a Haydn exposition. This feature is certainly not a defining feature of the symphonies produced at Mannheim and Vienna during the middle years of the eighteenth century. Burney's comment upon their expressive range and their style of performance includes no comment upon their forms. He merely rated them higher than the epigonic concertos played in England; but once the Mannheim style of performance became known it must certainly have affected orchestras in Italian theatres and the performance of works not actually called symphonies. Just as it is inconceivable that Albinoni's and Vivaldi's concertos were played without a new fire and passion so it is inconceivable (merely during examination of printed music) that the concertos of Italians after Vivaldi were not performed more and more as the Mannheimers performed symphonies.

Our primary concern here is the history of the genre, not an account of all known composers of concertos. We shall have little or nothing to say about most concertists, however prolific, who did not advance the forms of concerto movements beyond those of Vivaldi's first sets. Therefore we pass by one or two admirable

[1] See Pincherle's *Vivaldi*, English version, pp. 167–82.

composers. Scarlatti's twelve *Sinfonie di concerto grosso* are also of little importance for our purpose, but they should be briefly discussed because they are unusual and because the British Museum (Royal Library, g.1052) has a manuscript copy that was sent by a friend in Italy to Benjamin Cooke. We have Dent's expert assurance that 'each is numbered in the hand-writing of the composer',[1] who sometimes signs his name on the title-pages with the added 'Cavaliere'. These works and the string concertos, 'Sonate a quattro', may have been com-posed originally for the Arcadian Academy in Rome to which Corelli, Pasquini and Scarlatti were all elected members in 1706. The date is given on the first page of the first sinfonia thus: 'Cominciate al Po. Giugnio 1715. Sinfonia Prima, di concerto grosso con due Flauti.' Only the first has two flutes; the third and Nos. 5–12 add one flute to the strings, the second adds a trumpet and a flute, the fourth an oboe and a flute. There is no Vivaldian ritornello technique about these pieces although they have lyrical slow movements. They follow a unique scheme of two composite movements: (a) a short spirited allegro ending at a half close, leading to an adagio in saraband tempo, leading to a fast and lengthy fugue in the style of Handel's fugues on two subjects; (b) an adagio which begins and continues like the slow middle movements of other concertos but proves introductory to the final allegro. The general style is decidedly conservative, but the works are remarkable for the persistent development of motives and the composer's unwillingness to present five disjoined movements. The sections are not thematically related.

The first considerable virtuoso and concertist after Vivaldi was Tartini. All the Tartini Concertos which one has heard or seen are in three movements and follow Albinoni's and Vivaldi's simplest procedures. Several have been recorded recently, includ-ing some for solo flute as well as some for solo violin. Their terse rhythms make them superficially attractive, but one soon tires of them. When harmonic progressions are unorthodox the listener is not always able to tell if the composer is wilfully leaving well-trodden paths that he knows thoroughly or if he is hitting and sometimes missing because he has lost his way. Vivaldi himself sometimes fails to integrate his forms and makes us feel that his

[1] Edward J. Dent, *Alessandro Scarlatti—his Life and Works*, London, 1905.

chromatic progressions are insecure, and one sympathizes with Avison's attitude to Vivaldi although one does not share it. Tartini, though a great violinist and teacher, was rarely as strong a composer as Vivaldi at his weakest, and although his violin technique attracts our interest we cannot think of him as an orchestral genius comparable with Vivaldi. As a concertist he is simply a follower who does not advance the early Venetian forms beyond a more persistent recurrence of an engaging theme than is found even in Albinoni. Tartini's concertos were published in three books by Le Cène during 1730 and were called *Concerti a cinque e sei stromenti*, but there are said to be many more than these. The fact that the Grauns were Tartini's pupils may explain why printed copies of his concertos are found in German libraries along with some of his manuscripts. We need only notice one point about Tartini—his habit in fast movements of economizing ideas and composing entirely by repetitions and sequences of his one, two or three ideas, which he often asserts without filling the rests between them.

Veracini is even less important than Tartini. No printed sets of his concertos have been found. He may have written few or many. The only specimen which the present writer has seen was in manuscript parts at Florence. It gave the strange impression of being earlier than any concerto by Vivaldi, yet Veracini was still alive in 1745, in which year Burney heard him as leader of the orchestra in a concert at Hickford's Rooms.

Two Italians of the generation following Vivaldi's, both symphonists as well as concertists, notably help us to trace some of the links from the last phase of the concerto grosso to the beginnings of the classical symphony and solo concerto. They are Locatelli and G. B. Sammartini of Milan. Pietro Locatelli (1695–1764) came from Bergamo but was a pupil of Corelli in Rome. He travelled as a virtuoso violinist whose technical feats caused as much admiration and censure as did Paganini's a century later. They are reflected in the unprecedented twenty-four *Caprices*, which were published along with twelve concerti grossi in an Op. 3 entitled *L'arte del Violino*. Locatelli settled from 1729 in Amsterdam, and all his printed compositions except Op. 1 must therefore have been composed at Amsterdam for dissemination and for the concerts he began there. Arend Koole[1] gives a full catalogue of the library which Locatelli gathered at his house in Amsterdam. It included not only a valuable collection of instrumental music but also many books which indicate that their owner was a man of wide culture and interests, able to read Latin, French, Spanish, German, Dutch and English as well as his native language.

Burney's comment that Locatelli was 'a voluminous composer of Music that excites more surprise than pleasure' has been since echoed because the caprices seem the prototypes of showy violin studies which well merit Burney's comment. Like some passages in Locatelli's sonatas they draw attention to multiple-stopping, arpeggiando harmony, extremely difficult bowing and 'tricks' generally. An Op. 9 which has been lost and was entitled *L'arte di nuova modulazione; caprices énigmatiques* may have been extremely bizarre, but there seems little reason to regard Locatelli as a charlatan if he intended these simply as studies. Dittersdorf in his autobiography[2] specially commended Locatelli's works to students of the violin 'for practice, not for show pieces', and there is nothing of the charlatan in Locatelli's concertos. All were printed by Le Cène at Amsterdam:

Op. 1. *Concerti Grossi.* (Twelve concertos published in 1721 before the composer himself had settled in Amsterdam.)

Op. 3. The twelve concerti grossi in *L'arte del violino*, 1733.

Op. 4. Six symphonies (called *Introduzioni teatrali*) and six concertos, 1735.

Op. 7. *Concerti a quattro*, a set of six, 1741.

Op. 10. *Contrasto armonico; concerti a quattro.* (Date unknown.)

Some of the concertos in the first two sets are issued in a modern edition by Zanibon (Padua) edited by E. Bonelli. Their style is what we should expect from a pupil of Corelli who outstripped his master and admired Vivaldi and Leo. The movements are longer than Corelli's and fewer in number, but they are

---

[1] Koole, *Leven en Werken van Pietro Antonio Locatelli da Bergamo*, Amsterdam, University Press, 1949.

[2] *The Autobiography of Karl Ditters von Dittersdorf*, translated by A. D. Coleridge, London, 1896.

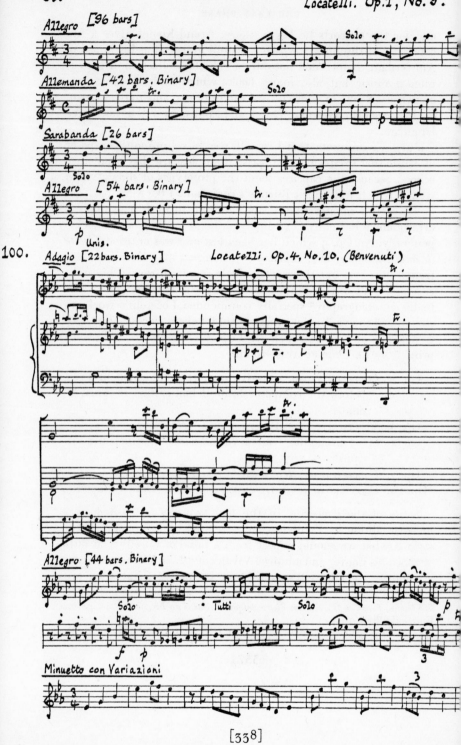

rarely as long as Vivaldi's, and at this stage Locatelli showed impatience with slow movements unless they came at the opening, not as introductions but as full binary first movements. 'Middle' slow movements are never of more than 8–12 bars, usually in the relative minor. These concertos contain no example of the Albinonian chaconne slow movement or of the Vivaldian pathetic aria, both of which Locatelli used later. His early manner may be judged from the extracts at Ex. 99 which gives the openings of movements in Op. 1, No. 9. However great the debt of this Op. 1 to Corelli we certainly cannot call it one of 'the dull and servile imitations' disliked by Burney.

Yet how great a development is observed as we pass to Locatelli's Op. 4! Here in 1735 is a rhythmic and harmonic verve which we do not expect before we reach music composed by Haydn in the second half of the century. This concerto (Ex. 100) was composed before Handel's Op. 6 and only fourteen years after the Brandenburg concertos. Vivaldi was still active. The brilliantly elaborate variations of the finale would cause surprise at a public performance, and they will surprise the solo violinist who does not already know the work; but it is the length of the first two movements and their wealth of ideas that seems to bring us almost into the classical period. The chief evidence of the early date is the absence of a clearly defined main 'second group' in the dominant.

Among the concertists discussed in this book Locatelli is one of the few whose music should have early consideration for reprinting and more frequent performance. The remark is not cynical. Most music published in this century or any other is by minor talents, and the student of a particular genre or period need not lose his scale of values merely because he recognizes anew the historical significance of certain works. It is a pity that Locatelli was ever thought freakish or showy, and that so little supremely great music was composed between Bach's last years and Haydn's middle years, for not many listeners are ready to give great attention to a composer who is vaguely called galant, rococo or pre-classical when their ears pall so quickly even of much C. P. E. Bach at a time, and when it seems incredible that visitors to Mannheim could tolerate more than three symphonies by Stamitz or Holzbauer in one evening. Locatelli and Sammartini were

101.

Locatelli. Op. 7, No. 12 [Brussels, Tr. Jenkins]
Concerto for 4 violins. There are no
ripieno violins, but two viola parts.

better composers than most of their German and Czech contemporaries, and both need thorough exploration. Lacking opportunity to undertake it, one can suppose from the few Locatelli
works which one has seen that we could postulate three periods,
as we do with Beethoven. Two of them are represented by the
two concertos already quoted, the third by the work quoted at
Ex. 101.

At first this concerto may seem less interesting than the specimen from Op. 4. Young listeners who have come to love the first
movements of Beethoven's first eight symphonies are sometimes
secretly disappointed at their first experience of the first movement of the ninth. If they immediately recognize a greater
imagination in its sublime economy, control and spread than they
do in previous symphonic movements, then they are enviably
intelligent young listeners. Despite an apparent simplification,
the movements of Locatelli's final period show a similar change.
The first snippet at Ex. 101 is proof of Locatelli's harmonic
range, yet in his last concertos he withholds modulation, retards
chord change, and builds by persistent motives and few themes in
order to achieve big paragraphs and large-scale design. The whole
of the first movement which begins as at Ex. 101 is derived from
the few materials of the initial tutti, some brisures and bariolage
for the solo violins, and the little extra figures shown at Ex. 101(a).
The slow movement has now become long and rhapsodic, opposing
an 'inexorable' ritornello (unison effect between violins and bass)
to a pleading and ornate aria which is shared by all four solo
violins. The finale is a rondo with only two themes, the episodes
being of motivic development. Again one stresses the mistake of
calling the *particular* means of composition 'a symphonic style'
rather than 'a concerto style'. Some classical symphonies and
sonatas are taut, some show a rich spread of ideas and some
concerto movements by Mozart and Beethoven are as compact as
any in their symphonies.

In his last sets of concertos Locatelli used only the three-
movement scheme, the finale often being a minuet with variations—a feature which survived until Mozart's early work. Most
of us cannot avoid listening to Locatelli's and Sammartini's first
movements with our minds prejudiced by the first-movement
plan of the classical epoch. Repetition, *wholly in the tonic* and in
the middle of a movement, of what sounds like the classical exposition seems queer. Bach could write a satisfying long movement by following the cycle of keys, setting out towards the
dominant and returning via the subdominant, with the main
theme coming at least four times—in tonic, dominant, subdominant, and again in tonic; sometimes the third occurrence was in a
different mode (minor or major) from that of the piece as a whole,

and sometimes the main theme was not finally stated in the tonic. We cannot but wonder why the transition from this high baroque smoothness to the ease of classical 'sonata form' incurred growing pains which are made obvious by the persistence of baroque full closes at the ends of sections. This impression is like the one which we receive from movements in Vivaldi's concertos which proceed like classical structures and lead us to expect a classical recapitulation, or perhaps a variant in which the order of expository ideas is reversed; instead one hears an improvisatory finish which does not seem weighty enough to balance the exposition. Binary movements with double bars better satisfy our sense of balance, and we ask: 'Why did it not occur to composers merely to omit the double bar and insert "a middle section"?' Composers whose best work was written between 1750 and 1775 need very special sympathy, especially when they are most admirably adventurous.

After Saint-Foix's valuable chronology, a general study of the music of G. B. Sammartini (1698–75) is much to be desired; its accomplishment will be a difficult task, not only because of the muddle of opus numbers and the confusion of his works with his brother's, but because copies of his sonatas, concertos and symphonies are widely dispersed in French, German, Dutch and Italian libraries. The following are the only London publications of concertos attributed to Sammartini and considered to be his by Saint-Foix, unless otherwise stated:

1751 Walsh. 'Six Concertos in 8 parts for Violins, French horns, hoboys, &c., composed by St. Martini and Hasse.' Nos. 2 and 3 are identified as Hasse's.

1755 Walsh. 'Concerti Grossi. . . . Opera Sesta di Gio Batta St. Martini.' This collection has already been mentioned as containing arrangements of sonatas by the London St. Martini. The items which have a minuet finale are probably all from sonatas by G. B. Sammartini of Milan.

1757 Walsh. 'Concerti grossi con due violini, viola e violoncello obligati, con due altri violini e basso di ripieno. . . . Questi Concerti sono composti da diversi Notturni del St. Martini da Francesco Barsanti.' Both brothers composed *sonate notturne*. The designation being new to

[342]

Londoners, Walsh explained it on a title-page of sonatas by G. B. Sammartini in 1762: 'Six Sonatas called Notturnis in 4 parts for a German Flute and two Violins with a Bass. . . .' The Geminianian concerti grossi advertised in 1757 were arrangements by Barsanti of such sonatas, but Saint-Foix is certain that none of them was by G. B. Sammartini.

1764 Bremner. 'Three Concertos for Violins, French Horns, etc. Compos'd by Sigr. Gio Battista St. Martini of Milan Opera 11da. N.B. These concertos may be play'd as Sonatas by leaving out the French horn parts.' (The works might as well have been called symphonies.)

1766 Bremner. 'An Overture and Two Grand Concertos Composed by Sigr. Gio Battista St. Martini of Milan. Approved and Recommended by Sigr. F. Giardini. Opera 4.'

Saint-Foix had 'the gravest suspicions concerning the authenticity, at least in their present form, of the Two Grand Concertos', and feared a fraud on the part of Giardini, who may have been abetted by Bremner in fobbing off his own work as Sammartini's.

Apart from these, the only works by Sammartini which the present author has inspected are those in the Blancheton Collection and those which have been transcribed, chiefly by Newell Jenkins, and reprinted in modern pocket scores. They are enough to show that, however many concerti grossi were composed after Sammartini's, his fully represent the last phase. Mishkin's internal evidence in support of Saint-Foix's doubts concerning Walsh's 1787 publication is worth quoting, because it tells us what distinguished Sammartini from older composers, even from his brother in London:

'The writing . . . is not in the galant language of G. B. The use of a binary-allegro procedure, the vigorous concerto grosso style of string figuration, the characteristic motivic patterns of a Baroque cast to "animate" inner voices, and the occasional expositions in trio sonata counterpoint relate this more to the Baroque quality of Giuseppe's Opus 3 than to the style pursued by G.B., in spite of

[343]

the superficially modern aspect of the two-movement structure and the implied *sensibilité* of the tempo indications.'

One has seen no work by Sammartini that is known to have been composed before 1740. He may have begun in a musical language that Burney would have thought 'ancient', but after 1740 he is definitely *galant* and often *empfindsam*. Because Gluck, both by his own declaration and by the evidence of his music, greatly valued his four years of study with Sammartini and learnt how to sustain long movements, many writers have considered Sammartini to be the most important composer of the short pre-classical stage of music except C. P. E. Bach. The reservation may have come through biographers of Haydn, who is said to have denied that he was influenced by Sammartini and 'owed everything to C. P. E. Bach'. There might have been no reservation if historians had thought of Mozart rather than of Haydn, for Mozart was certainly influenced by Sammartini, both indirectly through J. C. Bach and directly through the divertimenti and concertini[1] which were obviously the models for Mozart's early quartets and symphonies. Count Firmian, the governor of Lombardy, first introduced Mozart to Sammartini in Milan during 1770. Mozart's first string quartet was begun at Lodi on the way from Milan to Parma, and some Mozart biographers speak of 'The Milanese Quartets' when they refer to K.155–60. Mozart was also influenced by Toeschi, the only well-known Italian composer engaged at Mannheim, and he mentions Toeschi more than once in his letters. Toeschi, born in Padua, was surely himself influenced by Sammartini.

Sammartini remained all his life as organist and church composer in his native Milan, but his chamber and purely instrumental music was greatly admired in Vienna. Milan was the headquarters of the Austrian Government of Lombardy. Naturally favour with the many musical aristocrats of Austria had been one way to general fame in the German States from before the ascendance

---

[1] The word 'concertino' was used by Sammartini, Pergolesi and others to indicate what the seventeenth century would have called a 'concerto a quattro'. It is usually a string quartet, and it can be regarded as the beginning of the classical quartet, from which it differs by retaining the cembalo part. This means that a 'concertino' could be played as a domestic sonata, either without 'cello or without a keyboard instrument. On the other hand it could be played by a string orchestra. There are several 'concertini' in the Blancheton Collection.

of the concerto grosso, but it was evidently a very quick way from about 1730 onwards, to the benefit both of Sammartini and of his pupil Gluck. Sammartini's first four-movement symphony, which was performed at Milan in 1734, was received with such extraordinary enthusiasm that both it and other symphonies by Sammartini were in constant request for some years by Count Morzin and other grandees.[1] In symphonies, sonatas and chamber works for few instruments Sammartini had a clearer grip of design than in concertos. He tried to fertilize the concerto by some of the principles which guided him in these other works, but the provision of tutti and solo sections, as well as combined sections, complicated his work by giving him many choices of procedure among which he did not secure the ideal, at least in the important opening movement.

Before examining a concerto by Sammartini we should study carefully the first movement of one of his symphonies, but as that would be too long for much music quotation, we shall instead use the first movement of a concertino. A concertino by Sammartini gives us a symphony in miniature, and enables us to see why we can regard his concertos neither as belonging to the old tradition nor as being the first of a new harvest of concertos that were influenced by symphonies.

We notice from Ex. 102 that when Sammartini is not committed to composing under the title 'Concerto' or 'Concerto Grosso', his first-movement design is exactly what we suggested to be the most obvious transition from the longer and more elaborate baroque allemande or initial allegro to the classical first movement. Free development, beginning with thematic reference, follows the double bar, and leads to a reprise of the opening which is not, however, dramatically prepared or high-lighted. The finale is an almost similar construction, but there is no 'middle section'; after the double bar it goes straight to the reprise. The second movement is a binary andante—a 'sonata' exposition and recapitulation in which no idea in the second group is a clearly defined theme.

Sammartini's general style in a concerto is like that of the symphonies and quartets—nothing resembles extemporization or

[1] Evidence collected by Torrefranca, op. cit., and by Robert Sondheimer in *G. B. Sammartini*, Zeitschrift fur Musikwissenschaft, 1920.

Fortspinnung. A main theme is followed by sequences and shapely, well-phrased figurations; all is clear, neat, and easy to analyse. Yet the design as a whole is less satisfactory than that of first movements in his symphonies. After an initial tutti on such a scale that it suggests a first movement as long as one of Mozart's, the first solo section begins with new material; but the figuration is soon punctuated by the ubiquitous second idea of the initial tutti and develops like the solo exposition of a classical concerto, reaching the equivalent of the classical full close with shake in the dominant followed by a full ritornello from the initial tutti; but Sammartini does not maintain this ritornello. After six bars it is abandoned for new, lightly accompanied solo bravura, which is

developed by sequences at great length (47 bars) passing slowly
back to the tonic. Thus what promises to be the first full ritornello
of a classical concerto resembles the 'free fantasia' in the middle
of a sonata first-movement. At the reprise the solo rests until the
end of the movement, which is only 28 bars ahead, so that an
expected recapitulation proves to be only a truncated form of
the initial tutti.

It is not suggested that Sammartini was aware of groping
towards J. C. Bach's, Wagenseil's or Mozart's plan for the first
movement of a solo concerto, but that we, knowing the later
organization, feel that the implications of the initial tutti go un-
fulfilled, and we wonder why he did not simply compose a symphony or an ensemble sonata with solo, as Schumann and Grieg
did in piano concertos which dispense with the classical initial
tutti and its procession of ritornello ideas. It is fashionable in
some quarters nowadays to denounce as unscholarly the regret
that an artist did not reach the design of a later generation, and
to regard historical interest not merely as compensatory for but
identical with aesthetic satisfaction. The present writer faces daily
an Early English window of two lancets under one curved dripstone. The form is sufficiently infrequent to interest the connoisseur, but it remains ugly to eyes which imagine the simple
piece of tracery that is lacking between the heads of the lancets
and the point of the dripstone, and one asks why what was introduced only a few years afterwards did not commend itself to the
builders. Sammartini's work is never ugly, but his neat, lively
style and his feeling for orchestral texture cannot disguise the fact
that in his main concerto movements he was trying to graft
features of the baroque concerto on to features of the new symphony, and that the forms of these movements as wholes are
inferior to their parts. The same judgement can fairly be passed
upon the interesting but often sprawling movements in some of
C. P. E. Bach's keyboard concertos, for he seems to be using
'sonata' and 'rondo' principles with no basic plan of tonalities.
In short, both these great men were dealing with the last phase
of one set of concerto designs and the first phase of another.

The concerto grosso in Germany lasted longest in the Berlin
court and in Telemann's Hamburg. Elsewhere such composers as
Graupner and Zelenka worked for young and progressive patrons.

Graupner was only two years older than Bach and Handel, but unlike those sturdy giants he was anxious to please a private employer at Darmstadt. One intends no adverse judgement, for Graupner seems to have been an admirable man and was among the better musicians of his day, and in following new fashions he sincerely shared the ideals of his employers.

For smoothness, neat scoring and immediate attractiveness the Graupner concerto from which Ex. 63 is quoted is the best in Schering's collection; it is also the one which could be most easily passed off as an early symphony by Monn, Wagenseil or the elder Stamitz. Monn at Vienna and Stamitz at Mannheim were composing concert symphonies in the 1740s, and the new style had been accepted in most of Germany long before 1750. Riemann's *Musikgeschichte in Beispielen* includes a symphony by Graupner which no average English student could be expected to attribute to an exact contemporary of Bach and Handel. The same remark, however, could be made about many of Rameau's longer instrumental pieces, especially the scene-setting prologues to ballets like *Naïs* and *Zoroastre* which come as late as 1749. (Rameau was two years older than Bach and Handel.)

In England alone the oldest design of concerto, either with Corelli's string concertino or with the concertino replaced by organ or harpsichord, could frequently have been heard along with symphonies from Mannheim, Paris or Vienna. Old-style concertos were still being reissued for the music societies and academies of ancient music while J. C. Bach was delighting audiences with galant concertos for harpsichord or fortepiano in the styles through which Mozart was soon to achieve greatness. More than this, Vienna heard the very greatest of Mozart's piano concertos from 1784 onwards while London publishers were still printing keyboard arrangements of concerti grossi; yet in England as elsewhere the performance of concertos, if not their composition, was affected by the styles of the new symphonies. We can judge this matter at first hand from a gramophone record which gives us the original version of a Geminiani concerto and also its composer's 'corrected and revised' version of some thirty years later.[1] The oldest forms of baroque concerto, even the concerto

[1] OL.50129. The Boyd Neel Orchestra, directed by Thurston Dart, playing the original and revised versions of Geminiani's op. 3, no. 3, concerto in E minor.

grosso for strings with continuo, outlived the baroque style. The baroque concerto did not die, for its life flowed into the first concert symphonies and into preclassical concertos. If I strove to close this account of the baroque concerto with an elegant valediction my pains would be misapplied. The list of composers and works has already gone past the years of Mozart's childhood, and although there is no clear line of demarcation between the baroque concerto and the preclassical, the account should surely close before it leads to an examination of C. P. E. Bach, J. C. Bach, Wagenseil, Raupach, Honauer, Schobert and Vanhall, whose concertos, whatever they retain of the baroque, are best regarded as the foothills to Mozart's peaks.

Bibliography

This list of books has been strictly limited to sources consulted or quoted during the writing of this book. The exclusion of a title does not signify that the present writer doubts its value or its bearing upon the baroque period or the baroque concerto. General histories of music and standard works of reference are not mentioned except when they were found specially useful during the writing of one or more of the chapters.

Abbreviations

AM	*Acta Musicologica*
AMW	*Archiv für Musikwissenschaft*
AMZ	*Allgemeine musikalische Zeitung*
DDT	*Denkmäler deutscher Tonkunst*
IMG	*Internationale Musik Gesellschaft*
JAMS	*Journal of the American Musicological Society*
MA	*The Musical Antiquary*
MfM	*Monatshefte für Musikgeschichte*
MGG	*Die Musik in Geschichte und Gegenwart*
ML	*Music and Letters*
MMR	*The Monthly Musical Record*
MQ	*The Musical Quarterly*
MT	*The Musical Times*
RM	*La Revue Musicale*
P(R)MA	*Proceedings of the (Royal) Musical Association*
RMI	*Rivista Musicale Italiana*
SIMG	*Sammelbände der internationalen Musikgesellschaft*
VfM	*Vierteljahrschrift für Musikwissenshaft* (1884–93)
ZIM	*Zeitschrift der internationalen Musikgesellschaft*

THE BAROQUE PERIOD AND CONCERTO IN GENERAL

Bonaccorsi, A., 'Contributo alla storia del concerto grosso', *RMI*, xxix, 1932.

Boyden, D., 'The Violin and its Technique in the Eighteenth Century', *MQ*, xxxvi, 1950.

Bukofzer, M., *Music in the Baroque Era*, New York, 1947.

Burney, C., *A General History of Music (1776–89)*, ed. C. Mercer, in 2 vols., New York, 1935.

The Present State of Music in France and Italy, London, 1771.

The Present State of Music in Germany, London, 1773.

Carse, A., *The Orchestra in the Eighteenth Century*, Cambridge, 1940.

Clercx, S., *Le Baroque et la musique*, Brussels, 1948.

Dent, E. J., *Alessandro Scarlatti*, London, 1905.

Engel, H., *Das Instrumentalkonzert*, Leipzig, 1932.

Haas, R., *Die Musik des Barocks* (Bückens Handbuch der Musikwissenschaft), Potsdam, 1928.

Krüger, W., *Das Concerto grosso in Deutschland* (orig. dissertation, Berlin, 1932), Wolfenbüttel, 1937.

La Laurencie, L. de, *Le Goût musical en France*, Paris, 1905.

L'école française de violon. Paris, 1922.

Mattheson, J., *Das neu-eröffnete orchestre*, Hamburg, 1713.

Der volkommene Capellmeister (Hamburg, 1739), Bärenreiter facs. reprint, Kassel, 1934.

Grundlage einer Ehrenpforte (Hamburg, 1740), M. Schneider's edition, Berlin, 1910.

Mersmann, H., 'Die Kammermusik', 4 vols. in Kretzchmar's *Führer durch den Konzertsaal*, Leipzig, 1930.

Newman, W. S., *The Sonata in the Baroque Era*, Univ. of N. Carolina, 1959. (This book deals with so many composers who were concertists that, although it arrived after the present work was complete, it should be included in this list.)

Pincherle, M., *Les Violinistes*, Paris, 1922.

Praetorius, M., *Syntagma Musicum* (3 vols., Wolfenbüttel, 1614–19).

Vol. ii, English trans. by H. Blumenfeld, St. Louis, 1949.

Vol. iii, copy in British Museum.

Quantz, J. J., *Versuch einer Anweisung die flute traversière zu spielen* (Berlin, 1789, 3rd ed.), Bärenreiter facs. reprint, Kassel, 1953.

Raguenet, F., 'Parallèle des Italiens et des François (1702)', *MQ*, 1946.

Riemann, H., *Handbuch der Musikgeschichte*, vol. ii, 'Das Generalbasszeitalter', ed. Einstein, Leipzig, 1922.

Sachs, C., *Handbuch der Musikinstrumentenkunde*, Berlin, 1920.

Sartori, C., *Bibliografia della musica strumentale italiana stampata in Italia fino al 1700*, Florence, 1952.

Scheibe, J. A., *Der Critischer Musikus* (Leipzig, 1745), consulted only in anthologies, etc., by Strunk, Graf, etc.

Schering, A., *Geschichte des Instrumentalkonzerts* (Leipzig, 1905), 2nd ed. Leipzig, 1927.

Musikgeschichte Leipzigs, vol. ii, Leipzig, 1926.

Geschichte der Musik in Beispielen, Leipzig, 1931.

Preface to *DDT*, vols. xxix–xxx.

Smith, W. C , *A Bibliography of the Musical Works published by John Walsh during the years 1695–1720*, Oxford, 1948.
A Catalogue of Vocal and Instrumental Music published by John Walsh and his Successors, 1706–90, London, 1953.
Strunk, O., *Source Readings in Music History*, New York, 1950.
Walther, J. G., *Musikalisches Lexikon* (Leipzig, 1732), Bärenreiter facs. reprint, Kassel, 1953.
Walker, E., *A History of Music in England*, 3rd edn. rev. and enlarged by J. A. Westrup, Oxford, 1952.

BIBLIOGRAPHY PERTINENT TO SEPARATE CHAPTERS

CHAPTER I. THE PERIOD AND THE PLACES

Ambros-Leichtentritt, *Geschichte der Musik*, vol. iv, Leipzig, 1909.
Ogg, D., *Europe in the Seventeenth Century*, London, 1938.

CHAPTER II. 'CONCERTO' AND 'SINFONIA' DURING THE SEVENTEENTH CENTURY

Arnold, D., 'Music at the Scuola di San Rocco', *ML*, xl–iii, 1959.
Boyden, D., 'When is a Concerto not a Concerto?', *MQ*, xliii, 1957.
Vatielli, F., *Arte e vita musicale a Bologna*, Bologna, 1927, and articles under '*Konzert*' in *MGG* by Engel and Giegling.

CHAPTER III. STYLISTIC FEATURES OF BAROQUE CONCERTOS

Heuss, A., 'Die Instrumental-Stücke des Orfeo' within 'Die venetian-ischen Opern-Sinfonica', *SMIG*, iv, Leipzig, 1903.
Meyer, E., 'Form in the Instrumental Music of the Seventeenth Century', *PMA*, lxv, 1939.
Wasielewski, J. W., 'Instrumentalsätze', supplement to *Die Violine im XVII Jahrhundert* (Bonn, 1874), reprinted separately, Berlin, 1905.
Westrup, J. A., *Purcell*, 3rd edn., London, 1947.
Winterfeld, C. von, *Johannes Gabrieli und sein Zeitalter*, Berlin, 1834.

CHAPTER IV. STRADELLA. SONATA AND CONCERTO

Allam, E., 'Alessandro Stradella', *PRMA*, lxxx, 1953.
Crawfurd, F. M., *Stradella*, London, 1908.
Catelani, A., *Delle opere di Alessandro Stradella esistenti nell'Archivio musicale della R. Biblioteca Palatina di Modena*, Modena, 1866.
Evans, P. A., 'Seventeenth Century Chamber Music Manuscripts at Durham', *ML*, xxxvi, 1955.
Hess, H., *Zur Geschichte des musikalischen Dramas im Seicento: Die Opern Alessandro Stradellas*, Leipzig, 1906.
Roncaglia, G., 'Le Composizioni strumentali di A. Stradella', *RMI*, xliv, xlv, 1940–1.

CHAPTER V. BOLOGNA. SCHOOL OF ST. PETRONIO

Albini, E., 'Domenico Gabrielli, il Corelli del violoncello', *RMI*, xli, 1937.

BIBLIOGRAPHY

Berger, G., 'Notes on Some Seventeenth-century Compositions at Bologna', *MQ*, xxxvii, 1951.

Gaspari, G., *Musicisti Bolognesi nel sec. XVII*, Modena, 1875.

Haas, R., *Die estensischen Musikalien*, Regensburg, 1927.

Mishkin, H. G., 'The Solo Violin Sonata of the Bologna School', *MQ*, xxix, 1943.

Stevens, D., 'Seventeenth-century Italian Music in the Bodleian Library', *AM*, xxvi, 1954.

Tagliavini, L. V., *La Scuola Bolognese* (Accademia Musicale Chigiana), Siena, 1956.

Vatielli, F., *La scuola musicale bolognese* (Strenna storica bolognese), Bologna, 1928.

'Il Corelli e i maestri bolognesi del suo tempo', *RMI*, xxiii, 1916.

CHAPTER VI. CORELLI AND HIS CONTEMPORARIES

Busi, L., *Il Padre G. B. Martini*, Bologna, 1891.

Giegling, F., *Giuseppe Torelli, ein Beitrag zur Entwicklunggeschichte des italianischen Konzerts*, Basle, 1949.

Pincherle, M., *Corelli et son temps*, Paris, 1954.

Rinaldi, M., *Arcangelo Corelli*, Milan, 1953.

Sartori, C., 'Le quarantaquattro edizione delle sei opere di Corelli', *RMI*, lv, 1953.

CHAPTER VII. THE FIRST GERMAN (AUSTRIAN) SCHOOL

Hausswald, G. H., 'Johann Dismas Zelenka als Instrumentalkomponist', *AMW*, xiii, 1956.

Horneffer, A., *Johann Rosenmüller*, Berlin, 1898.

Nef, K., *Geschichte der Sinfonie und Suite*, Leipzig, 1921.

Riemann, H., 'Zur Geschichte der deutschen Suite', *SIMG*, vi, 1905.

CHAPTER VIII. THE VENETIAN SCHOOL

d'Angeli, A., *Benedetto Marcello, vita e opere*, Milan, 1940.

Eitner, R., 'Benedetto Marcello', *MfM*, xxiii, 1891.

Gentili, A., 'La raccolta Mauro Foà', *RMI*, xxxiv, 1927.

Giazotto, R., *Tommaso Albinoni*, Milan, 1945.

Kolneder, W., *Aufführungspraxis bei Vivaldi*, Leipzig, 1956.

Newman, W. S., 'The Sonatas of Albinoni and Vivaldi', *JAMS*, v, 1952.

Pincherle, M., *Antonio Vivaldi et la musique instrumentale*, 2 vols., Paris, 1948.

Antonio Vivaldi (English trans. of former work without the thematic guides of vol. ii), London, 1957.

Torrefranca, F., Article on 'Vivaldi' in *Enciclopedia Italiana*, Rome, 1937.

'Problemi vivaldiani', *IMG*, Basle, 1949.

CHAPTER IX. CONCERTO AND CONCERT

Dent, E. J., *The Foundations of English Opera*, Cambridge, 1928.

Elkin, R. S., *The Old Concert-Rooms of London*, London, 1955.

Girdlestone, C. M., *Rameau*, London, 1957.

Harding, R., *Origins of Musical Time and Expression*, London, 1938.

Laurencie, L. de la, *L'École française de violon de Lully a Viotti*, 3 vols., Paris, 1924.

Lubbock, C. A., *The Herschel Chronicle*, Cambridge, 1933.

Powys, T., One-volume condensation of Clark's *The Life and Times of Anthony à Wood* (orig. 5 vols., Oxford 1891–1900), Oxford, 1932.

Seiffert, M., 'Matthias Weckmann und das Collegium Musicum im Hamburg', *SIMG*, ii, 1901.

Scholes, P. A., Article on 'Concert' in *The Oxford Companion to Music*. *The Puritans and Music*, London, 1934.

Scott, H. A., 'London's Earliest Public Concerts', *MQ*, li, 1936.

CHAPTERS X AND XI. THE MAIN GERMAN SCHOOLS

Büttner, H., *Das Konzert in den Orchestersuiten Georg Philipp Telemanns*, Wolfenbüttel, 1935.

Dittersdorf, K. D. von, *Lebensbeschreibung* (1795. Edited Schmitz, Ratisbon, 1944). Eng. edn. trans. A. D. Coleridge, *The Autobiography of Karl Ditters von Dittersdorf*, London, 1896.

Gräser, W., *Zur Geschichte von Telemanns Instrumental-Kammermusik* (dissertation, Munich, 1924). Rev. in *Telemanns Instrumental-Kammermusik*, Frankfort, 1925.

Hausswald, G. H., *Johann David Heinichens Instrumentalwerke*, Berlin, 1937.

Krüger, W., *Das Concerto grosso Joh. Seb. Bachs*, Bach Jahrbuch, 1932.

Mennicke, C., *Hasse und die Brüder Graun als Symphoniker*, Leipzig, 1906.

Seiffert, M., 'G. Ph. Telemanns Musique de Table als Quelle für Händel', *ZIM*, i, 1900.
See also introd. to *DDT*, lxi and lxii, pub. separately as *Telemanns Musique de Table*, Leipzig, 1927.

CHAPTER XII. THE ENGLISH SCHOOL

Avison, C., *An Essay of Musical Expression*, London, 1752.

Boyden, D., Edn. of Geminiani's *The Art of Playing on the Violin* (London, 1731), London, 1852.

Hernried, R. F., 'Geminianis Concerti grossi op. 3', *AM*, ix, 1937.

Langley, H., *Dr. Arne*, Cambridge, 1938.

McArtor, M. E., *Francesco Geminiani, Composer and Theorist* (dissertation), Univy. of Michigan, Ann Arbor, 1951.

Milner, A., 'Charles Avison', *MT*, January–February 1954.

Westrup, J. A., 'Amateurs in Seventeenth-century England', *MMR*. lxix, 1939.

CHAPTER XIII. HANDEL'S CONCERTOS

Abraham, G. A., (Ed.), *Handel*, A Symposium, London, 1954.

Burney, C., *An Account of the musical performances in Westminster Abbey and the Pantheon, May 26, 27 and 29; and June 3 and 5, 1784*, London, 1785.

Chrysander, F., 'Händel's zwölf Concerti grossi fur Streichinstrumente', *AMZ*, xvi–xvii, 1882.

'Händel's Instrumentalkompositionen fur grosse Orchester', *VfM*, iii, 1887.

Cummings, W. H., *Handel*, London, 1904.

Dean, W., *Handel's Dramatic Oratorios and Masques*, London, 1959.

Delany, M., *Autobiography and Correspondence of Mary Granville, Mrs. Delany*, 6 vols., London, 1862.

Deutsch, O. E., *Handel: A Documentary Biography*, London, 1955.

Leichtentritt, H., 'Handel's Harmonic Art', *MQ*, xxi, 1935.

Schering, A., 'Zum Thema: Händel's Entlehnungen', *ZIM*, ix, 1908.

Swinyard, L., 'Handel's Organ Concertos', *MT*, January 1933.

Young, P. M., *Handel*, London, 1947.

CHAPTER XIV. BONPORTI AND LECLAIR

Barblan, G., *Un musicista trentino, F. A. Bonporti*, Florence, 1940.

Ecorcheville, J., *De Lulli à Rameau: L'Esthetique musicale*, Paris, 1906.

Laurencie, L. de la, 'Le rôle de Leclair dans la musique instrumentale' *RM*, iv, 1923.

Pincherle, M., *Jean Marie Leclair l'aîné*, Paris, 1952.

CHAPTER XV. THE LAST PHASE

Combarieu, J., 'Les Origines de la Symphonie', *RM*, 1903.

Dounias, M., *Die Violinkonzert Giuseppe Tartinis*, Berlin, 1935.

Farmer, H. G., *History of Music in Scotland*, Edinburgh, 1947.

Music-Making in Olden Days: Aberdeen Concerts, Edinburgh, 1951.

Fischer, W., 'Instrumentalmusik von 1750–1828', in Adler's *Handbuch der Musikgeschichte*, 2nd. ed., Berlin, 1930.

Koole, A., *Leven en Werken van Pietro Antonio Locatelli da Bergamo*, Amsterdam, 1949.

Laurencie, L. de la, *Inventaire critique du Fonds Blancheton*, 2 vols., Paris, 1930.

(With Saint-Foix) 'Contribution à l'histoire de la symphonie française', *L'Année musicale*, i, 1911.

Mishkin, H., 'The Published Instrumental Works of Giovanni Battista Sammartini', *MQ*, xlv–3, 1959.

Saint-Foix, G. de, 'La chronologie de l'œuvre instrumentale de Jean-Baptiste Sammartini', *SMIG*, xv, 1914.

Torrefranca, F., 'Le Origini della Sinfonia', *RMI*, xx–xxii, 1915.

Index